D1559143

FICHTE,

MARX, AND

THE GERMAN

PHILOSOPHICAL

TRADITION

TOM ROCKMORE

SOUTHERN ILLINOIS UNIVERSITY PRESS

Carbondale and Edwardsville

FEFFER & SIMONS, INC. *London and Amsterdam*

Copyright © 1980 by Southern Illinois University Press
All rights reserved
Printed in the United States of America
Designed by Richard Hendel

Library of Congress Cataloging in Publication Data

Rockmore, Tom, 1942–
    Fichte, Marx, and the German philosophical tradition.

    Bibliography: p.
    Includes index.
    1. Fichte, Johann Gottlieb, 1762–1814. 2. Marx, Karl, 1818–
1883. 3. Philosophy, German. 4. Act (Philosophy). 5. Philosophical anthropology. I. Title.
B2848.R63   193   80-13194
ISBN 0-8093-0955-6

CONTENTS

ACKNOWLEDGMENTS

M Y debts are too numerous to detail, but the most important ones should be mentioned. My greatest debt is to John Lachs, who interested me in this topic and suggested the relevance of Aristotelian activity. I should also like to acknowledge the encouragement of my colleague, John E. Smith, the secretarial aid of Anne Granger, and the help of my wife, Sylvie. I am further grateful to my colleague, Seyla Benhabib, and especially to Dick Howard for detailed comments on an earlier version. The award of a Morse Fellowship from Yale University freed me from teaching duties during the academic year 1974–75, and enabled me to do research in Heidelberg where much of the writing was done. An award from the Griswold Fund defrayed expenses in the preparation of the manuscript.

The present study is the result of several years of reflection, during which my understanding of Fichte, Marx, and their relation has matured. A small portion of the discussion has already appeared in print in article form. I refer to the following two papers: "Activity in Fichte and Marx," in *Idealistic Studies* 6 (May 1976) and "Fichte's Idealism and Marx's Materialism," in *Man and World* 8, no. 2 (May 1975). I thank the editors of these journals for permission to reprint the very few passages I have not seen fit to rethink or at least to rewrite.

T. R.

New Haven, Connecticut
January 1980

FICHTE, MARX, AND

THE GERMAN

PHILOSOPHICAL

TRADITION

CHAPTER I

ON COMPARING

THE POSITIONS OF

FICHTE AND MARX

*Mir hilft der Geist! Auf einmal seh ' ich Rat. Und schreibe
getrost: im Anfang war die Tat.*
                              Goethe, *Faust* I

*Tätig zu sein, sagte er, ist des Menschen erste Bestimmung, und
alle Zwischenzeiten, in denen er auszuruhen genötigt ist, sollte er
anwenden, eine deutliche Erkenntnis der äusserlichen Dinge zu
erlangen, die ihm in der Folge abermals seine Tätigkeit
erleichtert.*
                              Goethe, *Wilhelm Meisters Lehrjahre*, bk. 6

MY intention in this book is to compare aspects in the positions of Fichte and Marx, two thinkers often but mistakenly viewed at opposite ends of the intellectual spectrum, in order to disclose an important and largely unsuspected parallel. The discussion of this parallel will develop in two ways, thematically in terms of analysis of several related concepts in the two positions, and historically with respect to the genesis of the parallel in the wider context of the nineteenth-century German tradition.

The presence of a relation between the two positions is by no means obvious. Fichte was a professional philosopher, writing in the Kantian tradition, and interested in the epistemological concerns which constitute a major strand of the modern philosophical tradition. Although Marx received extensive philosophical training, he was not a professional philosopher. His thought cannot be labeled as philosophy without further qualification, since after an early brush with Hegelianism he professed to abandon the realm of abstract thought for the more concrete terrain of political economy. It further seems difficult to relate Fichte and Marx in terms of the usual classificatory schemes. As an idealist, Fichte has been thought to oppose all forms of materialism. Conversely, it has been held that Marx was at odds with all kinds of idealism. In fact, from the Marxist perspective a perhaps stronger point has often been made concerning the relation of Marx to the philosophical tradition. Since the publication of Engels's *Anti-Dühring* (1878), followed by his *Ludwig Feuerbach and the Outcome of Classical German Philosophy* (1888), the tendency has been to regard philosophy as nonscientific ideology and Marxism as nonideological science, although there are signs that a revision in this attitude with respect to Marx's position is now under way.[1]

Perhaps for these reasons, although there are some exceptions to be mentioned, for the most part there has been little attention to the possibility of a relation between the two positions. Books on Fichte rarely mention Marx. Discussions of Marx, if they mention Fichte at all, usually go no further than to stress that although Fichte's influence is perceptible in the thought of the Young Hegelians, it is absent from the Marxian position.[2]

If the usual view of the positions of Fichte and Marx were to be accepted, it would indeed be difficult to argue for a relation between them since there would not be any relevant common ground. To be sure, both thinkers were interested in socialism, social progress, and radical social change, but this limited area of common concern is hardly sufficient to suggest an important relation between two of many others in the nineteenth century who held similar views. But a stronger indication of the presence of a relation, if not a parallel, between Fichte and Marx, is given by the same person who did so much elsewhere to suggest that Marxism makes a clean break with the philosophical tradition. In the foreword to the first German edition of *Die Entwicklung des Sozialismus von der Utopie zur Wissenschaft*, Engels writes "that German socialists are proud to be descended not only from Saint Simon, Fourier, and Owen, but from Kant, Fichte, and Hegel as well."[3]

Although Engels does not state that Marxism is philosophy, he suggests here that German socialism, including Marxism, is in part indebted to three of the most important German philosophers. But for the most part, this suggestion has been followed up in a selective manner only. In the early part of this century, attention was directed to the relation between Kant and Marx by a number of writers.[4] And since the appearance of Lukács's *History and Class Consciousness* (1923), there has further been wide discussion of the genesis of Marx's position in relation to Hegel and the Young Hegelians. But although Engels also indicates the relation between Fichte and Marx, this aspect of the Marxian debt to the philosophical tradition has been mainly passed over in silence.

The presupposition of any comparison is that there is a resemblance between the positions to be studied. In general the existence of a parallel can be established in at least two main ways, although variations are possible. One procedure is simply to juxtapose all facets of the positions in question. But unless the contention is that the views in question are at least partially alike in all relevant aspects, a claim which will not be made here, there seems little reason to employ such a cumbersome method. Another procedure, to be utilized here, consists in the comparative analysis of one or more concepts. An approach of this kind is useful for the determination of the nature and limits of a parallel in terms of a central point or points, thus focusing the discussion more than might otherwise be possible. Further, since concepts are interrelated within a position, analysis of any concept, especially a central one, permits additional comparison of related ideas within the positions under study.

In the present study, I shall concentrate on the concept of activity, since this concept is, I believe, central to the positions of both Fichte and Marx. The discussion will develop in the following manner. The initial task is to outline the role of activity, and in particular of the concept of man as an active being, in the respective positions through consideration of each separately. Once this has been done, it will be possible to demonstrate a parallel between the respective views of activity, and then between the concepts of man which follow from these views. But theory corresponds to and exemplifies theory of theory, or metatheory. Accordingly, the third stage in the discussion will be to extend the analysis to the metatheoretical level in order to exhibit the parallel between the two views of metatheory. After the thematic analysis of the parallel has been studied on the levels indicated here, its origin in the development of the modern German philosophical tradition can be discussed. As a final stage, two problems arising out of the discussion will be considered: the apparent tendency to interpret nineteenth century German philosophy in a manner which obscures the parallel to be analyzed here, and the intrinsic philosophical worth of the approach to man as an active being as exemplified by both Fichte and Marx.

The parallel to be discussed turns on the concept of activity. This term, including its homonyms and related concepts, is used in different ways in numerous contexts. We speak, for instance, of active versus passive, action versus inaction, activity in the sense of radioactivity, *actus purus*, an act of Congress, and so on. Even superficial inspection reveals that although there may be a family resemblance in the intended meanings of these terms and others which might be added to the list, the precise denotation is not always the same. It is hence useful to differentiate in a preliminary manner the concept of activity, as here understood, from other similar terms, but at the same time it seems unnecessary to anticipate more than the general lines of the discussion to follow.

This inquiry is based on the Aristotelian concept of activity (*energeia*). In simplest form, in this view activity is distinguished from passivity as that which acts is distinguished from that which suffers or is acted upon. Activity is understood as providing the unity which underlies and relates together certain concepts often held to be separable and separate, such as potency and act, ends and means, subjectivity and objectivity. In activity, potentiality is transformed into actuality. But as actuality and potentiality are inseparably conjoined within the activity through which the transformation takes place, this form of change is to be differentiated from that in which ends and means cannot coexist. Activity further presupposes an agent or active subject, which develops through its activity and which can be understood as an active being. As I shall presently show, the approach to man as an active being in a quasi-Aristotelian sense is fundamental to the positions of Fichte and Marx.

A final point concerns terminology. A word needs to be said in support of the decision to employ "activity" as a neutral term to designate the views of both thinkers. This choice is, I think, an obvious one for Fichte's thought, since he is explicit in his use of derivatives of the term "Act" (*That*), such as activity (*Thätigkeit*) and active (*thätig*) to describe the self. Marx is however less explicit in the selection and use of his terminology, and not altogether consistent. But in consequence of the frequent employment of the word "praxis" (*Praxis*) in the "Theses on Feuerbach" it has become the custom, at least since the end of the nineteenth century, to describe Marxism as a theory of praxis.[5]

I intend to resist the tendency to refer to Marx's own position, as distinguished from Marxism, as a theory of praxis for several reasons. In the first place, Marx never formulates an explicit view of praxis, even if it is possible to piece together a Marxian concept of praxis from his writings.[6] Nor does he designate his own theory by this term, so one should be careful in making the designation for him, although this has often been done.[7] Further, even if the term "praxis" does occur frequently in the "Theses on Feuerbach," there is no evidence that Marx ever employs it systematically, so its occurrence in a single short text does not seem to justify its application to his entire theory. Far more likely is that Marx is here making use of Feuerbach's term against the latter's view, as was Marx's practice, in effect attempting to hoist Feuerbach with his own petard. But praxis is merely one form of activity and activity in several forms is a major theme in Marx's thought. For these reasons, to avoid misunderstanding, it seems preferable to utilize the wider and less prejudicial term "activity" to refer both to Marx's position as well as Fichte's.

CHAPTER 2

FICHTE'S THEORY OF

MAN AS ACTIVE SELF

M Y intention in this chapter is to state Fichte's view of activity in the context of his wider position. In Fichte's thought, the concepts of activity and man are inseparable, although neither is well understood. Accordingly, my task here will be to outline as clearly as possible Fichte's understanding of man as an active being. Although I shall refer to the relevant literature as the need arises, the primary emphasis here will be less on a definitive discussion of Fichte's concept of man as an active being than on the general exposition of this view in order to permit its analysis below.

There is good reason to believe that Fichte understood man as the central concern both in his own philosophy and in all human thought. In an early text, Fichte writes, "All philosophy, all human thought and teaching, its entire study . . . can be directed toward nothing other than the answer to the questions posed, especially to the last and highest: What is the vocation [*Bestimmung*] of man in general, and through what means can he best attain it?" [1] But somewhat paradoxically, aside from this single passage, Fichte only rarely mentions man. Rather, he formulates his position in terms of a concept of the self (*Ich*), which has no obvious connection with man. Perhaps for this reason, Fichte's contribution to the problem of man has received only scant attention. [2] It follows that, if we are to understand his view of human being, our immediate task is to grasp the concept of the self as Fichte's response to the problem of man.

Although this aspect of Fichte's thought has not attracted much notice, there is an interpretative tendency which should be indicated, since for the most part my own discussion will run counter to it. Fichte's thought begins from an analysis of the contents of consciousness in terms of a theory of the self. There are basically two schools of interpretation in the literature devoted to Fichte. One school, certainly the majoritarian tendency at the present time, holds that Fichte's thought is limited to the level of consciousness and self-consciousness, since it is unable to make the transition from subjectivity to objectivity. According to this view, which is largely but not wholly inspired by Hegel's reading of Fichte, the external world is no more than the result of the individual's mind. The German poet Friedrich Schiller's comment in a letter, that the individual is the complete source of all reality, is an early, but representative instance of this interpretative tendency.[3]

Needless to say, this way of reading Fichte is closely related to a widespread, but, in my opinion, unfair view of idealists in general, in which Fichte is frequently singled out as a chief offender, as purveyors of a patently ridiculous theory in which each individual plays the role of the divine creator. On the other hand, there is the less frequent tendency to interpret Fichte's view of the self as a theory of man. This can be represented by Dilthey's comment that what is new in Fichte is his grasp of the self, not as a being, but as an active principle.[4] My own sympathies lie with this second approach. It will be my task here to indicate how, from an analysis of the contents of consciousness, Fichte develops a continuous argument which include such areas as ethics and social organization, as different aspects of the problem of man.

Prior to beginning the exposition, a textual matter should be mentioned. Fichte developed his theory of the self primarily in the *Wissenschaftslehre* (WL),[5] and in other texts related to this book. Fichte published several different and only partially compatible editions of this work during his lifetime, and there are several additional versions in his *Nachlass*. Since this book exists in different and in part incompatible editions, it will be necessary to choose one as a source of his views. In the following discussion, I shall rely heavily on the first edition of the WL, which appeared in 1794. Although to some extent arbitrary, this decision is not merely so, for this text is widely recognized as Fichte's major contribution and, despite subsequent revisions, it remained the fullest version of his view. It further continued to play a central role in the later development of his thought, since Fichte made abundant use of the position developed here as the theoretical basis from which to address other, more practical questions.

Although the theory of the self arguably receives its most ample discussion in the WL, this text is not sufficient by itself. It will need to be supplemented by others in order to reveal the full scope of Fichte's view of man as an active being. The justification is Fichte's apparent intention. Shortly after the appearance of the first edition of the WL, in a semipopular article Fichte wrote, "On the basis of the current [form of the] WL next Easter a detailed theoretical and practical science of knowledge will follow."[6] In fact the proposed publication took the form of a series of works addressed to related questions in terms of the analysis already developed in the *WL*. Just as in the *Phenomenology of Mind* Hegel moves from an analysis of consciousness and self-consciousness to society, morality, and history, so Fichte's thought ranges outward from a theory of consciousness to related problems. The difference is that while Hegel is able to state the related aspects of his theory in a single, encompassing work, Fichte develops his own view in a number of interrelated writings. But to isolate the *WL* from these related texts, as is sometimes done, is in effect to consider merely a fragment of the position.[7] For this reason, I shall emphasize the manner in which selected, later writings complete the view of the self first sketched in the *WL*.

HISTORICAL BACKGROUND

To understand Fichte's thought, it is helpful to place it in historical perspective. In the period following Kant's elaboration of the critical philosophy, a number of thinkers, among them Beck, Maimon, Schulze, and Reinhold, subjected it to criticism, often in view of its amelioration. Although there were others who shared his desire to reformulate the Kantian doctrine, Fichte was distinguished by his belief that he was the legitimate successor to Kant.

Fichte's identification with Kant easily surpassed a mere academic interest. His first publication, the *Kritik aller Offenbarung* [Critique of all revelation], through accident appeared anonymously. When published in 1792 it was almost immediately mistaken for the long-awaited Kantian work on religion. This instance of mistaken identity brought Fichte immediate fame when he was identified as the author. More to the point, Fichte thought of himself as a Kantian, indeed as the only one who really understood the critical philosophy, a claim he clearly carried to indefensible lengths. For instance Fichte even goes to the extreme of alleging that he understands Kant better than the latter understands himself, although the excessive immodesty of the remark is perhaps moderated if we recall that Kant made a similar comment about his relation to Plato. Kantian premises are further everywhere present in Fichte's thought. Indeed there seems to have been some confusion in Fichte's mind concerning the relation between Kant and himself, such as when in a letter Fichte suggests grandiosely that the critical philosophy in fact follows from his own premises. "It is the same with Kant, whose writings I firmly believe I have understood. It seems more and more likely that he reasons on the basis of my basic principles." [8]

But there is a touch of irony in his assertion that his own view is the completion of the critical quest. Kant, of course, prided himself on the painful architectonic form in which he couched his thought as necessary to its rigorous exposition, although it is precisely this side of the critical philosophy which numerous post-Kantian thinkers, including Fichte, found least appealing. For if he could agree with Kant's conclusions, Fichte found the manner in which they were stated to be lacking in systematic form. Fichte's task, as he saw it, was to give rigorous structure to the Kantian theory by restating it in systematic form.

The source of Fichte's revision of Kantianism can be understood through his relation to K. H. Reinhold and G. E. Schulze. Reinhold is important in the post-Kantian tradition as the first to suggest that a philosophical theory should be based on a single, self-evident principle. He developed this view under the title of Elementary Philosophy (*Elementarphilosophie*) in a number of works. Schulze was a skeptic who, writing under the pseudonym Aenesidemus, objected to the attempt to develop an epistemological theory in this manner on the grounds that no such principle could be found.

The immediate occasion for Fichte to state the first version of his theory was provided by his review of Schulze's study of Reinhold. In his *Elementarphilosophie* Reinhold had attempted to formulate the Kantian position through the introduction of a principle of presentation (*Vorstellung*). "In consciousness the presentation is distinguished by the subject from subject and object, and related to both." [9] Schulze properly objected to this proposition on the grounds that Reinhold had failed to observe the asymmetry in the relation of presentation to the subject and object of experience. Although the presentation occurs in and is in this sense identical with the subject, it differs from the object which it represents. In his review, although Fichte endorses Schulze's criticism, he rejects the skeptical conclusions the latter attempts to draw.

With Schulze's objection in mind, Fichte reformulates Reinhold's principle in his own language, as the claim that the "presentation is related to the object as an effect to its cause, and to the subject as an accident to its substance." [10] This statement is significant, because it gives, in the compass of a single sentence, the outlines of an ontology of consciousness in terms of two elements, subject and object, and their interrelation. It is this same ontology which Fichte further develops in the *WL* and which is the basis of his entire position.[11]

Fichte's reworking of Kantian thought in terms of Reinhold's principle of presentation can be introduced through a comment on the aim of philosophy. If, as has been said, idealism is characterized by a simultaneous effort at total explanation and internal unity, then Fichte is an idealist.[12] In Fichte's view, philosophy must explain all experience, and an authentic or rigorous explanation can only be advanced on the basis of a single principle or hypothesis from which the remainder of the theory can be rigorously deduced. The concern to formulate a total explanation of experience in terms of a single concept is a constant theme in Fichte's thought. To grasp the attempt at total explanation in terms of a single underlying idea is to understand the intent motivating Fichte's position.

Like many philosophers, Fichte holds that the task of philosophy is coextensive with the explanation of experience. Fichte draws a basic distinction between two attitudes, that of philosophy and of life. According to Fichte, ordinary experience is insufficient to furnish its own explanation, which can only occur on a meta-experiential or philosophical level. The purpose of philosophy and indeed its only *raison d'être* is to run parallel to and to render everyday life intelligible. "The first standpoint is that of pure speculation; the second that of life and scientific knowledge [in a sense contrasted with that of the *Science of Knowledge*]. The second is intelligible only on the basis of the first" (*WL*, p. 31).

Fichte develops his theory in quasi-phenomenological fashion.[13] If we turn our attention away from the world and toward ourselves, we can see that our experience consists in the contents of consciousness, or presentations (*Vorstellungen*). Our presentations include two general classes. On the one hand, there are those presentations which are accompanied by a feeling of freedom. In contemporary terminology, perhaps the closest analogy would be imagining or free phantasy. Presentations accompanied by a feeling of freedom are contents of consciousness solely dependent on the individual, although in the post-Freudian world it seems doubtful that one would concede that anything occurs in consciousness for which the subject is wholly responsible. On the other hand, there are presentations accompanied by a feeling of necessity. These are contents of consciousness which, to an extent variable with the particular situation, may be said to have their origin in an external world. It is this latter form of presentation for which philosophy is to account. "The system of presentations accompanied by a feeling of necessity is also called *experience*. . . . Philosophy, in other words, must therefore furnish the grounds of all experience" (*WL*, p. 6). But since by virtue of his restriction of experience to these contents of consciousness accompanied by a feeling of necessity, Fichte has sharply limited the scope of his task, it is apparent that, at least initially, to explain experience is equivalent to accounting for one among the possible classes of the contents of consciousness.

If we take into account that Fichte conceives of the problem of experience in terms of a theory of consciousness, his approach has a certain plausibility. Just as, it has been argued, an infant can be aware of his surroundings as such only through the differentiation of the world from himself, so from the perspective of consciousness everything must be understood from the vantage point of the subject. The result is what might be called, in contemporary terms, a first-person ontology, or theory of being from the point of view of the experiential subject.

How is experience to be explained? According to Fichte, the ultimate constituent of reality, through which experience is to be understood, is the self (*das Ich*), a term chosen to designate the human individual as the conscious subject of experience. Using the interaction between subject and object as his basic experiential model, Fichte further distinguishes four kinds of self. From the perspective of the subject, Fichte recognizes both finite self and absolute self. Finite self is the human being as limited and hence defined through his interaction with the surrounding world. Fichte is unfortunately not entirely consistent in his use of this term, for which he frequently substitutes the word "self," but some misunderstanding can be avoided if it is realized that he apparently has in mind the finite human individual considered as the subject of conscious experience.

Absolute self, on the contrary, is Fichte's term for the individual considered in theoretical abstraction from the man-world interaction that is the setting of all human experience. Since the absolute self is not accompanied by a feeling of necessity, it can never be an object of experience. It follows that to the extent that it can be thought and hence present in mind, absolute self is a free presentation. More to the point, the concept of absolute self, or absolute being, is invoked as a theoretical construct only in order to explain the possibility of experience.

Since the absolute self has often been misconstrued, it is useful to note that Fichte's understanding of this concept underwent revision in his later writings. Schelling reformulated the Fichtean concept of the absolute as the *Indifferenzpunkt* in his *System des transzendentalen Idealismus* (1800). Beginning in 1801, in large part, one may speculate, as a reaction to the celebrated *Atheismusstreit*, Fichte redefines the absolute in a manner closely similar to Schelling's concept of the absolute harmony between subjective and objective forms of activity.[14] But it must be emphasized that earlier, and certainly in the initial version of the *WL*, this term refers merely to a speculative concept devoid of all religious overtones, as Fichte makes clear. "The *Science of Knowledge* makes a careful distinction between absolute being and real existence, and employs the former merely as a basis, in order to explain the latter" (*WL*, p. 245).[15]

From the side of the object, Fichte distinguishes not-self and absolute not-self. By the term "not-self," he refers to man's world as it is perceived in experience. Fichte also occasionally employs the term "absolute not-self" or even "thing-in-itself," although in a causal manner Kant could not sanction, to designate the surrounding world as that which does not appear in experience, but which may be thought of as the ground of experience. From this perspective, the absolute not-self can be said to provide the ontological underpinnings for experience in general.

It seems clear that Fichte's theory of the world, at least on the epistemological plane, is anything but detailed. In part for this reason, it was accorded a chilly reception by his contemporaries. Indeed, Fichte's failure to provide a more than highly abstract theory of the natural world is one of the reasons which led Schelling to develop his *Naturphilosophie*, and hence an important source of the controversy that separated Fichte from his contemporaries, Schelling and Hegel.[16]

SELF AND ACTIVITY

So far we have seen how Fichte developed an ontology in terms of concepts of self and not-self. He further attempted to comprehend man, understood as a self, as an active being. Since Fichte's aim is to understand the self in terms of its activity, it is to the latter view that one must turn in order to grasp his theory of man. The self's leading characteristic is that it is active or activity, and that this is so is the single presupposition to which Fichte will admit. "The self is absolutely active and merely ac-

tive—that is our absolute presupposition" (*WL*, p. 221). For
Fichte, selfhood and activity are synonymous terms. If we remember that in his view the term "self" stands for "human individual," it follows that, in a fundamental sense, one is not a
human being except as one is active and to be active is to be a
human being.

The claim that the self is active arises from the regressive nature of the discussion. The problem at hand is to explain the contents of consciousness accompanied by a feeling of necessity, or
facts of experience, in terms of the self or experiential subject.
Fichte's argument is based on the presupposition that experience
can only be understood in terms of an active self. But it should
be emphasized that Fichte's theory of activity is more than an assumption which he is constrained to make by the logic of his argument. For he claims that each of us can immediately verify our
own activity in what he terms "intellectual intuition" on the level
of self-consciousness.[17]

Fichte further develops a theory of the interactions between
self and world, and self and other selves. In terms of his basic in-
teractionist model of experience, he differentiates several forms
of activity. According to Fichte, subject and object stand in a relation of interdetermination, which may be understood as a restatement of Kant's concept of relation. Each element of the relation determines and is determined by the other. But since self is
defined as activity, only three basic forms of activity are possible.
Either the subject acts to limit the object, or it is limited by the
object, or it acts independently of the object. These three kinds
of activity are called respectively positing, striving, and independent activity. To posit (*setzen*) literally means to set, to place, or
to put (something). Positing is a positioning of something in regard to something else, and the verb suggests opposition. To
strive (*streben*) means to struggle or aspire to, for, or after.
Striving implies a perceived lack as well as an attempt to rectify
it. Independent activity (*unabhängige Thätigkeit*) is in no sense
determined by the subject-object relation, although it takes place
within the bounds of this setting.

Positing is the form of activity through which Fichte accounts
for consciousness. Fichte employs this concept in the sense of the
necessary condition. "It is intended to express that *Act* [*That-
handlung*] which does not and cannot appear among the empirical states of our consciousness, but rather lies at the basis of all
consciousness and alone makes it possible" (*WL*, p. 93). Fichte's
point here is that although positing cannot be experienced, it
must nevertheless be thought.

In a manner that recalls Kant's Copernican Revolution, Fichte further maintains that if the object of experience is to be known, the act through which it arises must be ordered according to the laws of the mind. Positing occurs according to three fundamental principles. The three fundamental principles, that is, identity, opposition, and grounding or quantitative limitation, should not be confused with the first principle, the hypothesis that the self is activity. The three fundamental principles may be characterized as quasi-logical laws in terms of which all experience must occur and hence can be explained. These principles invariably limit the manifestation of positing, and hence all experience, to a single paradigm of dialectically rational development. It follows that conscious experience must conform to laws of the mind, and there is no limit to our knowledge of the content of consciousness accompanied by necessity.

The regressive character of the inquiry resembles Kant's analytic approach in the *Prolegomena*. In this work Kant makes the key assumption that there is synthetic a priori knowledge and argues backward, or regressively, to its conditions. In the *WL* Fichte similarly argues from known facts to antecedent conditions or, in his terminology, from conditioned to condition. But since Fichte's theory presupposes that experience is limited to the contents of consciousness, he is obliged to proceed in terms of a specific fact, and not the existence of knowledge in general.

The problem which immediately arises is the selection of an appropriate fact from which to begin the analysis. Fichte begins in what can only be called pseudo-phenomenological fashion. To initiate the discussion, he proposes that we select any one fact of empirical consciousness "that everyone will grant us without dispute" (*WL*, p. 94) and, through abstraction, remove its empirical features. The difficulty is, of course, the specification of any such fact upon which general agreement could be obtained. But the problem is really no more than apparent, since it is patent that in his discussion Fichte is not so much interested in arriving at agreement regarding an initial fact, as in utilizing it as an example for the development of his analysis. In this sense, it makes no difference at all from what fact one begins, since the argument in no sense depends upon it.

The proposition advanced is none other than a form of the law of identity, which Fichte states as "A is A" and as "A = A" (*WL*, p. 94). Fichte uses this proposition to make a number of points in a very murky discussion, which can perhaps be summed up in two principal points. On the one hand, in a manner which partially echoes Kant's transcendental unity of apperception, Fichte maintains that a subject must be invoked as a necessary condition of any and all experience. From this perspective, the subject is no more than a quasi-logical concept which can and indeed must be thought of as accompanying all consciousness. With this quasi-Kantian point in mind, Fichte writes that the subject or absolute self is "a ground of explanation of all facts of empirical consciousness, that prior to all postulation in the self, the self itself is posited" (*WL*, p. 96). Thus, at least from the epistemological perspective, one must consider the subject qua logical principle as a prior and necessary condition of experience.

But Fichte has another, less Kantian card up his philosophical sleeve, a card which derives from his view of logic. It has been the usual practice, at least since Aristotle, to assume the validity of logical laws as a condition of all discussion. But Fichte parts company with the tradition by holding that the *Science of Knowledge*, which can in part be regarded as a logic of experience, is prior to logic *tout court*. This has certain consequences. For one thing, it means that, since the rules of logic must be assumed in all discourse, as Aristotle argues and Fichte concedes, philosophy is necessarily a circular enterprise, a conclusion Fichte readily acknowledges. But there is the further consequence that logical laws, which in Fichte's view can be derived only through abstraction from the content of experience, contain an implicit ontological reference. Applying this point to the concept of an epistemological subject, it follows that this concept is capable of an ontological interpretation.

Kant, as is widely known, laid great stress on the fact that the transcendental unity of apperception is a mere logical condition, in other words an epistemological subject only, to which no psychological interpretation can be attached. But Fichte argues that the logical concept at the base of experience is underlain by an actual subject, or finite human being. This can be seen in two ways. On the one hand, the proposition A is A is a judgment of personal identity, the validity of which can be confirmed by the subject in reflection. For in every case a condition of consciousness is that the subject can, through reflection, be self-aware. Further, the assertion of identity occurs through the coupling of subject and predicate in a judgment. Hence, the logical relation of identity must have as its basis the real subject which brings about the relation through mental activity.

The first or thetic principle, A = A, refers solely to the concept of the experiential subject. Fichte next introduces an antithetic principle, also called the principle of opposition. If there is to be consciousness, there must be something of which the subject is aware, something which stands out over against and opposes it and hence can be known. Now the principle of opposition cannot be deduced from the principle of unity. Accordingly, Fichte goes through a quasi-phenomenological analysis similar to that already described in order to deduce the concept of the object.

So far we have discussed concepts of thesis and antithesis, each of which was supposedly derived from the study of the conditions of consciousness. Now dropping any further pretensions to define his position from conscious experience, Fichte urges that if there is an antithesis, there must be a synthesis. As he puts it, analysis is the process of discovering the sense in which like things differ, and synthesis is the converse process of identifying the sense in which unlike objects resemble one another. Proposing that subject and object can be regarded as composed of scalar quantities, Fichte suggests that antithesis, or opposition between subject and object, can be overcome through a postulated mutual divisibility in which both poles of the subject-object relation limit and define their opposites through interaction. The advantage of this third principle is that it provides for the unity between subject and object requisite for the occurrence of consciousness.

After identification of Fichte's three fundamental principles, we can understand the use to which he puts them. In Fichte's hands, these principles are not a collection of logical rules, but the tools of a dialectical method, better known in its restatement in Hegel's thought. In Fichte's version of the dialectical method, the synthesis requires the antithesis and the antithesis the synthesis. The method is applied by developing two alternative ideas or propositions, both of which are shown to be true, but which are incompatible with one another. The synthesis of what, on closer inspection, is seen to be only apparently contradictory propositions, is achieved through the introduction of another proposition which "contains" the compatible elements of the other two propositions. This enables one to proceed to another synthesis, and so on. As a methodological device, the use of dialectic enables Fichte to generate his *Science of Knowledge* from the three principles discussed by constantly discovering new antitheses which require the introduction of new syntheses.

The topic to which Fichte immediately applies his dialectic method is the problem of consciousness. The argument here is too intricate to follow in detail, and I shall attempt to do no more than to summarize its main points. But if the discussion is to be understood, it must be borne in mind that Fichte's purported solution of this problem depends on the legitimacy of the analysis of the conditions of consciousness from both realistic and idealistic standpoints. Now this is perhaps a move which, on reflection, one may not want to grant Fichte, a decision which would rule his approach to the question out of order on strictly procedural grounds. But one must at least be aware that this is the method Fichte wants to follow if his argument is to be comprehended.

Fichte approaches the problem of consciousness through a quasi-visual image. Consider the following schema. The activity of the self streams outward until it is subjected to a check, at which point it is reflected back into the self. To the extent that its activity is hindered, the self is limited by the not-self, which may be considered as active in relation to a passive self. As passive, the self undergoes, or suffers, the activity of the not-self, of which it is the original cause. In more familiar terms, the relation between subject and object is that of cause to effect. What occurs in the subject is the result of the limitation of its activity due to the inter-action with the world. The relation is an opposition between self and not-self, which corresponds to the second principle. The op-position is in a sense overcome by the result of the interaction, the effect of which is the awareness by the subject of its surroundings. In the substance-accident terminology sometimes employed by Fichte, the subject is a substance in which accidents, which corre-spond to modifications of consciousness, occur as the product of the subject-object interaction. This latter relation is one of syn-thesis, in which subject and object unite as a condition of con-sciousness. Synthesis corresponds to the third principle. But the possibility of synthesis is guaranteed by free or unhindered imag-ination. For although the subject is limited to the extent that it is determined by its interrelation with the object, to the extent that it is undetermined it is free to act. Imagination, or independent ac-tivity, is the absolute power by which subject and object are united within a single consciousness. But this unity is made possible by the original thetic subject (the active being or finite person), that is, the first principle which underlies both antithetic and synthetic subject-object relations.

The theory just outlined errs perhaps by attempting to account for too much. Even if one grants Fichte his assumption that the self is the sole source of activity, a presupposition which seems as highly improbable as it is necessary for his attempt to explain ex-perience through a single proposition, at best Fichte can account for the facts of consciousness. What he cannot explain is the on-tology underlying his theory, a fact of which he seems occasionally aware. He is unable, for instance, as he is well aware, to cast any light on the source of either self or not-self. In this spirit he notes that his theory is limited "in that it shows how neither does the mere activity of the self provide the ground of the reality of the not-self, nor the mere activity of the not-self provide the ground of passivity in the self" (*WL*, p. 164), as do other views, which he, however, characterizes as dogmatic forms of idealism and realism. Fichte's point here is that at best a theory can describe and interpret the interaction which in fact occurs, but must leave unexplained the source of the elements of the interaction. The latter is a problem whose solution falls outside the scope of philosophy, as he defines it. But this momentary modesty is not only uncharacteristic of Fichte's writings. It is also incompatible with his ascription of activity to the not-self and entire explanation of presentation, since his initial assumption concerns the activity of the absolute self. For as Fichte writes, in a somewhat clearer statement of his position, "The absolute self must therefore be cause of the not-self, insofar as the latter is the ultimate ground of all presentation; and the not-self must to that extent be its effect" (*WL*, p. 22).

At this point, we might pause to evaluate what seems to be a patently circular argument. Fichte's explanation of consciousness makes use of both idealistic and realistic perspectives. From an idealistic perspective, the self is completely autonomous, and there is hence no need to appeal to an external force or principle. Self and not-self are merely determinations within the unity of the self, and self as activity is cause both of itself and not-self. But this idealistic view of self as activity does not "solve" the problem of consciousness, since it fails to demonstrate how the self can be determined by the not-self, as required by the theory of consciousness. This can only be done from a realistic perspective, on the assumption of the reality of the not-self. For consciousness is explicable only if we assume that there exists an external force which reflects the activity of the self back into the self. Not-self determines self, since it provides the real opposition necessary for the reflection of the self's activity. This is the realistic side of the argument.

As a result of the dual perspective, Fichte's position is both realistic and idealistic. Fichte relates this dual perspective to a necessary circle proper to the finite individual. His approach to this circle consists in an attempt to understand it within the context of his theory, rather than in an attempt to explain it away. On the one hand, he acknowledges the impossibility of a complete account of consciousness and experience without the assumption of an independent given. However, whatever is only is for the individual as a presentation on the level of consciousness, not as it is in itself. Since the self as active is self-determining, it can be regarded as the source of the given. In this way only the demand of reason, that the self, in its reflection upon itself, consider that it is the source both of itself and all reality, is fulfilled.

> Here, then, the principle: no ideality, no reality, and *vice versa* again receives confirmation or rather emerges into full clarity. As we can also put it, therefore: the ultimate ground of all consciousness is an interaction of the self with itself, by way of a not-self that has to be regarded from different points of view. This is the circle from which the finite spirit cannot escape, and cannot wish to escape, unless it is to disown reason and demand its own annihilation. (*WL*, p. 248)

The preceding account of consciousness contains a problem which should be addressed. The problem arises out of the one-sided nature of a theory which centers on the limitation of the individual by his surroundings and the nature of this limitation. The dual perspective from which this limitation is considered harbors a double view of the subject. From the realistic side, the subject is understood as a finite being, whose activity is limited through the opposition furnished by the external world. This is the finite individual, who is the subject of experience, the human being who in fact exists. From the idealistic side, the subject is understood as a theoretical construct, whose activity is, in accordance with Fichte's view of positing, entirely unlimited, or infinite. This form of subjectivity is of course not experienced nor is it experienceable. Rather, it has the status of a theoretical construct required to make the argument work. The problem is to relate the two sides of subjectivity in order to arrive at a single, coherent view.

As Kant before him, Fichte seeks the resolution for conflicts which arise within the context of a theoretical analysis on the practical level. According to Fichte, it is a fact of experience, verifiable through introspection, that the individual is confronted by a real and independent world, which stands over against and limits his activity. Fichte further suggests that it is a "fact" about human nature that the individual is unable to tolerate any restrictions to his activity. Human existence can be understood as an uninterrupted effort to overcome and to abolish all such restrictions. "The self strives to fill out the infinite" (*WL*, p. 254).

From the point of view of the human individual, the importance of striving is that it grounds a theory of self-development. As is his practice, Fichte considers self-development and self-realization from both real and ideal perspectives. The result is a quasi-Spinozistic deductive psychology. Realistically speaking, an individual can escape neither his context nor his limited status as a finite being. At best the surrounding world can be modified in ways consistent with the needs of individual development. The opposition of the individual and his world result in feelings, which Fichte defines as the subjective manifestation of the inability of striving to reach its goal. The feeling of the self's inability to act is accompanied by a longing for the required determination. Yet since a finite being can never actually expand out to infinity, satisfaction—or the real attainment of the desired determination—can be no more than partial. But on the ideal level, limitations are only apparent. Here it may be said that striving leads to complete realization or fulfillment, which Fichte calls harmony, through the generation of opposition to feelings. But a change in feeling signifies a change in that which opposes it. Harmony results from the fact that the drive and the activity are one and the same, although only ideally so. And it should be stressed, lest Fichte's view seem merely silly, that the fulfillment mentioned here is ideal precisely because the form of striving in question does not relate to a real object.

As an attempt by the individual to surpass what is in the direction of what should be, striving has moral implications. Thus, in Fichte's position as in Kant's epistemology theory leads to and is completed by morality. There is further an obvious comparison to be made between Kant's and Fichte's ethical theories. The similarity is that in both views freedom is a presupposition of morality. For Fichte, the human individual is limited to his relation to the world. It follows that man is free only to the extent that he is not limited by his surroundings. But insofar as man is unlimited, he is completely autonomous in the Kantian sense of the term. Morality is possible because, as a free but limited being, the individual can freely act within the limits of his surroundings according to the moral law. But Fichte's view differs from Kant's in that it preserves autonomy as a condition of morality without the requirement, unrealizable in practice, that the moral subject be thought of as a totally free and completely unconstrained being. Further it should be noted that Fichtean striving is wider than Kantian morality since all practical activity falls under this heading, whereas in Kant's view only activity based on the categorical imperative is moral.

But whatever advantage Fichte's ethical view might possess with respect to Kant's, it seems difficult to defend the concept of striving in the precise sense in which it is formulated by Fichte. Since striving is by definition deprived of causal efficacy, human agency can at best be limited to no more than rational self-orientation.

This overrestrictive definition can perhaps be explained in the following way. One may speculate that the residual rationalist tinge in Fichte's position, especially as related to Spinozism, would seem to prohibit a quantification of the causal principle. Yet Fichte's failure to see that causality is possible in a restricted form is nevertheless astonishing, given his own concept of mutual limitation and its relation to the grounding principle, as the latter depends upon the very concept of quantification here in question. The other reason may be that, following Kant, Fichte could not see his way clear, on pain of upsetting the possibility of natural science, to limit causality in the world of experience to make room for freedom, as Kant had limited knowledge to make room for faith.

Despite the evident difficulties with which Fichte's concept is beset, it would seem that a simple reformulation of its definition would resolve many of them. Fichte ought to have left open the possibility for striving to be causal or at least to attain causality, since it is manifestly true that in certain situations at least some actions are causally efficacious, even if all are not. He would still have been able to maintain that striving occurs in response to a desire constitutive of man's being and would not have lost the possibility of excluding certain forms of activity, such as positing, from the realm of conscious, voluntary action. He could then argue consistently, as he at times in the *WL* and frequently in other writings somewhat inconsistently attempts to do, that while complete domination of man over nature or himself is never in fact attained, this is a goal which is constantly and ever-increasingly realized in practice, as man expands the sway of his control of his environment.

But whatever the reason invoked to explain this definition, it would seem that it cannot be defended as it stands. In the short run it seems clear that the ability to act accordingly to principles is a human capacity, even if it is somewhat infrequently exercised. Further, it has been persuasively argued by many thinkers that in the long run human history records a gradually increasing mastery of man over nature as the cumulative result of the activity of many individuals, acting in concert or alone. In this connection, it is comforting to note that Fichte is rather consistent in his manifest disregard of the consequences of his definition of striving for his view of the self, which he regards, both in the *WL* and elsewhere, as a being able to undertake practical activity. Indeed, that man possesses this capacity is a necessary element of the attempt to relate the absolute and theoretical sides of the self through practical activity.

After this discussion of striving, we can understand Fichte's belief that practical activity provides the necessary junction between the absolute and theoretical perspectives previously described. Fichte makes this argument in two steps. On the one hand, as a practical being the individual attempts, in response to an inner drive, to overcome all possible obstacles to his activity and to become an actually infinite being. Hence the concept of self-development ment presupposes for its intelligibility an idea of the self as ideally unlimited, namely, an absolute self. In this way the practical side of human being may be said to relate to its wholly speculative or absolute aspect. On the other hand, through its striving the individual is constantly confronted by a real world, which stands over against and opposes it. But by virtue of the argument summarized in the deduction of presentation, that which opposes the self furnishes both the material and the opportunity for knowledge. So the practical aspect of individuality also relates to man's theoretical nature. In other words, both the absolute and theoretical sides of man are conjoined through practical activity. Hence Fichte can write that "we have at last discovered the point of union we were seeking between the absolute, the practical and the intellectual characters of the self" (*WL*, p. 244).

This phase of the discussion recalls Kant's similar preoccupation, but there is a difference which should be noted. Kant's intent is to determine the relative precedence to be accorded to different kinds of experience in order to avoid what he sometimes terms a conflict (*Streit*) between the various faculties. Fichte is interested in a somewhat different question. He is not so much concerned to avoid a conflict among faculties, although he certainly does not overlook this problem, as he is to demonstrate their possible coexistence in a finite human being. In this regard his primary motivation would seem to be to provide for a unitary conception of the human individual in terms of the various forms of activity which can be attributed to it in correlation with types of human experience.

MAN AS AN ACTIVE BEING

A résumé of the view of man which emerges from this complicated train of reasoning can now be rapidly sketched. In a discussion which begins with the problem of the conditions of knowledge and experience, Fichte considers man from two perspectives. As a finite human being, the individual person is both a theoretical, namely, a subject of consciousness, and a practical, or moral, being. As a real finite being, man is limited through his relation to the external world. The concept of absolute being is further invoked on the philosophical or meta-experiential level, as a philosophical concept useful in the explanation of experience. To the types of man or self Fichte associates kinds of activity. As theoretical man posits, as practical he strives, and as absolute he acts in theoretical independence of his surroundings. The concept of an ideally existent absolute being is justified as a means to understand the experience of the really existent finite being. Forms of activity need to be subtended by activity in general, and from the side of realism man is above all a practical being. But from the idealistic perspective, the concept of pure activity is identified with the absolute self, an acknowledged philosophical construct in Fichte's discussion. Yet since from this perspective a view of man follows from the concept of absolute self, Fichte may be said to "deduce" the concept of the individual from that of the absolute. As he notes in a letter: "My absolute self is clearly not the individual. . . . But the individual must be deduced from the absolute self." [18] But one should of course not lose sight of the fact that the pretended deduction only works since Fichte "smuggles in" the concept of the individual in abstract form as the presupposition of the theory.

So far we have been concerned with that portion of Fichte's position which appears in the first version of the *WL*, its introductions, and prior writings. It is obvious that the concept of man is here stated merely in the context of his relation to a featureless surrounding world, which has no apparent relation to a social context or other men. To be sure, in the *WL* there is a single passage in which the concept of interpersonal relations is obscurely invoked. "We thus envisage an activity extraneous to the self (= −Y), equal and akin to this activity of the self" (*WL*, p. 230). But this is hardly a full treatment of the problem. For this reason, it might be thought that Fichte somehow overlooks or fails to account for the social side of human being.

That Fichte does not at this point devote more attention to interpersonal relations is not surprising, but rather consistent with his understanding of his task. Although the narrow focus of the discussion has the effect of imparting a solipsistic tinge to his argument, the attempt to state a theory of experience solely from within the perspective of the individual's conscious awareness virtually precludes satisfactory discussion of man's social being. Yet one should be aware that Fichte's later emphasis on the interpersonal nature of human being does not mark a shift in the basic position. [19] There is rather a shift in emphasis.

The shift in emphasis has two major aspects. One aspect concerns the evolution of Fichte's original position, whose first full statement occurs in the *WL*. The further evolution of Fichte's original position can be attributed to several factors, including his own desire to improve the imperfect manner in which his theory was originally stated, his concern to respond to criticism raised by his contemporaries, and the development in his own mind of the goal and nature of philosophy. As a result, Fichte is perhaps the only major philosopher whose central work exists in more than half a dozen, only partially compatible versions, the consequence of his continued efforts to improve upon earlier statements of his own position.

The evolution of Fichte's position is not merely in degree, but in kind. In writings after the celebrated *Atheismusstreit*, for instance, he tended to emphasize the religious dimension of his thought in a manner which was not wholly consistent with his earlier position and further made stronger claims for knowledge in the traditional philosophical sense than can be defended in his earlier view. Accordingly, a consequence of the later change of his position was to bring it into closer alignment with the development from Kant to Hegel, in which his own thought is often, but erroneously, regarded as a mere transitional link, not worthy of consideration for its own sake.[20]

The complex issue of the later evolution of Fichte's position and its relation to his earlier thought represents an as-yet-unsettled problem which is the topic of much interest in the literature. But although an account of the later development of Fichte's philosophy would be interesting, it must be omitted since the ulterior modifications of Fichte's views tended to diminish the parallel between his and Marx's respective positions under consideration here.[21] But I do want to mention aspects of the later Fichtean view of man which are continuous with Fichte's earlier thought, since they are relevant to the present discussion.

In later works Fichte applies his view of man as an active being to various problems and gives increasing emphasis to social considerations. In the latter respect Fichte's basic point seems to be that "man . . . only becomes a man among men."[22] It follows that the concept of social interaction is built into the concept of individuality. For man is always in or must be considered in relation to a social setting, and hence cannot reasonably be conceived of in isolation from other human beings. Fichte develops his understanding of man's social aspect in several directions. One point he makes is that, as Hegel later observes, man is only fully aware of himself through the awareness of others. In other words, the condition of self-consciousness is that others recognize me as a human being. And Fichte goes on to stress that man develops only within a social context, although he notes that existing nations need fundamental reorganization if man is ever to reach the goal of becoming fully freely active among other freely active individuals.

Fichte further applies his view of man as an active being to ethics and morality. As Hegel will do later, Fichte draws a distinction between these two spheres. In Fichte's position, the distinction rests on the difference between independent and practical forms of activity. The former is completely unrestrained as to its occurrence and has no necessary effect on the individual's surroundings, since it is by definition independent of the subject-object relation of experience. It hence takes place on the level of mind only. The latter occurs within the space allotted to the individual by his context and is, again by definition, an attempt to enlarge the available space for man's free activity. "The concept of rights applies only to that which externalizes itself in the sensuous world; that which has no causality in the sensuous world, but rather remains within the interior of the mind belongs to another standard of judgment, that of morality." [23]

Fichte develops his theory of morality in *Das System der Sittenlehre* (1798). Although this work bears a strong Kantian imprint, it is essentially a critique of the Kantian position. Here, as elsewhere, Fichte is strongly concerned to give systematic form to what he regards as an unsystematic Kantian view. The discussion deals at length with the concept of duty (*Pflicht*) in relation to the concept of morality. Duty is portrayed as an abstract idea which has currency only within this realm, but within this realm it is the prime motivating force. Not surprisingly, Fichte even claims to provide the foundation for, as well as the correct deduction of, the categorical imperative.

But one ought not to overlook the critical thrust of this reworking of the Kantian position. It is significant that the locus of moral activity is restricted to the sphere of individual consciousness, since this is to imply that formal morality in fact has and can have no real application. Hence Fichte notes that moral freedom is merely a theoretical idea and he observes that the efficacy of morality is no more than that of the causality of its concept. For the restriction of its sphere of influence solely to the level of the individual's self-determination means that morality is deprived of a role on the social level. Morality is therefore an ideal concept which has meaning under the condition of perfect rationality only, and hence admits of no real application.

Fichte's criticism of the Kantian moral theory is elaborated from the perspective of social reality. A realistic analysis must proceed from the standpoint of free human relations. Its principal task is to understand the possibility of free human activity within a social context. Fichte elaborates his theory of social interaction in the *Grundlage des Naturrechts (Rechtslehre)* (1796). The title is, as Fichte later points out, somewhat misleading, since it implies erroneously that he holds a theory of natural right. But Fichte later corrected this impression in the second edition of the book when he writes that "natural right is a right of reason, and should be so called." [24]

Following Rousseau, Fichte maintains that the essential justification of community is the free association of individuals who come together on the basis of a contract. Now if there is a community, there must be rights. Rights include both the restriction of individuals' actions with respect to one another and the reciprocal recognition of certain privileges, or positive rights to something. Among the most fundamental rights is that of property, by which Fichte means the right to the means necessary for life. This basic right, which is grounded in the original contract, depends for its validity upon the ability of the individual to live from his work. In the event that this is not possible, then the contract is regarded as broken, which is another way of stating that under certain conditions the right to revolt and, if necessary, to revolution, exists. In practice this means the justification of individual rights is that in a social context, where each is limited, each profits from the existence of mutual limitations. But if and when the individual can no longer profit from the limitation of his range of action, then all such limits are to be regarded as removed.

As mentioned, the purpose of the *Rechtslehre* is to discuss the conditions of the possibility of the free association of social beings. A further question is the condition of the development of social freedom. Fichte addresses himself to this problem in a little-known book, *Der geschlossene Handelsstaat* (1800), which was intended as a continuation of the *Rechtslehre*. This work has unfortunately for the most part either been ignored or noticed only to point out its utopian character. Fichte was himself aware of this possible line of criticism, since he notes that it is highly unlikely that any state would freely agree to adopt the suggestions he makes here. And Struensee, to whom the book is dedicated, states in a letter to its author that "even you doubt whether this ideal can be reached." [25]

But it would be wrong to regard this book as wholly impractical. For the central idea, that the state must make use of economic closure in order to attain independence and hence provide for the real possibility of rational interpersonal relations, is not utopian.

The difficulty arises mainly in the transition to this kind of national organization. And although the details of Fichte's analysis have been improved on in subsequent political theory, this work retains permanent importance as the first serious discussion in the German tradition of the economic conditions of social freedom.

As the discussion has now reached the stage of the reorganization of social relations, this is perhaps an appropriate place to break off the exposition. In this chapter I have sought to outline Fichte's understanding of man as an active being in the wider context of his position. In rapid outline I have reconstructed the train of thought by which Fichte moves from a regressive and transcendental analysis of the conditions of consciousness to questions of individuality and human interaction. I have further stressed throughout the continuity of the argument in the earlier and later writings, through demonstration of the fact that in Fichte's position the attempted solution to the problem of consciousness requires a view of man as an active being. Marx's position is very different from Fichte's. But it is fascinating to observe that his conception of man as an active being is similar to Fichte's theory of the self. It is to Marx's view that I shall now turn.

CHAPTER 3

PHILOSOPHY AND POLITICAL

ECONOMY: MARXIAN THEORY

OF MAN

M Y intention in this chapter is to outline Marx's concept of activity. Since in Marx's thought, as in Fichte's, the concept of activity is inseparable from a related concept of man, the discussion will concentrate on Marx's understanding of man as an active being. Although little attention has been directed to Marx's grasp of activity, his view of man and his thought as a whole are the topic of an already vast and rapidly growing literature. It is clear then that one cannot hope to offer a definitive discussion of the Marxian position or even an aspect of it in relatively brief compass. Accordingly, my aim here, as in the preceding chapter on Fichte, will be neither to give a complete interpretation of Marx's thought, nor to discuss all the relevant literature, although it cannot be ignored. On the contrary, I shall limit myself to providing a preliminary exposition of the main lines of Marx's view of man as an active being within the context of his wider position in order to permit further discussion.

The present discussion can be related to the recent debate concerning Marx's view of man. Following the belated publication of certain of Marx's most important theoretical writings, in recent years there has been renewed interest in his understanding of human being. This interest has given rise to a three-cornered controversy. One side is represented by those who hold that Marx's early, so-called humanist phase was definitely superseded in his mature view. The protagonists of this interpretation are Althusser and his followers as well as some Eastern bloc philosophers, mainly in the Soviet Union. Against this tendency, Sartre has argued that Marx in fact has no theory of the individual and his position is hence in danger of collapse because of this lack. In disagreement with Sartre, Schaff has countered that there is a view of man implicit in Marx's position, but that it needs to be reconstructed and further developed.

My purpose in mentioning this debate is not to take steps to adjudicate it. Let me merely note that at the present time the evidence seems to be mounting in favor of the thesis that there is a continuity in Marx's early and later writings, and against the belief that there is a demonstrable discontinuity. A particularly forceful argument for the so-called continuity thesis has been recently made by Henry.[1] Although my sympathies for the most part lie both with the so-called humanist approach and with Schaff's concern to provide a viable retrospective reconstruction of the Marxian concept of man, I would like to differentiate the present discussion from either of these goals. My interest here is neither to defend portions of Marx's corpus against his other writings, nor to extend his view beyond the point at which he left it, nor, I might add, to understand it solely in terms of itself. Rather, I shall try to understand Marx's view of man in the wider setting of his overall position, and the position in the context of German philosophy. Although it would be foolish to argue that Marx's view does not develop over time, my basic contention is that there is a single theory in terms of which the early, more philosophical, and later, more economic writings can be understood as complementary phases of one and the same position. I would further like to suggest that central to this theory is a view of man as an active being comparable to the Fichtean view already discussed.

A good place to begin is by an indication of certain problems that arise in the discussion of Marx's position. Marx was apparently a slow and painstaking writer, who constantly revised and elaborated. Since he was rarely satisfied by anything he wrote, many of the texts we now have were never brought to finished form and fewer still were actually published by Marx. We further know that Marx quickly abandoned his early goal of an academic career, a fact which suggests that he may have felt no need to produce highly polished specimens of academic prose. Indeed, his writings lack the form customary for academic publications. As if this were not enough, it further often seems that Marx has simply not made up his mind on various questions, with respect to which he on occasion holds two or more demonstrably distinguishable views. In fact, the claim has recently been made that any given interpretation of Marx's thought can immediately be refuted by citing Marx's own writings.[2]

In view of these and other interpretative difficulties, if one is concerned to understand Marx's position, and not merely to proclaim its truth, a certain amount of retrospective reconstruction, quite unlike that necessary for Fichte, is essential.[3] In the latter case, to be sure, the concept of man needs to be elucidated from its position in the midst of Fichte's theory. But the theory itself is present in a highly developed, systematic form. Yet in the case of Marx, even the general outlines of the overall theory are subject to dispute. It follows that in the course of an interpretation of his understanding of man, texts which were often not destined for publication and ideas which were not fully developed or on occasion are merely implicit need to be assembled in a single position, whose coherence is a function of the variant readings which simply cannot be avoided at many points in Marx's position.

Perhaps in part because of the difficulty presented by the interpretation of Marx's writings, a frequent ploy has been to appeal to Engels. The two are often regarded as in effect a single personality, which presents the advantage of being able to interpret Marx's doctrine through Engels's writings. This ploy is useful, for where Marx is often hesitant and unclear, Engels is much the bolder writer, and is rarely encumbered by doubt. The justification for this practice is of course the intellectual companionship between Marx and Engels extending over some four decades. Engels further tended to portray himself as the official interpreter of his friend's position, and he has been often confirmed in that role by official organs of various East European communist parties. Thus, it should not be surprising that even serious academic interpreters of Marx's ideas often rely on Engels as a primary source.[4]

But to the extent that one is interested in Marx and not Marxism, none of these arguments is sufficient to justify a preference for Engels's writings over those of Marx. Indeed, the opposite seems clearly the case. Of course, a possible reason would be the absence of Marx's writings, but in fact we possess them in profusion. Further, there are demonstrable and important differences in Marx's and Engels's views.[5] With respect to philosophical background, this is easy to understand, for although Marx held a doctorate in philosophy, Engels's formal education stopped at the *Gymnasium*. And despite the fact that he was a gifted autodidact, a certain lack of philosophical sophistication is ever present in his thought. An example is his attempt late in life to extend dialectic to nature. So although it seems entirely feasible to attend to Engels as a source of information regarding Marx's interests, current reading, and possible intentions, and as an important influence on the development of his friend's ideas, it is essential to rely on Marx's own voluminous writings as the source of his position and ultimate test of its interpretation.

Since the present aim is to reconstruct Marx's view of man in the setting of his wider position, a good place to start may be by indicating his understanding of theory. Every position, even if often only on an implicit level, presupposes a theoretical paradigm. The kind of paradigm with which Marx operates can perhaps best be perceived through mention of his relation to the Young Hegelians, especially to Feuerbach.

One of Feuerbach's basic interests was to relate abstract, philosophic thought to life. One of his main points was the belief that the task for the philosophy of the future, which he opposes to the reigning speculative philosophy, is that of "pulling philosophy down from the divine, self-sufficient bliss in the realm of ideas into human misery." [6] In the attempt to relate philosophy and life, criticism has a fundamental role to play, for it is the tool by which we can become aware of the rightful place of man. Feuerbach was especially concerned to demonstrate this point in the sphere of religion. He developed it at length in a famous book, the *Essence of Christianity*. This work, which appeared in 1841, had an important effect in intellectual circles, where it was widely regarded as the definitive statement, which at least for the present generation brought to a close the criticism of religion begun by the publication in 1835 of David Strauss's massive two-volume *Das Leben Jesu*. Whereas Strauss was content to attempt to undermine the authority of the gospels, Feuerbach tries to show, well before Freud, that religion is no more than an idealized projection of man by man.

Although Feuerbach regards criticism as an essential tool to reform philosophy, it would be a mistake, despite his aphorism that his own philosophy is not philosophy, to consider that he transcends philosophy *schlechthin*. Rather, in his own mind, although he transcends a particular kind of philosophy, that is, its Hegelianized form, he remains a philosopher.

It is not difficult to discern a similar attitude in Marx's early writings. In his early writings Marx, like Feuerbach, is concerned mainly to restrict philosophy to its proper task, which he views as the criticism of the existing state of affairs, as opposed to its further employment in the service of speculative metaphysics. In particular, following upon the heels of Feuerbach's analysis of religion, Marx maintains that philosophy should reveal all forms of human self-alienation. "The immediate *task of philosophy*, which is in the service of history, is to unmask human self-alienation in its *secular form* now that it has been unmasked in its *sacred form*." [7] Indeed, in the Introduction to the *Contribution to the Critique of Hegel's Philosophy of Right*, Marx claims to be attempting just this kind of contribution. Referring to the need to unmask self-alienation, he writes, "The following exposition . . . is a contribution to this undertaking." [8]

Although philosophers frequently assert the relation of their thought to the external world, they rarely indulge in empirical discussion. On the contrary, Marx's writings are filled with concrete analyses rare in the philosophical literature, so much so that on occasion they may seem to be entirely unrelated to philosophy, a point of view which has often been expressed. This impression is fostered by occasional statements of Marx. For instance, in the Preface to the *Paris Manuscripts* he remarks that "my conclusions are the fruit of an entirely empirical analysis." [9] Yet if this is manifestly an inaccurate description of the *Manuscripts* taken as a whole, empirical material abounds there as in later texts.

Although Marx apparently accepts the need for critical engagement with social reality, he finds unacceptable the presumption, widely current among his Young Hegelian contemporaries that mere criticism suffices to bring about social change. This latter view is perhaps most visible in the writings of Bruno Bauer, who explicitly maintains that if we take care of criticism, history will take care of the rest. [10] This perspective amounts, in effect, to an apparently unwarranted optimism that the Idea, if somehow it can be brought to consciousness, can take care of its own realization in history. Marx, however, apparently rejects this supposition in the last and most famous of the "Theses on Feuerbach" when he writes, "The philosophers have only *interpreted* the world, in various ways: the point is to *change* it." [11] But it should be noted that this proclamation would seem to be directed as much, and perhaps more, against the understanding of criticism in Young Hegelian circles as it is against previous philosophy. For it is obvious that interpretation itself is usually, although by no means always, insufficient to alter social conditions, even if it may sometimes suffice to alter our understanding of them.

If we now attempt to sum up what has been said with respect to Marx's reaction to his Young Hegelian contemporaries, we can see that, in a first approximation, Marx's understanding of theory has two moments. To begin with, Marx retains the critical attitude of his contemporaries in two areas. He is critical of contemporary thought, including the Hegelian philosophy and the implicit quietism of the Young Hegelians, and critical also of contemporary social reality. But it would, I think, be an error to assume that by virtue of his critical attitude toward some forms of philosophy Marx is opposed to philosophy as such. As he himself notes, "In short, you cannot abolish philosophy without realizing it." [12] Second, if mere criticism is of itself inadequate to effect a change in social reality, then a further dimension to the theory is necessary which will show how the corrections are to be carried out.

The latter point separates Marx from his Young Hegelian contemporaries. Although Marx shares with them a critical interest in the human condition, he carries the criticism into another realm in his discussion of the economic dimension of society, a dimension that is largely lacking in the writings of the Young Hegelians, although not in Hegel. To be sure, in this respect Marx's view is not altogether dissimilar from the kind of critical analysis that Feuerbach, for instance, had attempted. What is different is that alone of all these thinkers Marx feels compelled to supplement the critical side of the theory, that is, the conceptual analysis of contemporary social reality in terms of an implicit model for man's full and free development in a social context, by a further analysis of how this can in fact be brought about. Achievement of this goal, as opposed to mere theoretical analysis, requires a precise discussion of real possibilities in terms of prevailing social conditions. As Marx puts the problem in a letter, "True theory must be clarified and developed within concrete situations and prevailing relations." [13] But it is in his refusal to be satisfied with mere criticism and his desire to understand the real possibility of a practical utilization of his criticism in order to ameliorate social reality that Marx's intent and position are unlike most and perhaps all others in the post-Hegelian tradition.

THEORY OF MAN

Although unanimity is not to be found in any phase of the Marx discussion, the account so far is relatively uncontroversial. But as has already been mentioned, a major controversy surrounds the problem of man in relation to Marx's thought. In part for this reason, discussions of Marx's position frequently begin with his critique of capitalism. Nevertheless, it seems preferable and indeed necessary to start with his view of man, both for chronological reasons, since this latter view is already apparent in the earlier writings which precede the mature economic discussion, but also for a logical reason. For if, as seems to be the case even in later writings such as *Capital*, Marx's aim is to expose man's social alienation and to strive for its correction, a concept of man is necessary as the standard by which present society is to be judged. This is a concept of man as he could be, if and when the necessary preconditions are met. It follows that even in the most "objective" moments of Marx's analysis of the evils of capitalism as he sees it, his position in fact and necessarily presupposes a normative concept of human being, which is, then, central to his position.

The claim that in Marx's position both normative and factual aspects are interrelated is highly controversial. The relation of Marx's view of man to his position as a whole, especially to his critique of capitalism, is not widely understood and the claim for a relationship of this kind has often been disputed. It has been frequently argued that the Marxian views of capitalism and political economy in general are independent of the philosophical trappings which a view of man might suggest, since otherwise Marxian political economy would be philosophy.[14] It has further been argued that since Marxian political economy is science, the concept of man is foreign to and in fact opposed to it.[15] But the possible consequence of a reason is not a ground for rejecting it with respect to the analysis of a given position. By the same token, merely because a particular conception of political economy as "science" does not include a concept of man is not an argument for the fact that this is not true for the Marxian position. Indeed, as we shall presently see, there is in fact a view of man in Marx's thought from which his view of political economy can be developed.

Marx is himself largely responsible for the confusion regarding the role of man in his wider position. In the first place, he never explicitly formulates a theory of human being, although on inspection such a theory would seem to be plainly present, at least implicitly, in many of his writings. On the contrary, he sometimes goes to great lengths to divorce his position from any philosophical view at all by stressing the empirical side of his position, as mentioned above. But since Marx's thought is never solely empirical, one may speculate that the reason behind this emphasis is his desire to dissociate his own thought from that of thinkers such as Feuerbach, who constantly proclaim their interest in man, but disregard concrete analysis of historical reality in favor of what, in Marx's opinion, can be no more than flights of theoretical fancy. But the fact remains that if Marx's thought is approached solely through the empirical side, one cannot grasp the point of view from which the empirical discussion develops and which alone gives it meaning.

In part the genesis of Marx's understanding of man can be seen in his reaction to Hegel. Although it is a serious mistake to view Marx's thought merely in terms of its relation to the speculative system, it must be conceded that his attempt to come to grips with Hegel's thought provided both the starting point of his own position and a number of ideas which are more familiar in their Marxian restatement. Marx's immediate goal in his criticism of the Hegelian system seems to be to restore human being to its rightful place as the central causal factor in human history. This restoration has three aspects. To begin with, the absence of an acceptable understanding of man's role in the historical process must be singled out in the Hegelian position. Following this, an appropriate concept must be advanced to fill the need perceived in the Hegelian discussion. It must further be shown that the role which in Hegel's thought is attributed to other factors, especially to the absolute spirit, is in fact played by man.

But although the immediate genesis of Marx's view of man is to be found in his reaction to problems perceived in Hegel's philosophy, it should be stressed that his own concept of man remains indebted to Hegel's discussion at several crucial points. This indebtedness is underlined by Engels, who notes that in his study of Hegel's *Philosophy of Right* Marx for the first time was able to perceive that the sphere of bourgeois society offers the key for the understanding of man's historical development.[16]

Although Marx remains heavily influenced by Hegel, the relation of his understanding of man to Hegel's is ambivalent. To be sure, Marx adopts many of the points present in Hegel's analysis of bourgeois society, especially in the discussion entitled "System of Needs" (*Philosophy of Right*, pars. 189–208). Marx, for instance, follows Hegel's insistence here on the fundamental importance of man's mediation of his reproductive needs through work, as well as the suggestion that the anatomy of bourgeois society should be approached through the science of political economy. Since Hegel emphasizes the politico-economic approach to human productive activity, in a sense it is even permissible to state that the Marxian view of man remains basically Hegelian in inspiration and specific doctrine. This is so even if it must be conceded that Marx carries the original theory, especially in its economic aspect, well beyond the point at which Hegel left it, which is indeed the case. But in another sense Marx's view of man is un-Hegelian. Since Marx in part develops his view in opposition to Hegel's overriding concept of the absolute, the result is to explode the Hegelian synthesis from inside his own position by emphasizing one phase of the view against the whole.

The outline of Marx's theory of man can be sketched through a series of dichotomies. Experience teaches us that man has a double character, through which he belongs simultaneously to the realms of nature and society. As a natural being, man depends upon his relation to nature for the satisfaction of his natural needs. As a social being, man lives and functions in society with other men. Any attempt to consider man apart from either his natural or social contexts presupposes each of them as its point of reference. Since the natural world provides man with the context of all life and the material required to sustain it, and the social setting provides a locus in which men strive together to meet their respective requirements on a collective basis, both realms are united through the concept of need.[17]

Human needs can be further divided into two classes. The more basic are the reproductive, or subsistence, needs, which must be met if the individual is to continue to exist as a physical being and if he is to continue to be able to meet his needs. Such needs, for instance hunger, are not peculiar to man, but are common to all living beings. What is specifically human is the manner in which men respond to their basic needs, through the production of "their own means of subsistence," which is, according to Marx, "the act by which they distinguish themselves from animals."[18]

Human needs are immediately less vital, but in the long run more important than reproductive needs. Unlike the former, whose satisfaction is not in itself a goal, the satisfaction of human needs is an end in itself and not the means to another end. Just as human social existence assumes different forms at different historical moments, so the precise form of human needs as well as their possible satisfaction is a historical variable. But what is invariable is that man has desires which transcend his simple subsistence in the direction of full individual development. In this way, we are each of us like the "wealthy man who *needs* a complex of human manifestations of life, and whose own self-realization exists as an inner necessity, a need."[19] It should further be noted that in a real sense the drive to meet human needs, which transcend the requirements of continued physical existence, is one of the central forces of human history.

The concept of need points beyond the present by relating the realization of man's desires to history. If man has real needs whose satisfaction is possible, he must also possess corresponding real potentials. In the first place, there must be a potential, common to all human beings, to meet reproductive needs. This potential in fact exists, since it is actualized daily in numerous ways. But in another sense, it is only gradually brought to actuality in the course of man's increasing domination over his natural environment. By the same token, there must be a potential for human needs, a capacity which Marx sometimes refers to by the term "species-being" (*Gattungswesen*) or the associated term "species-life" (*Gattungsleben*). It is further a fundamental tenet of Marxian theory that in capitalism human needs cannot be met either individually or collectively, but that they will be able to be satisfied in communism This suggests an additional potential, or the capacity of mankind to develop beyond the stage of capitalism, in which the person can do no more than meet his reproductive needs, to communism, in which man will be able to meet his human needs. For it is only in this stage that full human individuality, whose manifestation Marx understands as the terminal point of natural history and the precondition of human history, will become a real possibility.

A comment should be made about species-being, since this concept is controversial.[20] Marx takes over the term and the related concept from Feuerbach. In the *Essence of Christianity* Feuerbach employs the term "species-being" to designate a kind of consciousness supposedly peculiar to man, to wit, an awareness of his kinship with other members of the same species. Feuerbach's argument here reflects the belief, widespread as early as the late eighteenth century, that self-consciousness is man's distinguishing trait. In Feuerbach's writings this term has the double meaning of essential characteristic and intrinsic potential.

In his early writings, Marx apparently adopts both meanings of the Feuerbachian term in uncritical fashion. At this stage, the term occupies a prominent place in his discussion of alienation. But in the sixth "Thesis on Feuerbach" Marx objects that "human essence is no abstraction inherent in each individual. In its reality it is the ensemble of social relations."[21] This statement, coupled with the absence of the term in Marx's later writings, has sometimes been seen as evidence that he abandons this concept as his theory develops.

Although Marx did in fact abandon the term "species-being," it seems questionable that he could relinquish the concept for which it stands. To be sure, Marx quickly unburdens himself of the idea that consciousness is in itself a distinguishing human trait. This should not be surprising, since it would have been inconsistent to champion a theory of false consciousness, as Marx does in the *German Ideology*, and put much faith in individual awareness. Indeed, in the same work Marx notes that it is not in fact consciousness which distinguishes man from animals, but the production of his means of subsistence. But it is important to emphasize that it does not therefore follow that Marx rejects the idea that there is a distinguishing human characteristic. Rather, in effect this is to substitute one such criterion for another. It is hence in character when Marx returns to the concept of human essence in *Capital*, where in the context of a note on Bentham he comments on the need to distinguish between "human nature in general" and as "modified in each historical epoch." [22] The immediate effect of this passage is to reaffirm Marx's reliance on the concept of specific human potential. Indeed, he cannot do otherwise, for the price of the suggested renunciation of the concept of species-being would be to abandon the idea which in his position is meant to justify the possibility of individual human development as a historical goal, something which Marx is of course loath to do.

SOCIAL RELATIONS AND ACTIVITY

The mediation of needs and potentials in the context of society and nature is provided through a theory of activity. Marx underlines the sense in which, as an active being, man literally is his activity when he writes, "My *own existence* is a social activity." [23] In Marx's writings, activity is teleological, quasi-physical, and productive. Special attention is devoted to the latter aspect, especially as it relates to the physical process of production within the confines of the economic structure of society. Marx's argument is that since the form of activity possible at a given time is a function of the kind of society in which it occurs, the structure of the economic process is crucial in determining the way in which man relates to others and to his natural world. Marx further stresses the concept of agency, since whether a given person is himself the agent of or responsible for his activity is not unrelated to the social role he assumes. Further, through his occasional evocation of the concept of historical inevitability, Marx at least implies that history possesses a suprapersonal dialectic. The development of this dialectic comes to light in human activity, but the dialectic itself is beyond conscious human control.

The relation between human activity and society is mediated by social relations. Marx's understanding of this concept is general. "By social relations we understand the cooperation of several individuals, no matter under what conditions, in what manner and to what end." [24] The generality of Marx's definition enables him to attribute to this concept a wide range of functions. To begin with, social relations are produced and reproduced in each human social act. Since whatever I do is inevitably performed either directly with or in reference to others, my every move is in effect the constitution or reconstitution of my relations to them. Otherwise stated, either my social activity results in the generation of relations of one kind or another between myself and others or, if these relations already exist, the result of activity within an already defined social context is to regenerate the social relations by which it is defined. It follows that there is a dependence of social relations on the prior manifestation of activity. On the other hand, such relations provide a fixed locus for one's activity. For by virtue of their existence, an element of stability is introduced into social situations, which channels the ways in which individuals act and hence the manner in which they can and do interact. Accordingly, a person is defined by the kind of activity in which he engages, both as such and in relation to other people.

Marx further attaches special importance to the "economic factor" in social relations. The reason is simply that it is imperative to meet one's subsistence needs above all else. In normal circumstances, unless one has aspirations to martyrdom, if a choice presents itself, continued physical existence is that interest which takes precedence over any other. Thus for most of us the economic form of social relations assumes an overriding importance in our daily lives. Indeed, Marx carries the argument one step further, when he argues that awareness itself is largely determined by the need of individuals to provide for material subsistence. Hence, he is consistent when he remarks with respect to his own theory that "it does not explain practice from the idea but explains the formation of ideas from material practice." [25]

In Marx's view, society is nothing other than a dynamic ensemble of social relations. It has been pointed out that his approach here presupposes the Hegelian category of the whole, or totality, as the general concept for the analysis of a social complex. [26] The immediate advantage of this category for Marx is that it enables him to emphasize, against the possibility of the reductionism, functional interrelation of the various social relations within the unity of society, instead of being restricted to approaching it through isolated analyses of its structural elements. For although society as a whole can and must be understood in terms of the relations which compose it, it cannot be reduced to a mere sum of its parts. On the contrary, it can only be understood through their interaction.

The argument thus far has been perfectly general in that nothing has been said about the kind of society in which we live. The discussion to this point hence applies to all forms of social context. But the relation between activity and society is asymmetrical. For although society "rests" on human activity, the form in which activity can appear is restricted by the form of the social context. Now bourgeois society is characterized by private ownership of the means of production. In what is doubtless one of his most important arguments, Marx attempts to assess the effect of the form of distribution of the means of production on social life through a theory of alienation.

ALIENATION

Marx states his theory of alienation in a single, dense passage in the early, more philosophical *Paris Manuscripts*, although it would seem to be presupposed also in the later, more economic writings. The discussion, which is difficult, by no means answers all the questions which have been raised about it. Indeed, it has given rise to a specialized literature concerned merely with this facet of Marx's thought.[27] Although a full analysis of this concept would need to consider the literature about it, such reference does not seem indispensable in regard to the rapid outline of Marx's view of alienation to be given here. In simplest terms, Marx's point is that in capitalism man is able to meet his subsistence needs only, but is deprived of the possibility to satisfy his human needs.

The terminology of Marx's discussion of alienation presupposes a distinction between objectification (*Entäusserung*) and alienation (*Entfremdung*). *Entäusserung* refers to externalization, presumably of the worker in the form of the product. If I physically make something, my activity can be said to be "concretized" or "objectified" in the physical object which results from the productive process. Objectification gives rise to a physical separation between the human being and an object external to him. *Entfremdung* refers not to objectification, but rather to making "foreign" or "estranged" and hence "alien" to the person. In certain circumstances, to be specified, objectification is accompanied by a further, nonphysical separation which occurs between a person and his real capacity to satisfy human needs. This latter separation, which constitutes alienation, presupposes objectification as a necessary condition, although not all objectification gives rise to alienation.

The outlines of Marx's theory of alienation, as stated in the

Paris Manuscripts, can now be sketched. In view of the difficulty of Marx's discussion, it seems advisable to remain close to the text. Marx distinguishes four related forms of alienation. He begins with a consideration of alienation of the worker from the product of his work. As already mentioned, the product is separated from the worker in both a physical sense, in which it is external to him, and in a nonphysical sense, in which it is alien to his self-development. Marx develops the consequence of this form of alienation on the several planes of the object, the work itself, and the worker as a human being. According to Marx, the worker experiences his alienation as a vitiation, in which his life-activity is drained in the formation of the object; as a loss, in that the "crystallization" of his activity is taken from him; and as a servitude, in that the worker is controlled in his alienated activity by the object. In sum, in a manner which recalls Feuerbach's so-called transformative criticism, Marx points out that in alienated productive activity a subject-object reversal occurs as a result of which the worker is controlled by and hence passive in respect to the product.

Marx further maintains that the worker is alienated from his productive activity. He obscurely comments that work is in a sense "external" to the worker and foreign to his nature. He seems to mean that the work itself is not a possible vehicle for the development of man's human characteristics referred to by the term "species-being," but is rather forced on the person by the requirement to respond to his minimal, or subsistence, needs. Marx further observes that the worker is not freely active in his productive activity, but only in his "animal functions," such as "eating, drinking, and procreating, or at most also in his dwelling and personal adornment." [28] Hence, Marx can claim that in the alienation of the worker from the process of production he is reduced to the level of an animal whose activity sustains its physical existence, but is useless with respect to the satisfaction of further specifically human needs.

From the two types of alienation discussed so far, Marx infers that the worker is alienated from his species-life. The possibility of manifesting one's species-life in one's activity is blocked by the alienation of the worker both from the product and the productive process. In consequence, work activity merely represents a way to satisfy survival needs, which Marx describes as "a *means* for his *individual existence*." [29] Marx further maintains that the result of this form of alienation is to reduce man to a being alien to himself. As he notes, the individual is alienated from his body, from external nature, from his mental life, and from human life in general. The significance of this point is that each of the "things" from which the person is alienated would normally represent a possible means for man to satisfy human desires above and beyond mere subsistence needs.

In terms of the first three forms of alienation, Marx goes on to argue that man is alienated from other men. The argument here is based on a schematically stated view of capitalism which will later be developed at length. As stated here, Marx's point is that in this form of society there is a broad class division depending on the relation to the means of production. In an argument that echoes Kant's insistence on human being as an end not a means, Marx maintains that from the perspective of the owner of the means of production, the worker represents no more than a potential source of profit, not a human being valuable as an end in himself. In the same way, even within the working class, people tend to relate to one another as expendable units in the productive process, but not as real human beings. The result is a generalized estrangement in all human relations.

Although some have viewed the Marxian concept of alienation as a brilliant achievement, indeed the centerpiece of his theory, it has not always been perceived even as worthy of a permanent role in Marx's thought. Now on a purely linguistic level, this contention is contradicted by the fact that Marx continues to employ substantially the same technical vocabulary utilized for the discussion of alienation throughout his later writings.[30] There is further a conceptual point to be made, through reference to the concept of fetishism.

Although the only full description of Marx's theory of fetishism under that name occurs in *Capital*, there are scattered references to the concept in the writings which lead up to that work.[31] The concept of fetishism further needs to be understood in relation to the concept of alienation. As already mentioned, in the discussion in the *Paris Manuscripts* of the fourth form of alienation Marx points out that in capitalism individuals are estranged from each other by virtue of the private ownership of the means of production. In *Capital* he goes on to argue that personal interaction is in general mediated by products, which come between and make possible the relation between individuals. He remarks that those who consider products will observe that "there is a definite social relation between men that assumes . . . the fantastic form of a relation between things."[32] Accordingly, the commodity tends to usurp man's social role even as it assumes a mysterious social character.

One need only compare the discussions of alienation and fetishism to notice the change in perspective. In the former analysis Marx is concerned with the effect of capitalism on human being, whereas in the latter he is concerned with the effect of capitalism on the object. But the change in perspective should not obscure the basic similarity of the two analyses. For in capitalism commodities can only assume the social role reserved for people because the latter are in effect reduced to the status of mere thinghood. In other words, the theories of alienation and fetishism are two elements in the more general, quasi-Feuerbachian argument that in capitalism there is a role reversal, or transformation of the "natural" relation between man, his world, and other men, as a result of which subject and object tend to switch places as each takes on the characteristics and role usually associated with the other.

MARXIAN POLITICAL ECONOMY

The major emphasis in the exposition of Marx's position has so far been on the early writings, whose distinctly philosophic flavor is recognized by most commentators. Although political economy plays a role in Marx's thought as early as the *Paris Manuscripts*, in his later writings he increasingly orients his thought in this direction. For this reason, it has sometimes been argued that there is a hiatus, or radical discontinuity, between the early "philosophic" and the mature "economic" sides of Marx's position. In one version of this argument, which has been debated extensively in recent years, Marx is said to have later developed an entirely new position, which first appears in the *German Ideology* (1845–46), whose main theses are different in kind from his earlier views. Although it is conceded that the early writings are basically philosophical, proponents of this reading of Marx urge that his later position is scientific.[33] Against this interpretation, others have argued that a discontinuity cannot be demonstrated, and a strong case has been made for the *Grundrisse* as a bridge between the early and late works.[34] It has further been noted that most if not all of the doctrines supposedly typical of the later period are already present in the early attempts to come to grips with Hegel.[35]

But although the discussion which tends to demonstrate the continuity in Marx's position is helpful, the shift in emphasis needs to be explained. I believe that this shift can be attributed to the logic of Marx's position. I have suggested above that Marx's attention is primarily directed toward the real possibility of human social development and that in his view man is defined by the ensemble of his social relations. I have further suggested that the central importance of the economic dimension of man's social context follows from Marx's implicit distinction between human and subsistence forms of need. If these points are accepted, it would seem that the next step in the elaboration of the position is to formulate a theory of contemporary society, or capitalism, in order to grasp the general nature of the present social context and the real possibility of its transformation. It follows that Marx's own politico-economic theory of capitalism is continuous with and a further development of his earlier philosophical anthropology.

The general theory of capitalism plays a double role within Marx's wider view. In an obvious sense, if man is defined by his social relations, an analysis of the social context can contribute to a more profound understanding of man. From this perspective, there is a sense in which Marx, like the Plato of the *Republic*, can be said to attempt to view the state as man writ large. Marx further preserves the Platonic interest in bringing about the kind of social context in which each man will perform those tasks which best correspond to his innate capacities. But it should not be overlooked that, whereas Plato offers a theory of the best possible state, in the first instance Marx, as does Aristotle, limits himself to an account of the present form of society. Yet to a greater extent than either of his Greek predecessors, Marx is oriented toward changing a form of society which, in his view, is unjust for reasons which depend ultimately on contingent economic factors. Hence, another reason to formulate a theory of capitalism is to inquire under what conditions the present form of society can be advantageously transformed. To put the same point in Hegelian terminology, although capitalism is the negation of man, it may yet give rise to its own negation in a further social form more congenial to human development, in terms of which the present stage is a necessary condition. But from the Marxian perspective, if the real possibility of social transformation is to be grasped, it must be understood on the level of concrete social reality, and not only on the level of abstract thought.

In his analysis of capitalism, following Hegel, Marx distinguishes between the political state, and bourgeois or civil society. The immediate aim of Marxian political economy is to determine the anatomy of bourgeois society. But since civil society is only that state of economic evolution which corresponds to private ownership of the means of production, a general theory of capitalism is necessary. In Marx's writings, this task assumed the dimensions of a lifelong project, whose size steadily increased and whose completion continually receded into the future. Judged by the intention outlined in the *Grundrisse*, the published portion of *Capital* (which has been called Marx's unfinished masterpiece), and the thousands of pages of additional material left behind at Marx's death represent no more than a fraction of his initial project.[36] Accordingly, instead of a completed theory, we possess only a series of partially complete expositions of an ever more-detailed, but never fully stated view.

Although some of the doctrines characteristic of Marx's later, more economic writings are to be found as early as the *Paris Manuscripts*, the first indication that Marx's economic studies were to result in a major politico-economic theory was not given prior to the controversy with Proudhon, in which Marx submitted the latter's economic views to scathing criticism. A decade later Marx was ready to advance the outlines of his own theory in the form of a more than eight-hundred-page manuscript, the *Grundrisse* (1857–58), whose full text was published for the first time in a nearly inaccessible, wartime edition in Moscow during the years 1939–41. A restatement of a portion of that theory reappeared in the following year as the *Critique of Political Economy* (1859), and a newly revised and amplified version was later to become *Capital*, whose first volume was published in 1867.

Marx's analysis of capitalism, which is inseparable from his own theory of political economy, has been subjected to extensive discussion in a specialized literature.[37] It is beyond the scope of the present inquiry to provide either a full exposition or a detailed analysis of Marxian political economy. But I do wish to comment on selected aspects of the Marxian politico-economic theory of capitalism as it relates to the earlier writings in order to demonstrate the essential unity in the philosophic and economic dimensions of Marx's overall theory.

Although the position itself underwent extensive modification in the course of Marx's further study, a constant concern was to view society as a whole in terms of its economic structure. Following Engels, Marx's basic procedure seems to be to make use of previously available economic categories, appropriated from the writings of classical political economy, in order to reach different conclusions. This is not of course to imply that Marx does not introduce new concepts of his own, but rather to indicate that much of the originality of his discussion consists in an attempt either to refute or at least to rethink the conclusions of classical political economy by a reexamination of its own arguments in terms of its own concepts.

Marx makes conscious use of this tactic as early as the *Paris*

Manuscripts, where he writes, "From political economy itself, its own words, we have shown that the worker sinks to the level of a commodity."[38] Here as elsewhere Marx's basic point seems to be that the optimism latent, for instance, in Adam Smith's doctrine of the invisible hand, which is, as has often been observed, a secular form of Leibniz's theologically optimistic belief that this is the best of all possible worlds, is unwarranted by study of the social context. Indeed, the increasingly empirical orientation of the older economic writings seems designed to show that the price of industrial progress is great and largely unsuspected human suffering.

A central aspect of Marx's political economy is the theory of the commodity. It is known that Marx believed the theory of the commodity to be his fundamental contribution to political economy. In both of the mature economic works published by him during his lifetime, Marx begins with commodity analysis, out of which he then "deduces" the remaining portions of his theory. A commodity is defined as any object produced for sale in the marketplace which results from a privately owned productive process and which, by means of its properties, satisfies some human need.[39] In general, commodities have qualitative and quantitative properties.[40] The qualitative property is the use value. The quantitative property is the exchange value, which in the final analysis can always be expressed in financial terms. The production and exchange of commodities is an inherently circular process which, from the perspective of the market can be represented by the formula C-M-C′, where the initial and final elements stand for commodity values and the mediating factor is money or, conversely, from the perspective of capital can be stated as M-C-M′, where the first and last elements stand for money and the mediating factor is the commodity. In either case, the circular process depicted in this formula represents the dual conditions of bourgeois society's continued existence and self-development. For, by this means capitalism produces and reproduces its own necessary conditions, while at the same time the constant interconversion between commodities and capital results in the augmentation of the latter through the accumulation of surplus value.

A distinctive feature of Marxian political economy is the attention devoted to the effect of a particular distribution of the means of production, especially the capitalist institution of private property, on well-being. Marx is constantly concerned, especially in the later, more economic writings, such as *Capital*, to supply the concrete details which are suggested by the earlier theory of alienation. If the means of production are privately owned, the worker exchanges his labor-power for an hourly wage which he applies toward his own needs and those of his family. In exchange, the capitalist receives a product which he sells in order to meet fixed expenses and to realize a profit. The latter is the difference between expenses of all kinds and the commodity's sale price. Now, according to the labor theory of value, the inherent worth of a commodity is a function of the labor-time necessary in its production. To the extent that the worker fails to receive full value for his work, he is exploited.[41]

Exploitation is not a contingent factor, but is constitutive of capitalism. Wages represent a variable part of the cost of production. In the theory of surplus value, profit is increased as variable costs are diminished. There is hence a divergence of interest between the worker, who furnishes the labor-power necessary for the productive process to function, and the capitalist, who owns the means of production. Simply put, according to this view society tends to divide itself into two classes as a consequence of the individual's position relative to the means of production, and this division of society along class lines results in either latent or overt class war, that is, a conflict inherent to capitalism in which worker and capitalist are pitted against each other. Just as the worker desires to increase his wages to the maximum extent consistent with the continued existence of the enterprise for which he works, so the owner of the means of production strives to reduce wages to the minimum level consistent with the continued physical existence of the worker. The owner is aided in this endeavor by the forces of the marketplace, which subordinate all extrafinancial values to the tendency to maximize capital, which tends to become a law unto itself. Accordingly, both for reasons relative to enlightened self-interest and the structure of a free market economy, worker exploitation is the unavoidable consequence of private ownership of the means of production.

Although the purpose of the present discussion is more expository than critical, I would like to point to one of the difficulties in Marx's analysis. He doubtless renders an important service through his insistence on the human toll exacted by the development of industrial potential through private ownership of the means of production. But implicit in the argument is the premise that if it were possible to eliminate the profit motive, for example, through the substitution of collective ownership of the means of production for private property, the situation would be basically transformed. Yet, if we apply the standard of real possibility with which Marx constantly operates in his own theory and in terms of which he criticizes others, an ambiguity arises. Since the growth of an economy depends on the generation of fresh capital for investment purposes, a positive difference between what a product brings on the open market and what it costs to produce must exist in order to avoid stasis and perhaps even economic collapse. The ambiguity concerns the kind of remedy that Marx has in mind. If his intention is to reduce profits in order to stem exploitation, even at the cost of a reduction in economic development, then he would seem to have a strong argument. Indeed, it has often been maintained that a beneficial change in the financial situation of the worker has beneficial consequences for the economy as a whole. But if Marx is merely equating profit with exploitation in order to suggest the simple elimination of the profit motive, then his argument should be resisted as inconsistent with capitalist or, it would seem, any other form of economic reality.

CAPITALISM AND COMMUNISM

Marx does more than merely strive to bare the anatomy of bourgeois society. He further goes on to argue that capitalism harbors an inherent structural flaw which will result in its eventual replacement by communism. His point is that by its nature the institution of private property, which renders capitalism possible, will finally undermine the continued existence of that form of society, since private property represents a permanent, increasing, and finally intolerable source of tension reflected throughout society. This tension, which tends to increase, will eventually result either in economic collapse, political revolution, or some combination of both. On the most basic level, there is the already-mentioned class contradiction between the self-interest of the proletariat and of the bourgeoisie. This contradiction can be restated as a conflict between the forces of production and the means of interaction, which Marx clearly regards as the key source of conflict in human history. "In our view all collisions of history have their origin in the contradiction between the productive forces and the form of interaction." [42]

These tensions continually increase as, for instance, the rate of profit tends to fall, wages decline, and the labor pool increases. In consequence, as the contradiction ripens over time it spawns a series of crises, until finally a cataclysmic crisis occurs which sounds the death knell of capitalism. It follows that in the long run the institution of private property tends to destroy the very society it has helped to bring about. Marx puts this point strongly in the *Manifesto*, when he writes: "What the bourgeoisie, therefore, produces, above all, is its own gravediggers. Its fall and the victory of the proletariat are equally inevitable."[43]

Marx's argument for the internal self-destruction of capitalism is by no means clear. Unclarity attaches, for example, to the time span in view. In a well-known passage, Marx writes that "no social order ever disappears before all the productive forces for which there is room in it have been developed."[44] But since we neither know what constitutes the full development of such forces nor the residual potential at capitalism's disposal at any given moment, it seems difficult to predict when, if ever, it will be forced from the world's stage. Indeed, the possibility must be faced that there is in fact no intrinsic limit to the development of capitalist productive forces, in which case the time span in view would by definition become infinite. Analogously, there has been considerable recent interest in the manner in which bourgeois society tends to shore up its own defenses by reducing internal tensions and hence stabilizing its existence.[45]

Another ambiguity concerns the force of Marx's claim. He on occasion seems to suggest that the demise of capitalism can be foreseen with absolute certainty. In the Preface to the first edition of *Capital*, he states that "it is a question of these laws themselves, of these tendencies working with iron necessity towards inevitable results."[46] This is the strongest possible claim that can be made. But at other times Marx seems to hedge his bets somewhat. Toward the end of the first volume of *Capital* he writes that "capitalist production begets, with the inexorability of a law of Nature, its own negation."[47] This is a substantially weaker claim, since natural laws concern events which occur normally unless they are prevented from taking place. If this is Marx's position, then the demise of capitalism is not at all inevitable, but only likely if nothing occurs to prevent it.

Communism will follow upon the heels of capitalism. The precondition of this change is the abolition of private ownership of the means of production, although not necessarily the abolition of private property as such. The details of the transition remain somewhat vague, since despite the Marxist concern for the relation of theory to praxis, Marx paradoxically displays little interest in such practical matters. But he intends that communism be preceded by a period of socialism, during which time political power would be exercised by a dictatorship of the proletariat.[48] Since Marx makes only a few scattered references to this concept, it is difficult to specify the proper interpretation of the term "dictatorship." But the argument has been made that Marx conceived of proletarian class dictatorship as a democratic government of the working class, which is, of course vastly different from the kind of government developed by Lenin and his heirs.[49]

Marx's view of the relation of capitalism and communism has obvious Hegelian overtones. As is well known, Hegel was fond of asserting that there are no gratuitous moments in historical development. In the same way, although critical of capitalism, Marx continues to view it as a blessing in disguise. Despite stressing the short-range trauma which is attendant upon private ownership of the means of production, Marx realistically affirms that from a long range perspective this stage of social development has an important role to play, as capitalism makes possible the development of the means of production to an extent not otherwise attainable.[50] Capitalism is hence a necessary condition of communism, since a stage in which unrestricted financial gain holds sway is the precondition of a later stage in which financial gain no longer motivates social activity.

The differences between capitalism and communism are, in Marx's eyes, fundamental. If the means of production are not privately owned, the profit motive disappears since it will cease to be possible to exploit workers through the extraction of surplus value from labor-power. This should not, of course, be taken to imply that efficiency becomes unimportant. On the contrary, it remains of importance to the extent that it has a socially useful role to play. But other motives, such as the effect of certain forms of work on human individuality, can be given equal billing and certain social practices, for example division of labor, can be eliminated or reduced to a necessary minimum in order to dissipate the constraints exercised on capitalism by the association between profit and the imperative of personal survival.

A thorny point in Marx's view is the relation between freedom and necessity in communism. Marx has been criticized for occasionally sounding as if he expected labor to be abolished in communism since there will no longer be a realm of necessity. In the third volume of *Capital* he writes that "the realm of freedom actually begins only where labor which is determined by necessity and mundane considerations ceases."[51] This passage and others like it have on occasion been taken as an indication of a residual utopianism in Marx's thought.[52] This is, I submit, a serious misreading of Marx's view. Admittedly Marx is sometimes inconsistent in his terminology, but he never confuses the activity necessary to respond to basic human needs and the form such activity takes by virtue of the historical epoch in which it occurs. Although it will continue to be necessary to meet one's needs, according to Marx, the advantage of communism is that the social organization through which this is to be accomplished can for the first time be given a form that is rational with respect to human development. Hence, in the same paragraph Marx continues on to remark that "freedom in this field can only consist in socialized man . . . rationally regulating their [sic] exchange with Nature."[53] In other words, the realm of necessity will be reconciled with freedom, since the form taken by activity within the productive process will be, to the extent consistent with the adequate function of the economic process, rendered socially inoffensive.

It seems clear that from the point of view of individual development, communism represents a significant social chance since a reduction in the division of labor makes possible increased flexibility in the average person's relation to the productive process. But it seems unlikely that division of labor can ever be entirely eliminated. For who would want his car fixed by a neurosurgeon, or his brain operated on by a garage mechanic? Yet specialization and the social immobility it induces can certainly be reduced. Further, Marx insists on the importance of free time made possible by shortening the length of the work day. He even goes so far as to identify free time and wealth in a posthumously published text when in his special mixture of English and German, he states that "free time, *disposable time*, ist der Reichtum selbst."[54] Of course, by wealth Marx means time free of external constraints, in which man can do as he will, and not monetary value. In sum, the intrinsic interest of communism is that man will supposedly be able to develop as a human being, or fully individual person, at the same time as he meets his basic needs.

The concept of individuality is further worth emphasizing, since there has been some confusion on this point. It has been argued that Marx's genius is to be able to transcend the standpoint of the mere individual, which is hence unimportant for his position.[55] Of course, in one sense the class perspective is essential in Marx's thought, but only because it is helpful in determining the conditions through which it can be sublated. For when communism comes on the scene, private ownership of the means of production, which generates this contradiction, will have disappeared. Yet it should be observed that the essential reason for which change in the prevailing form of society is desirable is to bring about the real possibility for the development of human individuality. In this respect, the abolition of society's class structure is not in itself a final goal, but only the means to a further end. For it is only when each man is fully himself and hence has fully developed his own individual potentials that he is a whole man. Hence, with communism in mind, Marx writes, "Man appropriates his manifold being in an all inclusive way, and thus as a whole man." [56]

This marks the end of my brief discussion of certain of the main ideas in Marx's position. As should be apparent, consideration of his position requires a precarious attempt to construct an only implicitly unified doctrine out of often seemingly disparate texts, many of which were not intended for publication and which further reflect frequent shifts of opinion. Yet as there is no generally recognized account of Marx's position, there is also no generally recognized interpretation of it. Any discussion, including the present one, is thus necessarily controversial. Accordingly, my aim has been less to provide a definitive statement or interpretation of Marx's position as a whole than to sketch, as already indicated, his understanding of the concept of man within it. I have sought to show that central to Marx's thought is the problem of how through his activity, man can develop his potentials as an individual within a social context. This problem relates both philosophical and economic aspects of the wider theory: the anthropological view of man as a self-developing social being; and the politico-economic analysis of why this is not now the case, but can become a real possibility, as man radically transforms the form of the social context in which he lives. Since, as we have seen, a similar view is also central to Fichte's position, grounds for a comparative discussion of the two views of man as an active being would seem to be present.

CHAPTER 4

ACTIVITY IN FICHTE

AND MARX

SINCE the discussion has so far disclosed that Fichte and Marx both understand man as an active being, the next step is to compare their views of activity. But for views to be comparable, there must be a common ground in terms of which they are related. Accordingly, although the usual tendency has been to regard the positions of Fichte and Marx as poles apart, and therefore bereft of a common ground, the task of this chapter will be to show that in fact such a ground exists and to begin the comparative analysis of their views of activity.

It seems important to specify the kind of comparison to be attempted. It is obvious that in many respects the positions in question are dissimilar, and as the discussion proceeds I shall call attention to certain of the differences between them. But merely because two positions are in certain respects unlike does not mean that in other, relevant ways they are not alike. Positions dissimilar on a given level can well be similar on a deeper plane. Thus although conventionality about the non-comparability of the positions of Fichte and Marx does not necessarily preclude an attempt to compare them on a deeper plane, an attempt of this kind should not be taken to imply that conventional wisdom is entirely in error. It should rather be taken as an indication that the widespread manner of regarding these two positions is limited to a certain level only.

Although the aim of this discussion is to open the way for a comparative analysis of the two views of activity, some additional consideration is necessary before it can be undertaken. It has been shown that a view of man as an active being is central to each of the two positions, but it would seem that neither Fichte nor Marx ever tries to formulate his own view of activity. Indeed, it would have been surprising if they had, since ideas fundamental to a position cannot be discussed in terms of the theory they sustain. But this is not a significant obstacle, for as we shall see it is not difficult to provide a retrospective reconstruction of the views of activity implicit in each position.

But even if the two views of activity can be retrospectively reconstructed, it is not obvious how they can be brought into meaningful relation. Although the concepts of activity are themselves similar, the distinctions within the respective concepts are not isomorphic. But as Fichte and Marx are by no means the only writers who relate activity to subjectivity, it seems probable that if we appeal to the philosophical tradition a third view, or tertium quid, can be found in terms of which the parallel between the two views can be analyzed. Now, although Aristotle's concept of activity has been little studied, it is one of the most important attempts in the entire tradition to understand human being from this perspective. Accordingly, in this chapter, after some preliminary discussion in order to define and establish the relevance of the Aristotelian view of activity for the present context, I shall make use of it to explore the parallel between Fichte's and Marx's own views of activity. I shall argue that they are comparable because each is in effect a reformulation of the Aristotelian concept, and I shall further suggest that in this manner a parallel as striking as it is unexpected can be brought out between them.

SECONDARY LITERATURE

As activity is an important and perhaps central theme in the history of philosophy, it is surprising that more attention has not been devoted to this idea. In particular, this concept has for the most part been overlooked in studies of the German tradition. I am further aware of only two brief attempts to compare Fichte's and Marx's positions in terms of this concept. In each case, the emphasis is on distinguishing views that are at best only superficially similar, but in each instance the argument seems unconvincing.

In a dissertation, Peter Coulmas has observed that both Fichte and Marx stress the role of work (*Arbeit*) as the foundation of social and individual well-being. Coulmas's discussion is useful in calling attention to work as a theme common to both positions, particularly so since Fichte's concept of work has received almost no notice. But it is difficult to follow Coulmas when he maintains that for Marx work is something which will unavoidably remain as a necessary evil, whereas for Fichte it can presumably be abolished.[1]

On the contrary, Fichte's *Vernunftsstaat* and Marx's concept of communism agree at least in the supposition that what now takes the form of unfulfilling drudgery can be converted into a different kind of activity. Both argue for the importance of the transformation of work into a more rewarding form of productive activity, and for the creation of free time apart from work. But neither holds that the productive activity, upon which continued biological existence rests, ought or can be abolished. Hence, one cannot subscribe to Coulmas's assertion that Fichte and Marx respectively represent positive and negative, and hence basically different, views of work.

More recently Jürgen Habermas has offered a comparative analysis of Fichte's and Marx's concepts of activity. In the context of an extended discussion of the course of modern philosophy, Habermas distinguishes two aspects in Marx's view of work: the relation of man to nature and the self-production of the species in history. His claim is that in the former respect Marx follows Kant, whereas in the latter respect Fichte's influence is apparent. He further claims that Marx's view of the self-production of the species "betrays the paradoxical consequence of taking Fichte's philosophy of the ego and undermining it with materialism." [2]

Habermas's interpretation of the relation of Marx to the philosophical tradition, and especially to Fichte's thought, is apparently based on the frequently invoked premise that in the elaboration of his position Fichte in effect denied a presupposition of Kant's epistemology concerning the non-identity of subject and object. This interpretation is presumably on loan from Hegel, who, beginning with the *Differenzschrift* (1801) and in subsequent writings, maintained that Fichte posits a primitive, subjective unity of subject and object as a condition of knowledge.[3] But this Fichte interpretation, both in its original Hegelian form or in its restatement by Habermas, is simply not faithful to the texts. For Fichte repeatedly stresses the givenness of the material world, which implies a fundamental distinction between subjectivity and objectivity. But if the recognition of a natural given is already present in Fichte's position, then it is difficult to understand how Marx's view can be the result of undermining Fichte's idealism with materialism.

Habermas's reading of Fichte's position, and thence of the relation between Fichte and Marx, needs to be corrected to conform to the texts. When the needed correction is applied to Habermas's interpretation, it results in a transformation of his view of the relation of Marx to the tradition. Rather than a materialistic revision, Marx's theory appears to be a restatement of the basic Fichtean point that through his activity the self or finite individual "generates" his world and himself. By the same token, if it is seen that

Fichte's position includes both a theory of the relation of man to the natural world as well as a theory of the self-creation of the human species in natural history, then the need to appeal to a Kantian source in the genesis of Marx's position disappears. Now, it is to be expected that Habermas would find this latter consequence difficult to accept, since it tends to undercut the distinction between Marx's position and the German tradition, which is presupposed in so much of the secondary literature, including Habermas's own writings. But it must be emphasized that when the details of Habermas's Fichte interpretation are corrected, a parallel between Fichte's thought and Marx's view becomes clearly visible.

ACTIVITY IN FICHTE AND MARX

In order to compare the respective implicit views of activity, the outlines of each must be reconstructed retrospectively. This merely requires us to develop further the discussion already begun in the preceding chapters. When this has been done, it will be possible to confront the two concepts. But as each develops in a different direction, the confrontation can do no more than demonstrate an anisomorphism.

Fichte distinguishes, as already mentioned, three kinds of activity: absolute activity, associated with the absolute self; and positing and striving, associated with the finite self. The former kind of activity, although necessary for the deduction of presentation, is not relevant to the present discussion. For its status is, as had already been shown, that of a philosophical fiction which is, hence, not to be viewed as a real capacity of human being in Fichte's view. It follows that, in Fichte's discussion, on the level of the individual two basic kinds of activity are distinguished.

Positing is an epistemological principle invoked to explain the possibility of knowledge. In Fichte's theory, the self's capacity to posit permits what he refers to as the "deduction of presentation." In simplest terms, the result of positing is that the self generates both self and not-self, subject and object of knowledge. Further, since by this means all that is, that is self and not-self, is "brought forth," it follows that the act of positing must be unlimited, for the occurrence of an activity through which the contents of consciousness arise cannot be limited by its results. More generally, as the cause of all limited situations, positing is not restricted by any situation.

As Fichte's acknowledged epistemological aim is to base the

possibility of knowledge on human activity, it seems reasonable to expect that his theory contain an interpretation of this activity in terms of human capabilities. But it is not clear how Fichte intends his concept to be interpreted. As specific guidance seems to be lacking, a useful procedure is to compare this concept to various mental processes, such as the imagination. Fichte tacitly encourages this analogy by the quasi-psychological terminology he often employs in texts later than the *WL*. For instance, in the *First Introduction to the Science of Knowledge* self is called intellect and activity is designated as reason.

To develop the analogy, positing is similar to imagination in that it can bring into being an object either completely *ex nihilo* or on the basis of prior experience. A further resemblance is that the not-self, or result of positing, "opposes" the activity of the self by which it has been brought into being in much the same manner as an imagined object on occasion "opposes" or "resists" the attempt to think it away. But positing purportedly leads to knowledge, while this is not necessarily the case for imagination. So at most positing may be thought of as akin to a single form of imagination, to wit, that kind which spontaneously occurs as the result of the interaction of man and world, and through which the individual acquires consciousness of his surroundings.

Another analogy, not inconsistent with the first one, has been suggested by Lask, who helpfully points to the analogy between positing and emanation.[4] To develop the suggestion, positing shares many of the characteristics traditionally associated in philosophy with divine activity. In Spinoza's view, for instance, God as *natura naturans* is understood as externally unlimited, self-developing, creative activity, whose manifestation is limited only by the internal necessity of his own nature. Beyond the evident similarities, there is some textual evidence for such an interpretation, since Fichte describes the epistemological side of his position, for which positing is a key concept, as "Spinozism made systematic; save only that any given self is itself the one ultimate substance."[5]

But despite the various properties which can be inferred from this form of activity, the fundamental fact of its occurrence remains unexplained. One can do no more than to note that positing is spontaneous and nonvoluntary activity which must occur as a necessary condition of knowledge. Fichte never clarifies the mechanism of its occurrence. Indeed, it is difficult to understand how he could have done so and remained consistent with his own theory. In fact, in later writings he on occasion gives a rather unhelpful, mystical twist to positing, when he speaks of it as *projec-*

tio per hiatem irrationalem in order to imply that this phenomenon surpasses human understanding.

Striving, Fichte's term for what is essentially a practical form of activity, is the manifestation of a desire, supposedly constitutive of human being, to attain ever increasing autonomy through the overcoming of limitations posed by the surrounding world. As used by Fichte, the term suggests a meaning similar to Spinoza's *conatus*, namely, a drive, force, or urge directed on the part of or by the individual. The difference is that whereas in Spinoza the emphasis is on self-preservation, in Fichte it is on self-development. But as in the case of Spinoza's *conatus*, Fichte's striving is deprived of causality. "The striving of the self must be infinite, and can never have causality" (*WL*, p. 252). Hence striving is not in itself causal activity, but rather a longing or desire for causality.

It seems worthwhile to point out that positing and striving stand in a reciprocal relation. The latter forces the individual out of himself into an external world. In a sense, striving can be either real, if the person aims at an attainable goal, or ideal, if the goal is in principle unreachable. But in another sense all striving is realistic since it is by definition the reaction to the shock that results from the perception of a real external world. Positing, on the contrary, is ideal in a different sense, since it is inferred and cannot be shown through experience to exist. The effect of positing is the converse of striving, in that by attributing the subject-object relation solely to the self, it has the result of interiorizing the individual's surroundings, which are hence reduced to the status of a mere distinction within the unity of the self. Thus if striving may be said to lead the individual out of himself and hence to be a "centrifugal" activity, positing may be described as the opposed or "centripetal" force. Further, each form of activity evokes the other. Striving calls forth the need for positing, through its "recognition" of external reality, and conversely positing makes striving possible, through its "generation" of that reality as perceived. In a word, each form of activity apparently requires the other as its complement.

In commentary on Fichte's position, it is the usual practice to distinguish several phases in the course of his refinement and restatement of the original view. As in the earlier discussion, I have here purposely limited consideration of Fichte's concept of activity for the most part to the earlier writings, since, as already mentioned, his thought later underwent a significant change in emphasis as Fichte, in the aftermath of the *Atheismusstreit*, undertook to stress a religious side of his position. The religious theme, to be sure, is present throughout as an abiding interest. We recall that Fichte's first publication, the *Kritik aller Offenbarung* (1792), dealt with the problem of revelation. Despite this interest, for the most part his writing preserves an entirely secular character until the religious element resurfaces in the *Darstellung der Wissenschaftslehre* in 1801. But as this latter development takes Fichte ever further from a possible comparison with Marx and, it would seem, away from much of what seems to be of permanent value in his earlier position, for present purposes at least it seems reasonable to concentrate on the earlier writings.

Although it seems advisable to concentrate on Fichte's earlier position, this approach does not seem to be possible in the case of Marx. There is a sense in which his view of activity steadily developed throughout his writings. Less precise assertions with respect to labor and value, for example, are in the later writings replaced by a more rigorous and more carefully formulated theory of use and exchange value. But there is a difference since, although Fichte succeeded in formulating successive, nearly complete statements of his entire position, beginning with the *WL* of 1794, which is a seminal text, as already indicated in Marx's case early and later texts would seem to constitute different aspects of a single view. Topics in Marx's writings which are prominent in his early writings tend to recede into the background, although not to disappear, in later texts and conversely. For this reason, in order to comprehend the position as a whole, it seems advantageous to regard early and later writings of Marx as composing a conceptual unity. This is especially the case for his view of activity.

A constant dimension of Marx's position is his attempt to grasp man through his activity. As early as the *Paris Manuscripts*, we find him asking, "For what is life but activity?"[6] and as late as *Capital* we find him employing what is in its essentials merely a more sophisticated version of the same approach, as when he writes: "The purchaser of labour-power consumes itself by setting the seller of it to work. By working the latter becomes actually, what before he was only potentially, labour-power in action, a labourer."[7] Now if Marx's position is taken as a whole, we find two equally fundamental forms of human activity. One form, which Marx designates as *Arbeit*, will here be rendered as "work," which will further be taken as synonymous with "labor."[8] In the most general sense, work is the activity manifested by a person within the productive process. As work requires the use of preexisting material which is acted upon as part of the process, it is productive as opposed to creative, quasi-physical as opposed to mental, and active as opposed to passive. Marx, however, emphasizes that work is in another sense a "passive" activity, at least in capitalism, in that it is not under the control of the worker.

Work, the first form of activity, is epoch-specific to capitalism. It is a fundamental tenet of the position that when capitalism is replaced by communism, work in the traditional sense will cease to exist. Marx occasionally stresses this point, as in the following passage in the *German Ideology*. "In all revolutions up till now the mode of activity always remained . . . whilst the communist revolution [which] is directed against the preceding *mode* of activity, does away with *labour*."[9] It follows that in communism there will be a different form of activity. But unfortunately, just as Marx is rarely explicit in reference to communism, he only occasionally refers to this second form of activity, although its real possibility is everywhere presupposed as the perspective from which to criticize capitalism. For want of a better term, I shall designate the second form of activity to occur under communism, as "free human activity."[10]

Free human activity has properties which, for the most part, are opposite to those of work. Free human activity is of course productive, since in all historical epochs man remains a natural being whose needs require attention. But the emphasis is on free mobility, as opposed to the division of labor characteristic of capitalism. "In communist society . . . nobody has an exclusive area of activity and each can train himself in any branch he wishes, society regulates the general production, making it possible for me to do one thing today and another tomorrow, to hunt in the morning, to fish in the afternoon, breed cattle in the evening, criticize after dinner, just as I like, without ever becoming a hunter, a fisherman, a herdsman, or a critic."[11] Further, the free mobility indicates that the worker is no longer "passive" or controlled by the economic process. On the contrary, he is "active" in a variety of ways, with respect to his work, the product, his own potentials, and other men.

If we reflect on the distinction just drawn, it is apparent that work is a necessary precondition of free human activity. Work is necessary since, according to Marx, it is only through "exploitation" that the profit which is required to develop the means of production needed for free human activity to be really possible can be guaranteed. For it would seem that in view of the emphasis placed on individual freedom within the economic process, in this post-capitalist social form, it appears unlikely that the potential for economic growth in communism can approach that of capitalism. Yet without substantial prior development, increased freedom within the productive process is not practically possible. But economic development is not an end in itself; it is rather the means necessary to reach the goal of human happiness. It follows that as soon as the real possibility of free human activity has been brought about, the means to that end should be replaced by another and more satisfying form of activity.

If we now attempt to bring the Fichtean and Marxian theories of activity into relation, their dissimilarity in terms of the present level of the discussion is, I think, apparent. Positing and striving are respectively theoretical and practical forms of activity. They may be said to be two sides of Fichte's attempt to provide a comprehensive theory of human being in terms of the forms of activity that relate to two fundamental kinds of experience. The best, admittedly imprecise, equivalent in Marx's position of theoretical and practical kinds of activity is the structural distinction of superstructure and base to which Marx occasionally alludes. But it should be observed that for the most part, Marx's discussion centers on the analysis of activity on the level of the base only. Indeed, the distinction of work and free human activity differentiates two forms of the latter type of activity.

The anisormorphism of the distinctions each concept of activity contains is not necessarily a bar to comparison. Various compromises might be effected which would render a direct comparison possible. One might, for example, draw an analogy between positing and striving on the one hand and superstructure and base on the other. Or one might work out a parallel between striving in Fichte's position and free human activity in Marx's view. For the latter two types of activity might be said to be kinds of the more general concept of practical activity. But such mental gymnastics are inherently unsatisfactory since they do not permit us squarely to compare the ideas in question. But unless the two theories of activity can themselves be shown to be similar, any such parallel can be suspected of being merely artificial.

In order to compare two types of activity as such, two general avenues seem open. One could place the two views directly in conjunction with the aim of uncovering a basic similarity. The drawback of direct comparison in this case is that although a parallel could well be demonstrated, it would inevitably appear the result of mere philosophical legerdemain unless in the process questions concerning its intrinsic significance and genesis could also be answered. But the response to queries of this kind is only available through an appeal to the history of philosophy. Indeed, since a persistent theme is the attempt to relate subjectivity to activity, Fichte and Marx are in good historical company. For this reason, a more effective manner in which to explore the analogy between the two views of activity is indirectly, through their relation to a third attempt to grasp subjectivity in terms of activity.

ARISTOTELIAN ACTIVITY AND SUBJECTIVITY

The prevalence of the concern to understand subjectivity, or human being, in terms of activity is apparent in even a rapid glance at the history of philosophy. The link between subjectivity and activity was forged early in the tradition. An implicit example is found in the Socratic belief that to know the good is to do the good. In this view, theoretical and practical forms of the exercise of virtue are inseparable. In Plato's thought subjectivity and activity are interrelated through his approach to man in terms of his characteristic task or function. In the *Republic*, he writes, "Would you agree to define a thing's function as the work for which that thing is the only instrument or the best one?" (1. 352). And he further adds that "living—is not that above all the function of the soul?" (1. 353).[12]

Aristotle continues the Greek concern to understand human being in terms of activity, but he initiates a new stage in the discussion in at least two respects. He invents a new vocabulary in order to discuss activity, which he designates as *energeia*. In previous writers the adjective *energos*, meaning "to be active" or "at work," occurs. Like Plato, Aristotle also uses the term *ergon*, which can mean either "work" or "activity" in the sense of plowing a field, or "work" in the sense of "product" or "result," such as the bed made by the carpenter or the statue by the sculptor. Although the etymology of Aristotle's term *energeia* is uncertain, he himself suggests that the word is derived from *ergon*, which accords well with the wider, nontechnical meaning of activity in general.[13]

Aristotle further innovates in his theory of activity. Although, as noted, there are other implicit views of activity in the preceding philosophical tradition, Aristotle's is the first explicit view of this concept as such. His technical term, *energeia*, receives a narrow, technical meaning within his own thought. In this respect, it is surprising to note that, despite the attention which has been directed to virtually every aspect of the Aristotelian position, his concept of activity seems to have been little studied.[14]

Aristotle's writings contain numerous references to the concept of activity, especially in the *Metaphysics*, to a lesser extent in the *Nicomachean Ethics*, and to a still lesser extent in the *Physics*. In the fullest discussion, which occurs in the ninth book of the *Meta-physics*,[15] Aristotle contrasts activity (*energeia*) and movement (*kinesis*) as two forms of change. Although this distinction has recently come under attack,[16] it seems rather straightforward. Movement differs from activity as the incomplete from the complete, since in the former case means and end cannot both be present. It cannot be the case that one is becoming thin and is thin, is learning and has learned, or is building and has built. There is hence a necessary separation between the end result, for which the action is undertaken or performed, and the means for its attainment. But in activity the end is present immanently, so that there is no separation between means and end. Unlike movement, activity therefore has no parts, since means and end form an indivisible unity. Examples are that we are seeing and have seen, or thinking and have thought.

Activity can further be described in terms of the relation between potentiality and actuality. Since activity is teleological, it implies a potential to be realized and a result to be obtained. Potentiality (*dynamis*) is the possibility which is realized in or becomes factual through activity. The possibility is the condition of the activity, as the acorn is the condition of the oak. But since, as mentioned, activity is inseparable from the result, means and end form a unity. Hence activity and actuality constitute two aspects of the same "event." The coming to be and the being can no more be isolated than the oak can be isolated from the stages of its development. For the same reason, possibility and actuality are united, since the potentiality which is initially present in the activity as possibility is transformed into an actuality, or result, from which the activity is inseparable. There is thus a unity of potentiality and actuality which is brought about and preserved in and through activity.

If we reflect on this summary of Aristotelian activity, we can see that a principal characteristic, perhaps the central theme of this complex concept, is unity in diversity.[17] Thus, one use of this concept is to help us to understand that certain distinctions, such as those between means and end, potentiality and actuality, act and actuality, or potentiality and act are in fact not absolute, but relative, since they are merely distinctions in unity. In this respect, the importance of the Aristotelian concept of activity is that it enables us to perceive the deeper unity which underlies and makes possible certain forms of diversity.

Aristotelian activity is also important in at least three further ways. Although apparently little studied, this is a central concept in Aristotle's own thought. Aristotle invokes the concept of activity in various ways throughout his position: in the views of physical motion, in the biological theory of development, in the theological concept of eternal and mutable forms of being, and in the ontological ideas of being itself.[18] Two suggestions in particular are worth noting here. It has been argued that activity is Aristotle's response to the basic question raised in the *Metaphysics*, which can be rendered as what does it mean to be? or, what is being? (*to ti hen einai*).[19] In this interpretation, being would literally be activity.[20] It has further been argued that activity is the concept invoked by Aristotle in order to "heal" or otherwise "overcome" the Platonic duality of reality and appearance.[21] If we remember that in the Aristotelian ontology, particulars are composed of form, matter, and their interrelation, the plausibility of the latter suggestion is apparent, if matter is interpreted as potentiality and form as actuality. In this way, in Aristotle's view the concept of activity enables him to surpass the dualism to which he objects in Plato's thought.

Aristotelian activity is further a central concept in modern philosophy. Heidegger has claimed that through the translation of the Greek term *energeia* by the Latin *actualitas*, the Greek insistence on becoming was lost to the later tradition.[22] Heidegger has further claimed that as a result the original Greek impulse disappeared in later philosophy.[23] On the contrary, the Aristotelian view of activity as unity in diversity appears widely throughout the modern philosophical tradition, as three brief examples will show. In Spinoza's thought, Aristotelian activity reappears as the unity of God as both *natura naturans* and *natura naturata*.[24] In the nineteenth-century German tradition, Aristotelian activity takes the form of the unity of thought and being. Kant, for instance, stipulates as the condition of knowledge that phenomena must correspond to the categories of the mind. Further, in Hegel's thought we find a concerted attempt to show that, on the level of absolute knowledge, the distinction between subject and object, or thought and being, is overcome. Thus, Heidegger notwithstanding, it would seem that the Aristotelian concept of activity is widely represented in modern philosophy.

A third area in which Aristotelian activity is important is as an approach to the perennial philosophical question of the nature of man. In his own thought, Aristotle applies his concept of activity to understand subjectivity. In relation to human being, Aristotle distinguishes several types of activity, which, following his analytic approach, for the most part he studies separately, although there is some overlap. In the *Nicomachean Ethics*, Aristotle advances a teleological theory of human activity. The aim of activity (*energeia*) is happiness (*eudaimonia*), for which the prerequisite is independent, or autonomous, well-being (*autarkeia*). "Happiness" is specifically defined as "an activity." [25]

Aristotle's teleological theory of ethical activity is closely related to Plato's own view. As did Plato, Aristotle understands man as a being who exercises his activity in areas of his greatest competency.[26] But he modifies Platonic doctrine when he argues that although virtue requires activity, a person is virtuous, not in terms of a single act, but rather in terms of an entire life. It is with this in mind, that he makes the famous observation: "For one swallow does not make a spring, nor does one summer day." [27] Rather, the capacities for intellectual and moral excellence, the two basic forms of virtue, need to be manifested to the fullest possible extent throughout the life of the individual in order to achieve full virtue. But since both forms of virtue require associated forms of intellect, Aristotle is justified, within the limits of his theory, in describing man as a rational animal (*zoon logikon*).

This description has been enormously influential in the subsequent history of philosophy. It seems fair to say that most later attempts in the tradition to resolve either directly or indirectly the question of the nature of man are variations on this theme, which thus unites thinkers as disparate as Descartes and Pascal, Kant and Hegel, and others in the view that man is finally to be understood as a rational being. It is perhaps all too easy to overlook the fact that in Aristotle's view human rationality is associated with another, equally basic characteristic, that is, man's political being (*zoon politikon*).

In the *Politics*, Aristotle shifts the emphasis from man's rationality to this political side, or activity within a social context. Practice (*praxis*) is opposed to pure theory (*theoria*), or disinterested activity performed only for its own sake. With the Greek city-state specifically in mind, Aristotle further differentiates kinds of practice. In the narrow sense, practice is the free activity of the head of the household, as opposed to slaves, women, or children, within the context of the city-state. But Aristotle is careful to emphasize that political activity, or doing, has its basis in other forms of activity, such as *poiesis*, or making in the sense of production, and *techné*, which may be rendered as the technical knowledge or know-how required, for instance, by the doctor to heal the patient. For the possibility of pure contemplation, the highest form of human activity, and the existence of the Greek city-state itself depend on the other forms of activity through which man responds to his natural, biological needs.

If we now reflect on the discussion of man in the ethical and political writings, we see that taken together they represent two aspects of an approach to man in terms of his activity. In simplest terms, Aristotle would seem to be suggesting that man should be understood through his capacity for what, in current terminology, might be described as rational social activity. Such activity is wider than but includes doing and making as subspecies. But if, as has been proposed, for Aristotle "what it is for a thing to be, its mode of existence, turns out to be its mode of activity," then the theory of human being would turn out to be a special case of the wider theory of being.[28] By the same token, human activity is merely a species of the wider genus, activity in general.

ARISTOTELIAN ACTIVITY: COMPARISON OF FICHTE AND MARX

We have seen that a central characteristic of Aristotle's activity is unity in diversity. If we return now to the comparison between the views of activity in Fichte's and Marx's thought, it is apparent that in ways consistent with their respective positions both thinkers re-state or reformulate the Aristotelian concept if this criterion is ap-plied. As we shall see, in each case activity is both a means to an end as well as an end in itself. Each view thus offers a neo-Aristo-telian conception of activity and, from this angle, they are similar. This similarity can perhaps best be brought out through a point by point reexamination of the two views of activity in terms of the distinctions brought out in the discussion of Aristotle's view.

The basis for the comparison is that Fichte and Marx both view man as an active being. With an eye to Aristotelian activity, it is interesting to note that in each position there is a unity of human potential and activity. For the capabilities of a human being in the fullest sense of the term are inseparable from the activity in which they are manifested. Although Fichte does not directly address himself to a theory of potentials, the concept of human capacity is everywhere present in his position. Indeed, as already mentioned, the basic concerns which motivate his theory are the nature and limits of man. Further, the finite self, or individual human being, may be said to have a variety of potentials which are to be made explicit through its activity, such as those for self-consciousness and moral comportment. But the potentials cannot finally be sep-arated from man's activity, since to have such capacities is to be an active being and when one is active one is in the process of man-ifesting such capacities.

At first glance, Marx would seem to distinguish more sharply than does Fichte between human potentials and human activity, as for instance in the rare allusions to species powers, which represent capacities, and species activity, which is the activity of human being. This distinction is of real importance in Marx's position, since it enables him to specify historical circumstances in which man's activity is separated from the manifestation of potentials, which are hence unable to be developed in these circumstances. But from another perspective, it seems clear that to be a human being is to manifest one's species-being in what one does, so that a person's potentials to become a specific individual can be divorced from his activity only on pain of loss of his humanity.

It should further be noted that each distinguishes activity and its result, only to emphasize that on a deeper level the distinction is overcome. If on one level in both cases activity generates a result separate from it, on another level the result is merely the activity. In Fichte's theory, the self is an active being, whose activity results in a not-self, or representative physical object. Now, in one sense there is an obvious distinction to be drawn between activity and its result. But in another sense, this is no more than a distinction in unity, since from the perspective of the self the not-self is nothing but the activity through which it is generated. Similarly, in Marx's view, work gives rise to a product or physical object, which enjoys a physical status as a thing. But in another sense the product is the "concretion" (*das Konkretisieren*) of the activity which brings it about. Hence, in each case activity is finally inseparable from its result or, in other terms, the distinction of means and end can be seen to rest upon an underlying unity.

So far we have seen that in both positions there is a unity which underlies the distinction between human potential, and activity and its results. If we now pause, after the initial two moments of the comparison, we can see that both views are similar to the Aristotelian concept of activity. The presence of the analogy between each view of activity and its Aristotelian predecessor suggests that each is a perhaps unconscious "restatement" or "reformulation" of the Aristotelian concept, at least with respect to the theme of unity in diversity, and further suggests that since each resembles the Aristotelian concept in the same way they further resemble each other. But the similarity thus disclosed is not helpful because its relation to either Fichte's or Marx's position is not yet apparent. But if we now turn to the unity of potentiality and actuality, it will be easier to perceive the connection. A major theme in both views is that man develops through his activity. Now, in order for development to occur, possibilities must be realized in and through activity. But for a possibility to be realized, a relation must be established between potentiality or potency, and act or actuality. Understood in this way, it would seem that in the relation of potency and act Aristotle describes the nucleus of a theory of development in and through activity, a theme common to both Fichte and Marx.

But some further discussion of the Aristotelian concept of activity is necessary before we can make use of it as a standard in terms of which to compare Fichte's and Marx's views of development. There is an important difference between the Aristotelian conception of development and that in the latter two positions. With the highest, or contemplative, form of life in mind, Aristotle distinguishes between instances in which activity results in a product beyond itself, in which case it is said to be in the product, and those in which there is no other product beyond the activity, in which case the activity is said to be in the actor or subject.[29] But, perhaps because in his view human development is primarily in the excellent exercise of the rational faculty, he makes little or no effort to relate the two instances he distinguishes. But as we have seen, Fichte and Marx both insist that activity gives rise to a quasi-physical product. If Aristotle's theory is to be used to continue the comparison, it needs to be "adapted" in order to show how in the generation of an object or product of activity, the subject or human being develops.

To this end, it has already been shown that Fichte and Marx both understand man as an active subject, and it has further been shown that man's activity is in a sense identical with the object which is its result. If the relation of transitivity is to hold, it needs to be demonstrated that the subject as potential is in a sense identical with the object, or subject as actual. I shall call the relation between subject and object established through activity a "metaphysical identity," since it is only on an abstract or metaphysical level that it can be brought out.

It might be helpful to approach this concept by distinguishing it from homonyms with which it could easily be confused. Let me state at the outset that I am not claiming that what I call "metaphysical identity" is necessarily an identity in a strict logical sense. The point in comparing it to more familiar forms of identity is to avoid possible misunderstanding.

At least two concepts of identity are in common philosophical use. Numerical identity is the sense in which a given thing is self-identical. This form of identity is usually, if not always, a relation of something to itself. For instance, the feather pen Krug employed to criticize Hegel was identical to his writing instrument in this sense. Qualitative identity refers to the way in which two or more things share a property. If we abstract from any differences of shade, two things which are both red are in that respect qualitatively alike. This latter kind of identity is of course familiar to us from the history of philosophy, since it is basic to the Platonic theory of ideas.

On the contrary, as used here the term "metaphysical identity" refers to a nonnumerical, nonqualitative unity in difference, which is brought about by the subject between the subject and the object it generates through its activity. Although no doubt the term used to describe this relation is unfamiliar, this type of identity seems to be well anchored in ordinary experience. A well-known example is the German poet Schiller's discussion of the play instinct (*Spieltrieb*).[30] In observing that in a sense the sculptor is his statue, Schiller was merely reformulating a popular belief, which is sometimes stated in the form of the claim that "an artist expresses himself in his art."[31]

It would seem that the concept of artistic self-expression can be interpreted in at least two senses. In one sense, the artist's self-expression is nothing other than the objet d'art which comes into being as a physically distinct object in the manifestation of his artistic capacities. In this way, the object is there for all to enjoy as a public object to which each of us can relate as we will. But there is another, more private relation, which concerns the relation of the artist to his own work. In the latter sense, the artist can express himself in the course of his artistic endeavor because his artistic conception takes shape in the art object. For through translation of an artistic idea into wood, metal, stone, or some other material, as the case may be, as he gives rise to a piece of sculpture physically distinct from himself, the sculptor also gives concrete embodiment to the idea he has in mind, the idea that motivates his artistic creation. But since the sculptor or any other artist for that matter has an idea which functions as a possibility, and is then realized in an object which is actual, one can say that the sculptor as potential and the actual object are two aspects of the "same thing." For the art object is in fact the actual realization of the idea whose status was formerly confined to potentiality. It is in this latter sense, because there is a unity in diversity, that an artist expresses himself in his art.

The relation of unity in· diversity is a prominent aspect of Fichte's and Marx's respective attempts at understanding human development. Of the two, Fichte puts greater emphasis on the identity to be obtained through activity and less stress on development. In his view, as repeatedly mentioned, the individual, or finite self, is an active being, and the result of the activity, or not-self, is inseparable from the activity. It follows that although in one sense distinct, in another sense self and not-self are merely two aspects of an underlying unity. Fichte makes this conclusion clear, when he describes the self as "at once the agent and the product of the action; the active, and what the activity brings about" (*WL*, p. 97). But if a self, or person, is what he does, and if by acting he generates a product to which he stands in a relation of "identity" in a fundamental sense, then he develops as a person through his activity by virtue of the relation between himself and his object.

In Marx's position, a similar inference is implicit. The worker is his work activity, and the object is the work in concretized form. As emphasized, the object is physically distinct from the worker and, in certain historical circumstances, can "oppose" him. But the distinction between worker and product is overcome if we realize that on another level, the relation of worker to product is necessary for his self-development as the objectified form of the worker's potentials or species-being. This point can be made in a number of ways. For example, it is only if the object literally is the worker that the capitalist's appropriation of the product takes on the pathetic overtones of the appropriation of the worker himself. Again, it is because the product represents the possibility of the worker's self-development that alienation separates him from his species-being, or possibility to develop his specific individual capacities. But a change in the form of society from capitalism to communism will bring about the possibility of full human development because the individual will be able to manifest his potentials as a human being in his productive activity.

The demonstration of a similar unity in diversity in both views between man understood as an active being and the products, or results of his activity, is the final step needed to establish a basic parallel between the two views of activity in terms of the Aristotelian concept. The theme of unity in diversity has been shown to be central to the Aristotelian concept of activity. In terms of this theme it has further been shown that Fichte's and Marx's views restate a quasi-Aristotelian unity in diversity in the following ways: in the relation of human potentiality and human activity; in the relation of man's activity and its product, or result; and in the relation between man as the active object and the results of his activity, that is, as a "metaphysical" identity. Secondly, there is a parallel between Fichte's and Marx's respective theories of man's activity, which are similar in terms of their restatement of a funda-mental theme of the Aristotelian concept. But since the third kind of similarity represents, as we have seen, a theory of man's self-development in and through his activity, and since the views of activity are also analogous, it seems likely that the concepts of man which follow from the respective views of activity will also be parallel.

CHAPTER 5

ACTIVITY AND MAN

SINCE in both positions man is understood as an active being, and since the respective ideas of activity are similar, the next step in the comparison is to show the parallel between the concepts of man implicit in the two views of activity. Although the parallel in the theories of human being could be brought out in various ways, I shall use the concept of development as the initial clue for several reasons. In the first place, man's development is a central concern for each thinker. Fichte's intention to grasp the nature or limits (*Bestimmung*) of man has already been mentioned, and reference has also been made to Marx's interest in the real conditions of man's emergence as a fully human being. Further, the relation between activity and development has been discussed in the preceding chapter. But as each thinker approaches man in terms of his activity, as activity is related to development, and as development is a central theme in the respective positions, it seems plausible to utilize the latter concept to point to the parallel in the views of man. I shall argue that there is a basic similarity between the respective views of human development, as well as between related views of fulfillment and agency. For these reasons, it would seem that the concepts of man implicit in Fichte's and Marx's ideas of activity are also similar.

LOGIC OF DEVELOPMENT

Development is one of those words whose meaning is difficult to specify, certainly in a philosophical sense. The task is further complicated by the fact that this word is not only in wide use in everyday parlance, but in philosophy as well, where it recurs with modifications in a wide variety of contexts.[1]

But one must wonder whether the amount of information imparted by a given term is not inversely proportional to the range and frequency of its use. Whether or not this is a general principle, it seems clear that "development" and its companion term "fulfillment" are employed in so many senses that a precise meaning must often be inferred from context. If we restrict ourselves for the moment just to the word "development," we can note the existence of various synonyms. When we turn from the synonyms to the various denotations, the difficulty of finding a single meaning which encompasses all legitimate usages of the term is, if anything, still more evident. From the purely linguistic point of view, development can mean "to disclose" or "to reveal," "to unfold more completely," or "to form" or "to expand." The first definition alludes to the fact of something being uncovered, the second to further disclosure, and the third to a process, such as that of growth. Ingredient in all three definitions is an idea of latency, as that through which potential can be or is brought out.

One might further attempt to survey the different ways in which the term is used. One can speak of development in the sense of bringing under control, for instance the development of a natural resource. Technical development is also a possibility. Again development can have the sense of the continuation of a process in a predetermined manner, as in the expansion of a mathematical series. Still another meaning is to work out variations, for instance, of an idea or a musical theme. Development further has the sense of rendering visible, as in the development of a negative or photographic plate.

Even this brief survey of some among the various denotations of the term suggests how difficult it is to pin down a unique or even a central meaning from a linguistic approach. But from a conceptual approach, I would like to suggest that the idea of development is inseparable from an associated idea of an end or goal. For development presupposes something to be attained. This end or goal is both that toward which the developmental process tends as well as that point whose attainment effectively completes, or fulfills, and thus terminates the process. Accordingly, it would seem that development and, in the same way, the activity associated with it are by their nature teleological.

Since we have now specified a meaning for the concept of development, we can address the problem of the developmental process which both Fichte and Marx understand in similar fashion. It seems convenient at the outset to consider the developmental process from the vantage point of the subject or person who in fact develops, although later some qualification, especially with respect to the concept of agency, will be necessary. From the subject's perspective, there is a choice to be made between two types of description, which can be designated as "immediate" and "mediate" forms. Immediate development can be said to occur if the object, which is the product or result of activity, is the development *simpliciter*. Mediate development can be said to occur if the person relates to himself and thus develops through the object which results from his activity. Mediate development includes immediate development as a moment in the process, but the converse relation does not hold. Now since human development includes, but is not limited to, a relation between man or men and the results of human activity, it seems preferable to choose the rubric of mediate self-development in order to bring out the analogy between the two positions.

If we consider development as a process of self-mediation, two stages can be identified. In the first stage, the person becomes a definite being when through his activity he generates an object which stands over against and opposes him. In the second stage, the person overcomes the opposition as the condition of further development. The first stage is the necessary condition of the second one, and taken together the two moments represent successive phases of the same developmental process.

In order to understand the sense of the first stage of development, it seems appropriate to introduce certain additional distinctions. Although it is correct that as a result of his activity a person generates an object, some qualification is in order, for as a further result he also generates a social context, or social environment in which his activity is manifested. I shall use the term "objectification" to designate both the limited physical product as well as the secondary product or social context. The distinction between first and second order products in general plays a more prominent role in Marx's position than in Fichte's. Marx insists on the difference between physical objects and their effects on social relations to which they give rise in his analysis of alienation. But this distinction is at least implicit in Fichte's theory, since the term "not-self" covers both that which "naturally" exists, that is, nature, which is generated by the self, such as "things," as well as a further human product, that is, the social relations Fichte seeks to ameliorate in the *Rechtslehre* and in the *Handelsstaat*.

The phenomenon of objectification has a double significance with respect to the active person. On the one hand, when a person makes something he by the same act defines himself as the author of or responsible for a specific thing. The act of making is in itself inevitably an act of self-definition, for a person is what he does. On the other hand, the relation between the person and the objectification, either as a product or in a more extended sense as a social context, serves to limit further activity, which now has a context within which it not only can, but must occur. Hence, Fichte observes that man and his world or, in his terminology, self and not-self, stand in a relation of interdetermination. In the same way, Marx is attentive to the relation between man and all that is external to him, be it products or society in general. It follows that in both views as an individual generates an object he defines himself and limits his further activity by generating the context within which it can take place.

This brief statement serves to locate the concept of objectification within the framework of the present discussion of mediate self-relation. But if we desire to carry the analysis further, it is important to note that the relation between an individual and his "object," where by "object" is understood both the thing or things which result from the activity as well as the surroundings further generated in this way, can take two forms, that is, either active or passive. If the relation is passive, development is stalled or arrested, either temporarily or permanently, at the initial stage, since as the person is unable to "reappropriate" or otherwise make use of the results of his activity for his own purposes, the developmental process comes to a halt at this point. On the contrary, if the relation is one in which the person can actively relate to the results of his activity, then the process can continue. It follows, conversely, that if the process can be temporarily blocked because the relation assumes a passive form, then the condition for its resumption is that the relation becomes active.

Fichte and Marx each make this argument in a manner consistent with their respective positions. The problem of the active or passive relation of a person to his surroundings arises in Fichte's thought as the basic distinction between doing and knowing, or striving and positing. As has been repeatedly emphasized, Fichte holds that these two concepts and their associated forms of activity are inseparably connected. He also maintains that, although doing is prior to knowing, since life is essentially practical, the former needs to be completed by knowledge. Translated into less esoteric terminology, this means that if the problem of knowledge is to arise at all, it is only because of the need to overcome an obstacle, in other words, a practical problem. Otherwise stated, although doing is necessary for knowing, knowing is a precondition to further doing.

This doctrine finds application in Fichte's position on the twin levels of morality and politics. The conjunction of morality and politics recalls Aristotle, although the moral theory set forth in the *Sittenlehre* has unmistakable Kantian overtones. Following Kant,

Fichte defines the moral sphere as that concerned with the individual's self-limitation or self-prescription of rational laws in relation to duty. Since man is a volitional being, it is necessary to bring one's desires under control in accordance with reason. From the moral viewpoint, one must assume that one is free to act in a rational manner, even if this freedom cannot be demonstrated. As Fichte puts it, we must presuppose the "causality of the concept" as a condition of morality.[2]

An Aristotelian side of Fichte's view is clearer in his account of politics. Here Fichte goes beyond a quasi-Kantian satisfaction with mere formal possibility to urge that moral precepts have to be translated into actual practice. Politics is the science, according to Fichte, which bridges the gap between the concept of a rational society and that which in fact exists. Now, the goal of the human race is to be actually free in its social relations, since "the aim of man's earthly life is to organize his life freely in a rational manner."[3] Hence the role of politics is to bring about on an actual social plane the freedom that is merely postulated on the moral level.

Where are we with respect to this goal? In the *Grundzüge des gegenwärtigen Zeitalters* (1804), Fichte proposed a developmental schema of human history as a tool for the analysis of the contemporary social context. He claims that speaking generally human history can be divided on an a priori basis into periods, according to whether or not mankind actually possesses rational control of its relations. He further distinguishes five historical epochs, which run the gamut from a supposedly complete inability of man to direct human relations, or an absolute lack of freedom, to what he terms the complete victory of reason over instinct. Fichte's optimism is visible in his assertion that we are presently in the third of the five stages, namely, at a turning point in history when man is about to subject instinctive behavior to the control of reason.

A word should be said here about Fichte's understanding of the relation of religion to history, since it might be thought that his concern with religion marks a decisive difference between his and Marx's positions. In order to evaluate this problem, it is helpful to understand certain differences in personal background and social context. Fichte, like his great idealist colleagues Schelling and Hegel, had been in the seminary and, within the framework of the German university, was required to deal with the institutionalized form of religion. His failure to do so adequately in fact ultimately cost him his position at the University of Jena. The conditions for Marx were rather different. There was of course a possible personal reason for antipathy to religion, due to his father's conversion from Judaism to Protestantism, which was socially more acceptable. Again, one ought not to overlook the further factor that Marx, from his position outside the German establishment, was under less pressure than Fichte to adopt a tolerant attitude. We should also recall how easy it was to take a harsh stance toward religious phenomena in the period following Hegel's death and after the important critical publications of Strauss and Feuerbach.[4]

To be sure there is a clear difference in emphasis, for unlike Marx, who scarcely mentions religion except to condemn it, Fichte makes an effort, despite repeated accusations of atheism, to understand religious phenomena, and in addition he claims that there is a religious dimension to history. But it would be hasty to magnify this difference before understanding what Fichte means by the latter claim. Perhaps the clearest indication of his view occurs toward the end of the *Grundzüge*, where he makes the following remarkable statement, "*Religion* consists . . . in the following: that one must consider and recognize all life from the perspective of its necessary development out of a single primitive, perfect and blissful state."[5] On examination we see that, despite the religious terminology in which the definition is formulated, Fichte's concept of religion has less to do with theism or an organized system of theological belief than with the conviction, which he shared with Kant and Hegel, that for mainly epistemological reasons, history needs to be understood as a *unity* in order to interpret any phase of the process and that in the long run history reflects human progress. These are both views that Marx defended in his own position.

But we are still entitled to ask: How can this progress come about? Fichte's response is that reason is a force for freedom. Since philosophy is concerned with the rational analysis of reality, it follows that this discipline enjoys a political role as a means to bringing about human liberty. Hence, although he has often been criticized for an exaggerated chauvinism, it was perfectly in character for Fichte to attempt to make use of his educational role in a series of lectures published under the title *Addresses to the German Nation* (*Reden an die deutsche Nation* [1808]), to rally the beleaguered Germans against the French occupation during the winter of 1807–8. But it is entirely possible that reason is insufficient to bring about fundamental change, as Fichte was perfectly aware. For this reason in some of his earlier writings, such as the *Zurückforderung der Denkfreiheit* (1793), he was not above recommending revolution as a last resort. Though not content to assume the causality of reason on the moral plane, Fichte tried also to put his thought into practice in order to diminish the distance between reality and the concept of it as revealed in philosophical analysis.

In Marx's position, the problem of the active-passive relation of man to his surroundings appears in his analysis of the structure and growth of society. Much of this analysis is already familiar, so it can be sketched again rather quickly in order to see its relevance to the present stage of the discussion. Reviewing quickly, like Fichte, Marx divided human history, or in his terminology human prehistory, into different epochs. The relevant similarity in Marx's view is his distinction between capitalism, in which the individual has a passive relation to the results of his activity, and communism, in which the relation will be active. The present epoch, or capitalism, is, again in a Fichtean sense, a turning point, since it is the moment in which the transition to a more positive phase of human social relationships can finally be undertaken.

There is further a similarity to be observed in the respective understanding of social change. Although Marx's emphasis on the role of the proletariat has no equivalent in Fichte's view, his belief in the importance of theory in effecting social change stresses the role of self-consciousness in a manner similar to Fichte's view. An example is the pamphleteering in which Marx engaged, of which the *Manifesto* is only the most famous instance. Again, Marx's lengthy analysis of the mechanism of what he saw as capitalist repression can also be understood as an attempt, on a different level, to contribute to a change in self-consciousness and, by extension, as an educational application of theory in order to bring about a change in social practice.

But beyond the similarities, two specific differences in Fichte's and Marx's respective views of social development should be mentioned. One difference concerns the sense in which in Marx's view a given form of social organization has a tendency to maintain itself. In his indication that no form of social organization ever disappears before its possibilities for further development are exhausted, Marx made clear his belief that the process of the transition from one social stage to another may involve considerably more than a mere awareness of the limitations of the present moment. But just as Fichte's own economic analysis never reached the relatively advanced state it was to assume in Marx's position, in the same way detailed discussion of the "economic" auto-defense mechanism through which capitalism, or indeed any stage in the individual or society, endeavors to protect its existence and hence maintain the status quo is absent from his thought. In this respect, whatever the final verdict on the viability of Marx's political economy, his more developed grasp of the economic issues related to social progress constitutes a conceptual advance on the more primitive Fichtean model.

A second difference concerns alienation. Since in Marx's view thought is related to and indeed arises from a given social context, the phenomenon of human alienation is one of the most important obstacles in the way of the average person's awareness of his human condition. Alienation hence has the result of retarding social change. Now although this is a topic of considerable controversy, it has been suggested that the concept of alienation constitutes Marx's basic philosophical contribution. But Marx's priority in this matter has been challenged on behalf of Fichte by Arnold Gehlen. In an essay entitled "Über die Geburt der Freiheit aus der Entfremdung," he maintains that Fichte anticipates later views of alienation, including that of Marx.[6]

It is, however, difficult to give much weight to his argument. There is of course a superficial sense in which it has merit. Fichte's use of the word *Entfremdung* precedes Marx's later theory, in the same way as his own view is chronologically anticipated in Rousseau's occasional references to *aliénation*. But as there is in fact little trace of an attempt in Fichte's writings to elaborate a concept of alienation as a tool for social analysis, one must be careful in asserting that he anticipates the conceptual moment in Marx's view in any substantive sense. The closest Fichte comes to such an anticipation is when he writes that "this alien element stands necessarily in conflict with the self's endeavor to be absolutely identical" (*WL*, pp. 233–34). But one must, I think, distinguish Fichte's indication of the human tension which arises in the difference between unlimited aspirations and practical finitude from Marx's understanding of the source of man's contemporary social malaise. Although the former problem is rooted in human being itself and hence cannot be overcome in time, the latter is merely a painful, but ultimately transitory aspect of social existence. It is this latter sense of alienation which has no anticipatory echo in Fichte's thought.

But although there are undeniable differences in the two positions with respect to the logic of development, there is nevertheless a broad area of agreement. If we sum up the discussion we can see that in each case emphasis, in the transformation of man's relation to the results of his activity from passive to active form, includes stress on three general areas: the practical role of theory in overcoming the difference between concept and social reality, the educational role of theory in effecting social change, and the significance of self-consciousness as a force for change.

FULFILLMENT

The concept of development is conceptually inseparable from that of full development, or fulfillment. The nature of a thing is, according to Aristotle, that which it becomes when fully developed. Accordingly, development presupposes as its limit a concept of full development, or fulfillment, toward which the process tends. The *telos*, or end, that is, the full realization of the nature of the thing, is both the goal of the process and that stage whose attainment effectively terminates the process. To again cite the standard Aristotelian example, the end of the acorn is to become an oak and when the oak "emerges" from the acorn the potential to do so has become fully actual and the process has come to an end. In the same way, man's *telos* is the full development, or fulfillment, of his human potentials, whatever they may be. I want now to relate development to fulfillment in the two positions. In particular, two questions should be asked: What is human fulfillment, and to what extent can human fulfillment be attained?

Although neither Fichte nor Marx has much directly to say on the topic of human fulfillment, both positions contain hints that each understands the goal of human development as the full manifestation of human nature. As has already been remarked several times, Fichte's theory of activity is based on a distinction between its theoretical and practical forms. In broadest terms, fulfillment requires a harmony between both kinds of activity. This requirement can be met through the organization of practice according to norms suggested by theory and, conversely, by the restriction of theory to the domain of practice. Fichte's view of full human development can be brought out by retracing some of his by now familiar regressive arguments from conditioned to condition.

In the *WL* Fichte presents an argument in piecemeal form whose implications are only clear in later writings. If we distinguish between theory and practice, beyond consciousness and self-consciousness, theoretical understanding of experience is the end in view in terms of which both awareness and self-awareness function as means, and which results from positing. On the other hand, in the discussion of man as a practical being Fichte urges that the function of practical activity is to overcome obstacles through striving. The two forms of activity are complementary since theory has as its condition that the individual be opposed in his activity in order that consciousness can occur and the obstacle be known, while practical activity tends toward the elimination of the obstacle. There is hence a tendency of theory to turn into practice and practice to revert to theory, as the individual strives to understand himself and his environment in order to act in a moral manner.

The argument at this point is highly abstract, in accordance with Fichte's interest in *Ursprüngsphilosophie*. But as he applies the theory in later writings, it takes a form not unlike Marx's view. In the *WL* Fichte maintains that from the point of view of a rigorous philosophical deduction, self-consciousness is the ground of consciousness. In the *Grundlage des Naturrechts* (1796) he makes the related point, perhaps better known in its Hegelian restatement, that the condition of self-consciousness is to be recognized as an individual by other individuals. But in order for this recognition to be obtained, individual rights must be acknowledged. Indeed, the purpose of this text is merely to provide a theory of rights or, as he puts it, "to deduce the concept of right and its object as the condition of self-consciousness." [7]

The significance of the relation between rights and self-consciousness is that the latter is necessarily rooted in a social context, since that is the locus of human relations. But if rights are to be recognized within this context, it must be of a specific type. It is not sufficient for the context to exhibit the characteristics of society (*Gesellschaft*), since this does not in and of itself imply mutual recognition. It is possible and indeed frequently the case that individuals or even whole groups within a given society fail to achieve a relationship of mutual recognition. In order for it to be really possible, the society in question must form a community (*Gemeinschaft*) in which the people who compose it come together freely for a common purpose. But such community requires that my freedom be limited by equal freedom for others. In other words, mutual self-limitation through mutual recognition is the condition of self-consciousness.

If self-consciousness is possible only in a particular type of social context, one is entitled to inquire how the latter is possible. Fichte's answer is to be found in *Der geschlossene Handelsstaat* (1800). Here he argues that the condition of a rational social context and the mutual recognition by which it is characterized lies in respect for property rights. Since at first glance this response may seem confusing, it should be noted that Fichte here uses the word "property" (*Eigenthum*) in an unusual sense. It has often been argued that property rights are a necessary condition of social existence, but in most cases the term "property" is taken to refer to things or possessions. On the contrary, by "property" Fichte has in mind the right to activity, especially one's own activity within a social context. "I have described the right to property as the inclusive right with respect to *activity*, in no sense with respect to things [*Sachen*]." [8] In order to protect the right to property, as so defined, from restrictions arising out of economic pressures, which Fichte perhaps incorrectly views as developing only from a source external to the state, commercial closure must be introduced. In this way, the problem of economic domination, at least from without, is allegedly removed as a possible hindrance to the individual's free direction of his own activity. But when the right of the individual to his own activity is secured through the economic closure which guarantees respect for property, then the resultant freedom which is bought at the price of mutual self-limitation transforms work into something more nearly approaching pleasure. Fichte further observes that when economic domination disappears free time is created for man, as he puts it, to turn his gaze to heaven, a statement which can perhaps be best construed, once we remember that it was written after the *Atheismusstreit*, as an indication that in his free time the individual can cultivate his mental faculties.

Although the imprint of the critical philosophy is widely present elsewhere in Fichte's thought, in his conception of human fulfillment in a rational social context Fichte's primary debt is to Rousseau. Fichte's *Grundlage des Naturrechts* was published several months prior to the appearance of Kant's essay on *Perpetual Peace*. Indeed, in the second edition of his book Fichte justly points out that although there are a number of similarities, his own work gives a greater role in actual practice whereas Kant insists more on abstract theory. Rather, Fichte was here influenced by Rousseau, especially in his own distinction between society and community which can be traced to Rousseau's distinction between general will (*volonté générale*) and will of all (*volonté de tous*). [9] Although Marx knew Rousseau's work, the immediate influence on his understanding of human fulfillment can be seen in his attempt to come to grips with Hegel's *Rechtsphilosophie*. But although Fichte and Marx drew their respective inspirations from different parts of the tradition, their concepts of fulfillment have much in common.

Marx's conception of fulfillment is detectable in his famous, but never explicitly described theory of communism. Marx, as already noted, holds that capitalism is not a possible setting for human development. The main problem is that capital has an irresistible tendency to acquire an ever increasing autonomy relative to man. Now, since capital depends for its existence on private ownership of the means of production, Marx suggests that fundamental amelioration of the human situation requires the elimination of private property. So far this is merely a restatement of familiar themes. A difficulty arises when we try to pin down the end in view which Marx presupposes. Despite the fact that the theme of full human development as a real possibility in communism is omnipresent in Marx's position, he never provides a clear statement of exactly what is supposed to occur.

Although Marx did not formulate a single theory of fulfillment in communism, he refers to this concept in isolated passages virtually throughout his writings. Inspection of these writings yields a series of different but related analyses, all of which may not ultimately be fully compatible. In early texts, such as the *Paris Manuscripts* (1844) and the nearly contemporaneous discussion in *Excerpts from James Mill's Elements of Political Economy* (1844), stress is placed on a new and qualitatively different form of activity which is to occur in communism. This stress is perhaps most evident in the latter work in passages such as the following, when, in referring to communism, he writes: "In my production I would have objectified the *specific character* of my individuality. . . . Our production would be as many mirrors from which our natures would shine forth. . . . My labour would be the *free expression* and hence the *enjoyment of life*." [10] In the *German Ideology* (1845), attention shifts to free social mobility and constantly mutable choice of one's social responsibility, as in a well-known text already cited, in which Marx speaks in somewhat rhapsodic, visionary terms of each of us as free to do as we like: to fish, to hunt, to criticize, and so forth. The *Manifesto* (1848) underscores the possibility of free association, in which tasks are to be shared and in which each assumes a share of the responsibility for the welfare of society taken as a whole, as in the following passage. "In place of the old bourgeois society.—We shall have an association in which the free development of each is the condition for the free development of all." [11] Since it is difficult to imagine such an association as a practical solution for a large society, presumably Marx has some form of small-unit social structure in mind at this point. Later in the *Grundrisse* (1857–58) and in the posthumously published third volume of *Capital* Marx suggests that through the elimination of the profit motive the work necessary for the maintenance of life can actually be made more or less enjoyable, and that as a further consequence free time will become available in which people will be able to develop as individuals. Thus in the

Grundrisse he states that a long run effect of capital is to "reduce labour time . . . and thus to free everyone's time for their own development." [12] In *Capital* he writes, in ungrammatical fashion, in reference to communism, that although "it . . . remains a realm of necessity. Beyond it begins that development of human energy which is an end in itself, the true realm of freedom." [13] Again, in another posthumously published work, a fragment of *Capital* known as the *Theory of Surplus Value*, once more in a passage already referred to, by equating free time with riches Marx implies that the value of communism for human development is to be found not in the transformation within the work process, but rather in the possibility created external to the process.

But if one can point to so much variation in Marx's grasp of the consequences of communism for human activity, one is justified in wondering whether he in fact has a view of fulfillment at all. For clearly satisfaction within the work process is not to be equated without qualification to satisfaction external to this process. One way to explain the apparent discrepancy is to suggest that he never fully formulated his response to this problem, despite the fact that it is implicit throughout his criticism of capitalism as the positive standard, or that his view underwent evolution, or even that he changed his mind. But it would, I think, be mistaken to suggest that there is no view to be dealt with, for despite the variation, there is nevertheless a central theme which runs throughout Marx's thought on this topic. To put it in terms of his theory of alienation, in communism man's relation to his work, its results, himself, and other men will be different because the passivity associated with capitalism will be replaced by an active relation between man and his surroundings. Hence, the key to the real possibility of human fulfillment is that man may be active with respect to the work process, its result, other men, and as a consequence, he may further be active in respect to his own possibilities as a human being. It is this active side of human being which is sought in the transformation of capitalism into communism, and it is further this active side of human being which is the theme that runs throughout Marx's numerous references to human fulfillment.

Enough of each view of fulfillment has now been sketched to permit us to compare them. There is a basic similarity since in each case the key condition for human fulfillment is that man be able to transform the relation to his surroundings from a passive to an active form. In other words, what is important is the activity itself and not its result, even if activity and its product are finally inseparable. This is a somewhat surprising conclusion, since it rules out one kind of fulfillment, such as that in and through the object, as in the Schillerian example of the sculptor and the statue. Schiller was influenced in the formulation of his view by Fichte, who was a personal friend and colleague at the University of Jena, and it might be thought that Schiller's theory was a model for Marx's position. But on reflection, this conclusion is fully in accord with the concept of development as an ongoing process. If fulfillment were obtainable in any single act, the process would continually be being brought to a close. But if objectification of potentials is not itself the final goal of development, but instead a condition of it, then the process preserves its ongoing character. In other words, a person does not fully actualize his human nature in any single product or act, but rather in the continuing series of acts which may result in a succession of products.

The need to transform the relation of man to his surroundings constitutes a general framework in terms of which several more specific but interrelated similarities in the two positions can be noted. One area of similarity concerns the nature of a social situation in which full development can even be a real possibility. Fichte and Marx both emphasize that with the introduction of a change in the relation of man to his natural and social environment, important possibilities for individual development will open up. Neither, of course, holds that either the activity within the productive process or the process itself ought to be abolished, since the imperative of biological needs cannot be transcended. But both the nature of the productive process and the activity within it ought to be rendered as humane as possible to an extent consistent with the satisfaction of minimal social and biological needs.

But Fichte and Marx differ in the attitude each takes with respect to present society. The difference is in part due to the fact that Marx, who comes on the scene at a later date, was able to acquire greater knowledge of the specific problems due to the Industrial Revolution, especially in the English context. Although Fichte addresses himself to current political problems in a number of texts, beginning with the *Zurückforderung der Denkfreiheit* (1793), his writing nonetheless remains mainly on an abstract level, which is, however, paralleled by Marx's own early essays. But after Marx's move to England and his increasing acquaintance with the social problems attributable to industrial development, mainly developed through research and only occasionally through direct experience, Marx's writing takes on a concrete emphasis concerning human exploitation and misery, such as the descriptions of the abuses of child labor in *Capital*, which has no counterpart in Fichte's work.[14]

A further parallel is in the respective views of free activity which will supposedly become possible through social reorganization. The parallel between Fichte's claim that in his free time man can turn inward and in Marx's view that human faculties unrelated to the productive process can be developed in communism is unmistakable. For both agree that men have potentials which are not made fully manifest within the productive process and which have little directly to do with the ability to respond to biological needs. Indeed, it is precisely for this reason that the need for free time assumes such importance, since it is only in the time one spends outside the productive process that man's extrabiological capacities can be brought to full development.

So far we have been discussing the importance of activity for fulfillment in both views. An additional area of similarity concerns the practical preconditions necessary to make such activity possible. One such condition is the elimination of external influences which tend to remove the control of society, especially in the productive process, from the people who live in it. As we have seen, Fichte proposes economic closure as his remedy and Marx suggests elimination of the profit motive through the elimination of private property. The means may be somewhat different, but in each case the aim is for man to regain control over his social context. Now, it might be objected that Fichte is quite Platonic in his inattention to the crucial problem of the transformation of the current form of society, certain sectors of which are unlikely to give up their privileges unless obliged to, into a form more rational with respect to human development. But although Marx certainly provides us with a more detailed analysis of current society and hence goes far beyond Fichte in this respect, he has unfortunately little to say on the practical problem of the transition from capitalism to communism beyond occasional references to internal economic collapse and proletarian revolution. One must wonder if, in the final analysis, we can have confidence that this transition to communism, as Marx envisages it, is either likely to occur or in fact is really possible. For despite Marx's emphasis on the relation of theory to practice, this key aspect of his theory receives little attention in his writings, which contain no clear discussion of the problem or the real possibility of the transition from capitalism to communism. But whatever the conclusion to be drawn, the fact remains that the views are similar in their emphasis on the reduction of the pressure exerted by the economic side of social existence in order to free man for further development.

DEVELOPMENT OR FULFILLMENT?

Similar concepts of development and fulfillment have been identified in the two positions. But as yet little has been said about the real possibility of fulfillment. The relation of this problem to the notion of development is obvious. For if there can be fulfillment then in this way the developmental process can be brought to an end. The significance of this point is manifest, since as a social being man's development and fulfillment must occur within the historical process. If human fulfillment is a real possibility, then history itself can finally be brought to a close, or to a real beginning, depending on the point of view one wishes to adopt. But if, on the other hand, fulfillment cannot be attained, then this concept has the status of a regulative ideal toward which human history tends, and development is an ongoing process coextensive with but not completed in history. As we shall see, Fichte and Marx both hold that development is an ongoing process which draws ever nearer to, but can never attain, the goal which would bring it to an end.

Fichte's approach to the limits of human development derives from his understanding of man's activity as context-limited. Man develops only within the context which limits him, but to be human is to strive to overcome or go beyond all limits to one's activity. In Fichte's view it is characteristic of human beings that they constantly attempt to expand the limits of their control over the external world in order to approach the ideal of complete or total freedom. But as such freedom cannot be fully realized on the practical plane, it can only have the status of a mere regulative idea in the Kantian sense of the term.

Within the *WL* Fichte supports this point with an interesting technical argument. In the abstract terminology he employs in this work, Fichte distinguishes determinations as to form and content. Complete development would include both determinations. Yet although one can aim at fulfillment, it cannot be attained since at most the self can determine its form, but not its content, as content is the result of the self's relation to its surroundings. But since the self can only develop through an interrelation with the not-self, although not directly through a relation to itself, it can never transcend this relation.

This abstract argument can perhaps bear restatement in slightly less abstract form. Since practical activity is by definition moral, we can put this point in terms of the concept of man as a moral being. Striving is related to an infinite desire, or desire of the finite individual to be infinitely moral. As the individual progressively brings his environment under his control, he increases his moral capacity to act by widening its scope. But just as one can never completely subjugate the surrounding world, in the same way the radius of man's activity can never be infinite. Further, if it were practically unlimited, the result would be to make morality impossible. For morality requires an obstacle against which one strives, but at the limit all externality is wholly absorbed into the person as the real opposition of the external world vanishes. So by virtue of the fact that morality requires practical activity in a real world, man is condemned to being able to approximate ever more closely to an ideal that he can never attain.

Marx is never explicit on the topic of the limits of human development, but his probable reaction is easily inferred. It follows from his basic belief that man is a social being and that human development is a function of the social context. With respect to Marx's position, this point has a double significance. It is clear that the kind of development practically possible is a result of the kind of society in which one lives. Indeed, as has already been remarked several times over, the point in bringing about a communist society is to make human development a real or practical possibility. Communism does not, however, mark the end of the developmental process, since human history only commences at the time when man can become a human being.

There is further a kind of relativity which follows from the Marxian view of man as a social being. In a superficial sense, there is cultural relativity inherent in the fact that what counts as development is a cultural variable. But beyond mere cultural relativity, there is the element of historical change. Just as "the cultivation of the five senses is the work of all previous history,"[15] so also, as society changes, the form of social fulfillment cannot remain unchanged. Accordingly, although the goal of complete or fully developed human being is a historical constant, the manner in which this is to be attained and what in fact counts as the attainment of this goal vary through human history. Thus, there is a similarity between Marx's general position and the Fichte of the *Grundzüge* in the sense that each relates the form and extent of human fulfillment to human history. But Marx differs from Fichte in his relatively greater understanding of the relativity of the form which full human development can assume to the kind of social context which in fact exists.

The question arises: Can development be brought to an end? In terms of Marx's understanding of man as a social being, the response must be negative for man is dependent on his social context in at least two senses. As already noted, Marx refers repeatedly to an implicit distinction between reproductive and human needs. Now with respect to reproductive needs, man cannot transcend his social condition, regardless of the form society assumes. For his biological dependency on his surroundings can never be gone beyond, and these needs must be met in a social context. Neither can man transcend his social context with respect to human needs. Even if *per impossibile* one did not need the social context for reasons of inherent biological limitation, one would still need a social locus in which to develop as a human being, since man can only be fully human in relation to other human beings. It follows that as man must depend on his social context, he can never be entirely self-subsistent or completely free. Further, to the degree that one can never finally achieve a perfect organization of the social context within which one lives, the effort to achieve maximal freedom within society will always be underway with respect to the goal of perfect freedom and hence in relation to the real possibility of unlimited self-development.

POTENTIALITY

In the preceding chapter the concept of potentiality was briefly mentioned and it was pointed out that all development presupposes a potential to be manifested. But it is important to distinguish between general and specific forms of potentiality. To take an Aristotelian example, in the normal course of events all boys develop into men and hence share in this wider general potential of male children, but only some men have the further, person-specific capacity to become generals. The wider, general potential is the condition of the specific capacity, since only some men can become generals.

The importance of this distinction can perhaps be suggested in the following way. Fichte and Marx both relate the development of the individual to that of mankind in the course of which the form of social context necessary for further development is also evolved. The capacity to generate the requisite form of social context is thus common to mankind as a whole, but this general potential should be distinguished from each person's specific potentials, which he may or may not share with others.

In Fichte's position, potentiality is associated with the concept of the absolute subject. This concept is invoked, as has been mentioned, to describe the subject as a purely theoretical concept. Now, the defining characteristic of subjectivity is activity. In fact activity is at all times limited by the presence of the surrounding world, but in theory at least one can entertain the idea of the subject as unlimited and therefore as completely free. The absolute subject thus stands for the potentially fully developed, or absolutely free, human being. In this sense, the absolute subject is both the potential for and goal of all development.

The suggested interpretation of the absolute self as a source of human potential should not obscure a hierarchical order among human capacities. Certain capacities are the precondition for others. For example, the real possibility of the self to act morally and hence to be a moral being is conditioned by the prior attainment of consciousness and self-consciousness. It follows that although the concept of an absolute self generally implies the pure potentiality for development in general, implicit in this concept is a coordination and temporal order in which specific development, in line with the quasi-logical process already elucidated, can occur.

This last point may perhaps be restated in order to emphasize the dependency of the development of the individual on that of mankind. In Fichte's view, to be fully individual means to be fully moral, and the state of complete morality can be described as the realization of one's capacity to determine one's actions in full accordance with rational criteria. But rational self-determination depends on mutual recognition and self-limitation with respect to others. Although this stage of social interaction has not yet been achieved, its occurrence as a historical stage is both foreseen and necessary. But it should be observed that the development of a person into a real individual is dependent on the prior development of mankind.

Marx makes a similar argument, but there is a difference which should be noted. Although the tendency is by no means absent from his thought, Marx insists on the whole less strongly on the view of history as a process which unfolds with quasi-logical necessity. Even more than does Marx, Fichte seems to see history as a quasi-logical locus in which conditions for further development can and must necessarily be met. Marx at least evokes the possible failure of the historical process with respect to human development. Although this is certainly not a possibility that Marx could cheerfully entertain, it is nevertheless implicit in his belief that a form of society never disappears before all its developmental resources are exhausted and that capitalism could prove to be a stable system which successfully resists all efforts to supersede it. This is of course an aspect of his view that Marx never works out in detail. But despite the fact that the imminent end of our contemporary way of life is trumpeted by Marx time and again, there is no guarantee in terms of his own analysis that the present stage will ever fully exhaust further avenues for growth.

Another difference in Marx's position is his emphasis on class with respect to social change. In the early writings, especially in the *Paris Manuscripts*, Marx employs the term "species-being" and its cognates to designate human potentials which cannot be manifested in capitalism. As already noted, Marx argues that through human needs man differs from other forms of life. Human needs require human potentials for their satisfaction, and it is axiomatic that in order for this to be possible the social structure must be radically transformed. This last point is indistinguishable from Fichte's similar belief. The difference is that in Marx's view the transition from one stage to another requires the concerted activity of a given class, namely, the proletariat. This class analysis, which is of course so important in Marx's view, is entirely absent in Fichte's position.

Despite differences which should not be overlooked, there is nevertheless a discernible parallel in the two views of human potentiality. The parallel can perhaps be summed up in the observation that each distinguishes specific and general forms of potentiality in order to argue that the real or practical manifestation of mankind's general capacity to create a better social context is a necessary precondition for man's practical ability to realize his capacities as an individual.

AGENCY

The developmental process further presupposes a cause which makes it happen. Since man is the subject of his own developmental process, a notion of human agency is implicit in any discussion of human development. It is interesting to note that both Fichte and Marx are ambiguous about the sense in which man is the subject or agent of his own development.

In respect to human being the term "agency" refers to the sense in which the subject can be said to be the cause or moving factor of its own activity. Two kinds of agency can futher be distinguished. "Real" agency means that a person is the cause of his actions, as for instance when I voluntarily raise my arm. "Apparent" agency means that a person is not himself the immediate cause of his activity, as when I raise my arm because I am made to do so, for instance, by a hypnotist. It should be noted that, since the results of both kinds of agency can be indistinguishable, as in the examples given, different forms of agency can be differentiated only by the kind of causation involved. But both real and apparent forms of agency are further to be distinguished from reflex activity, in which agency can be properly assigned neither to the individual in question nor to another person, but rather to a vague concept such as biological heredity or evolution or nature, as when I raise my arm not because I or someone else desires the result, but because I am attempting to ward off a blow. Applying the distinction between real and apparent forms of agency, we can perceive two relations of the person to the developmental process, according as he develops himself or is caused to develop.

The ambiguity in Fichte's understanding of human agency can be attributed to a Kantian residue in his understanding of practical activity. Like Kant, Fichte has a tendency to consider man from a double perspective: as a completely free rational being, and as a completely determined physical being. Although aware of the problem, for which he has frequently been criticized, that we have no grounds for attributing causal efficacy to our moral determinations within the limits imposed by his theory, in his later writings Kant suggests more than once that it is at least not inconsistent to believe in our capacity to act morally. As Kant puts it, "Morality thus leads ineluctably to religion, through which it extends itself to the idea of a powerful moral Lawgiver." [16] But it should be pointed out that Kant's suggestion is less the expression of religious belief than a speculative attempt, within the framework of his epistemological analysis, to heal the bifurcation resulting from the distinction between noumenal and phenomenal perspectives.

Although Fichte appears to follow Kant in his appeal to divine agency, his view is probably closer to that of Hegel. Responding to the problem of the possibility of morality, in both the *Anweisung zum seligen Leben* (1806) and *The Vocation of Man* (1800), Fichte urges that the notion of morality rests on a concept of the divine. In the latter text, in relation to the will he writes, "It has results because it is immediately and infallibly perceived by another will to which it is related: *in Him* it has its first results, and *through Him* it acquires influence." [17] The language of this passage and others like it might lead one to infer that Fichte is here professing an orthodox theism, but this inference would, I think, be a grave interpretative error. Although his view is here admittedly somewhat disguised by its religious trappings, Fichte is making the point that all knowledge is ultimately grounded in faith, since knowledge cannot ground itself. We are accustomed to attribute this view to Hegel, who makes a similar point in numerous places in his writings.[18] But Fichte very clearly anticipates Hegel, when he writes that "no knowledge can be its own foundation, its own proof. . . . It is not knowledge, but a decision of the will to allow the validity of knowledge."[19] If we apply this dictum to the realm of ethics, we must assume that the moral will is effective, even if we can never know this. Hence Fichte writes, "We are compelled to believe that we act, and that we ought to act in a certain manner."[20]

The ambiguity in Fichte's conception of man's agency is, I think, quite clear. On the rational level the individual acts freely and in this respect can be said to be the real cause of his development, although on the level of the external world, man can only be assumed, but not known, to act freely. But if a concept of divine agency must be invoked in order to justify man's moral activity, through which he develops, then man is only apparently but not in fact the cause of his own development.

A similar ambiguity can be detected in Marx's understanding of man's relation to his development. Unlike Fichte, the ambivalence in Marx's position does not arise from a "two-worlds" theory of human being. For as a consequence of his theory of ideology, Marx is required to reject any claim to conscious ideas that are not in some sense influenced or limited by the social context. A problem for Marx's view arises in the justification of any freedom whatsoever within the social context. Marx's attempt to face this problem gives rise to a dual conception of social development as both determined by man and as beyond his control.

Although Marx is to some extent inconsistent on this point, the ambiguity in question is evident in a striking difference in emphasis in early and late texts. In the former, for example, in the *Introduction to the Critique of Hegel's Philosophy of Right* stress is consistently placed on man as the root of man's world. Slightly later, the possibility of fundamental social change is ascribed to conscious group action, as in the *Manifesto*'s famous invitation for the working class to unite in order to throw off its chains. But in subsequent writings, as Marx developed in ever more detail his model of capitalism, the emphasis shifts gradually to the self-sustaining nature of capitalism and of its independence with respect to individual or group intent. Although man is potentially at the center of his world, Marx strongly emphasizes that in fact the real subject in capitalism is capital, which tends toward self-accumulation regardless of our conscious desires. This in turn implies that the real possibility of social change lies less with man's decision to confront the evils of the present form of society than with the inherent tendency of capitalism to sublate itself. In his later writings, Marx accordingly devotes comparatively little attention to man's possible subversion of the capitalist system, but ever increasing interest is displayed in the possibility that the system will subvert itself.

Here again a comparison between Marx and Hegel is instructive. As is well known, there is a tension in the Hegelian position between the role of the individual and that of the absolute. Although in his early writings, Marx follows Hegel in his reliance on the capacity of reason to see through mere appearances, for the most part the emphasis seems to be on man as ultimately responsible for his own development or lack of it. Indeed, as we shall see, Marx strongly objects to Hegel's alleged failure to understand that man is the real subject of human history. But in later writings Marx gives increasing emphasis to the capacity of social reality to function as an autonomous unit in independence of man's will. Here Marx's view runs parallel to the Hegelian concept of the self-developing absolute which unfolds through individuals, but in independence of their desires. In sum, depending on which facet of Marx's writings is emphasized man is either the real or apparent subject or agent of his own development.

CONCEPT OF MAN

The purpose of this chapter has been to call attention to similar concepts of man implicit in Fichte's and Marx's similar concepts of activity. It might now be useful to bring together the points made in the discussion in order to indicate the extent of the parallel. The following, not insignificant measure of agreement has been detected in the comparative analysis of the two positions. In both cases man is viewed as an active but finite being in a natural and social context. As a natural being, man meets his needs through production of objects. The result of man's productive activity is not only to generate an object, but also to generate social relations and hence the social context in which he exists as a definite being. Both further emphasize the basic importance of the economic sector and the sense in which it can inhibit man's activity. But when man further acts to diminish the restrictions which impinge on his activity from the economic sphere, he frees his activity both within and without the productive process. This is the inherent logic of human development.

The developmental process has been further analyzed from three related perspectives. From the perspective of potentials, first and second order potentials were distinguished, that is, general human potentials shared with other men in virtue of which the social context can be transformed in a manner propitious for the manifestation of individual potentials and potentials for individuality. From the perspective of agency, although man cannot at the onset of the process act as he wishes, he can nevertheless set in motion a chain of events which will create the real possibility for being able to act freely. Thus in one sense he is the agent of his own development, although in another sense his agency only develops as a result of the historical process. Finally, from the perspective of human activity, man's development requires that through his activity he undertake to transform the existing social context in order to bring about the manifestation of his own potentials. If it were necessary to sum up the measure of agreement in a single phrase, one might say that through his own activity man limits himself and thus generates the possibility for further development in and through activity.

CHAPTER 6

THEORY AND METATHEORY

IT has so far been shown that there are parallels in the role of activity within the positions of Fichte and Marx, and between their respective views of activity and man. The discussion to this point, in which these parallels have been disclosed, has been on the level of theory. But theory corresponds to metatheory, a dimension clearly present in both positions. Reflection on the nature of theory and on possible alternatives to traditional philosophical theory and even to philosophy as such engages the attention of both Fichte and Marx. Fichte explicitly considers such questions, especially in several early texts, and Marx's writings contain occasional comments on this problem as well as one substantial passage devoted to it. Accordingly, it must now be determined whether the parallel disclosed on the level of theory carries over to the metatheoretical plane.

There is no standard definition of metatheory, although this has been a topic of increasing concern in recent years. But in general, one can say that metatheory is the moment at which theory reflects upon and hence becomes conscious of itself. For present purposes, it will be sufficient to understand metatheory as the reflection on theory in general, for instance, on its nature, purposes, and limits.

Metatheory and theory are interrelated. As the theory of theory, metatheory is conceptually prior to any particular theory, even if it is usually only elaborated after the fact in order to justify a choice of theory which has already been made. But although conceptually prior to theory, metatheory is not therefore independent of it. Indeed, metatheory cannot be independent of theory, since as a theory of theory, it is itself theory.

The interrelation of metatheory and theory is comparable to that of theory and practice. Theory is itself the practice for which metatheory provides the guidelines, since a given theory requires a metatheory in order to justify the kind of position it chooses to defend. But conversely, just as practice provides the *experimentum crucis* for and otherwise influences the choice of theory, so a theory can influence the kind of metatheoretical stance to be adopted.

The interrelation of theory and metatheory is of particular interest for the present discussion. Since, as has been shown, there is a parallel on the level of theory in the two positions, a similar parallel should be available on the metatheoretical plane. But if the similarity on the theoretical level cannot be extended to metatheory, then the original parallel would be difficult to maintain since any given theory depends on a conceptually prior concept of theory as such. Hence we can do no less than attempt to extend the parallel between the two positions to the respective conceptions of the nature of theory in general.

It is obvious that in the extension of the discussion to the metatheoretical level it will be necessary to determine Fichte's and Marx's respective views of the nature of theory as such. But prior to this phase of the discussion, there is an important obstacle which needs to be removed. It is often thought that the distinction between idealism and materialism reflects a choice between two basic kinds of theory. In the present context, this widespread belief is important since it has often been held that, in virtue of its alleged materialism, Marx's position is different in kind from any in the German philosophical tradition. Indeed, all too often the mere mention of materialism serves as a pretext to distinguish Marx's position from philosophy in general.[1] But if the distinction between idealism and materialism contains even a veiled reference to a further distinction between philosophy and non-philosophy, the comparison between the positions of Fichte and Marx must necessarily fail. Thus even before we attempt to develop the parallel between the two metatheories, it will be necessary to defend it against the challenge tacitly posed by the distinction between Fichte's idealism and Marx's materialism.

THE IDEALISM-MATERIALISM DISTINCTION

To analyze the significance of Fichte's idealism and Marx's materialism for the present comparison, we must also address the distinction itself of which their positions are examples. Accordingly, the analysis will proceed in two stages, in the first of which I shall consider the distinction between idealism and materialism as such, and then further discuss the importance of Fichte's idealism and Marx's materialism for the present study.

The importance of distinctions in philosophy or in any intellectual pursuit is almost self-evident. One is tempted to say that distinctions are a necessary means without which discussions of all kinds would necessarily cease to be possible. All thinkers, of whatever stripe or persuasion, constantly operate with a small, but relatively stable stock of ready-made distinctions which has been handed down to us as an important part of the legacy of philosophy and thought in general. It would seem that a significant part of the philosophical task is to add to and refine our usual distinctions. Progress in philosophy, if such a term is indeed at all applicable, often is the result of a new distinction or reformulation of an already familiar one, which are two ways of enabling us to see things with which we are familiar in new and different ways.

But although the benefit to be derived from the application of one or another distinction is obvious, the danger of an abuse is ever present. For once accepted, distinctions order our perceptions and thoughts about experience. As a result, a distinction which is badly drawn or false or otherwise imperfect can have a negative effect on our efforts to understand the world and ourselves. Hence, just as it is useful to coin new distinctions or to reformulate old ones, it is also useful to criticize those on hand as an aid in piercing the veil of illusion sometimes woven by philosophy. An example is the notion of a sense datum, which bears roughly the same relation to philosophy as does phlogiston to physical theory. It is well known that the concept of the sense datum led to a lively debate in related questions, culminating in an attempt by A. J. Ayer, which he later repudiated, to reconstruct objects of experience in terms of this mythical entity.[2]

Because of this example and others like it, it is helpful to examine our fundamental distinctions from time to time. It is sometimes the case that our most hallowed distinctions become problematic when subjected to examination. A case in point is the analytic-synthetic distinction, which Kant took over from Leibniz as a cornerstone of his own position, but which has recently come under sharp attack.[3] I would like to suggest that the idealism-materialism distinction may also be vulnerable.

It is beyond the scope of the present discussion to provide a history of the distinction in question, even in outline. But it is nonetheless useful to indicate something of the range of its application. It would be difficult to name a distinction which has been more frequently employed than this one, nor one which is more deeply rooted in the philosophical tradition. But even a superficial glance at the history of philosophy suffices to reveal how difficult it is to specify the difference to which it refers. Plato is usually thought to be an idealist, and for centuries his position has been known as Platonic idealism. But in the post-Platonic period, the term "idealism" has taken on many meanings whose interrelation is at best tenuous. Merely within the modern German tradition, it is usual to distinguish transcendental (Kant), subjective (Fichte), objective (Schelling), and absolute (Hegel) subforms of idealism. A similar variety arises also with respect to materialism. One of the earliest examples of materialism is the atomism associated with Democritus and Leucippus, which recurred in a related formulation centuries later in Hobbes's position. In the nineteenth century Marxists distinguished historical and dialectical materialism, although as Avineri has shown, these terms are never used by Marx to designate his own position.[4] More recent varieties include epistemic materialism, associated with Carnap and Neurath, and central-state materialism, which gave rise to the mind-brain identity theory in the work of J. J. C. Smart, D. M. Armstrong, and others.

It is more than obvious that this abbreviated list of thinkers associated with one or another of the varieties of idealism or materialism is incomplete. The list could be greatly extended, but that would be unnecessary for even this reduced catalogue is sufficient to indicate the problem which arises when an attempt is undertaken to specify what exactly is meant by this distinction. The proliferation of species of a given genus is sometimes a sign that their relation is becoming ever more distant and hence that their continued grouping under the same heading is increasingly questionable. Although both are called idealists, the differences between Plato and Hegel, for example, seem at least as important as the similarities, even if it is difficult to know how to demonstrate this point without undertaking a full-scale analysis. Indeed, the point is often made that Hegel has more in common with Aristotle than with Plato, which in turns calls into question the use of the term "idealism" in this particular case as a common denominator. Similarly, it is unclear what feature the positions of Democritus, Marx, and Armstrong have in common, although each is supposedly representative of one or another form of materialism.

Nor is it especially helpful to turn to the literature. Despite the attention devoted to the idealism-materialism distinction and the extent to which it is ordinarily presupposed in philosophy, or perhaps even because of these reasons, it is significant that the distinction in question seems never to have been drawn in either a universally accepted or even widely acceptable manner. A comparison of some among the many attempts to define and discuss idealism, materialism, or the difference between them reveals important divergences. In most instances, common to the discussion is a presupposition of their incompatibility, although there is an important difference of opinion on this point. Opinion is further divided on whether these two viewpoints divide the philosophical universe between themselves, or whether either or both must in turn be differentiated from further alternatives.

To consider several representative examples, both the *Dictionary of Philosophy* and the *Philosophisches Wörterbuch* view idealism and materialism as exclusive alternatives, whose principal difference concerns the relative priority accorded to consciousness or to matter.[5] This position is also followed by Georg Lukács in his posthumously published work on social ontology.[6] On the contrary, the *Enciclopedia Filosofica* opposes idealism to realism and materialism to both idealism and spiritualism.[7] From a slightly different perspective, *Baldwin's Dictionary of Philosophy and Psychology* opposes idealism to materialism or naturalism, and materialism is defined as that theory which argues for the reduction of mental events to physical processes.[8] In the "Refutation of Idealism," G. E. Moore considers the opposition between idealism or spiritualism and commonsense realism.[9] Kemp Smith and H. B. Acton, following Smith, maintain that the distinction refers to whether matter is primary to mind and to spiritual values, and both argue that idealism has to be distinguished not only from materialism but from naturalism and objectivism as well.[10]

Other writers presume that a strict distinction between idealism and materialism cannot be drawn. Hegel, for example, maintains that in virtue of its concern with concepts all forms of philosophy are forms of idealism and that, as he puts it, the opposition of idealism and materialism is without significance.[11] On the contrary, Santayana claims that all idealists are in fact crypto-materialists and that a self-consistent theory of idealism is impossible.[12] Bosanquet opposes idealism to realism and argues that they are not sharp contrasts, but perspectives which have much in common.[13] More recently, Rorty has suggested, in a discussion of alternative conceptual frameworks, that the distinction in question cannot be defended, since it rests on a prior and untenable distinction.[14]

I have so far identified two levels of approach to the idealism-materialism distinction. Taken together, these two general approaches suggest that the distinction in question is not unproblematic. Prior to its utilization, certain questions need to be answered. Among these questions are the following: Are idealism and materialism mutually exclusive, or complementary theories? Is there a "normal" way of drawing this distinction, or can it only be drawn normatively? Can the different forms of the distinction be reduced to one another or to a central paradigm, or are they irreconcilably dissimilar?

Unless the problems posed by these queries can be satisfactorily resolved, it would seem that the wisdom of the continued usage of the distinction in question is doubtful, since the distinction itself may not be tenable. This last point is worth pondering, if for no other reason than that this distinction is often assumed to be valid without further consideration. For present purposes it is important to note that the supposed distinction has frequently been employed for the description of nineteenth-century thought.

Even a rapid review of the schema usually employed in descriptions of nineteenth-century thought suggests heavy reliance on a possibly untenable distinction. Classical German philosophy is often divided into three, temporarily unequal segments: the critical philosophy of Kant; idealism, represented by Fichte, Schelling, and Hegel; and materialism, Marx's perspective. The result is the "identification" of a triple-methodological opposition in classical German thought, comprising three methodologically distinguishable theories.

This tripartition of German philosophy is based on several assumptions. On the one hand, Kant's statements, as early as the first *Critique* and as late as the *Opus Posthumum*, that his thought is an idealism are unaccountably ignored, thus establishing an "opposition" between the critical philosophy and idealism. On the other hand, assertions by Fichte, Schelling, and Hegel to the effect that their positions are idealistic, and by Marx to an extent, but even more so by the Marxists, that Marx's thought is materialistic, are taken at face value, thereby generating a further "opposition" between idealism and materialism.

FICHTE, MARX, AND THE IDEALISM-MATERIALISM DISTINCTION

So far, I have tried to show that the idealism-materialism distinction may well be problematic. After this review of the distinction as such, we can turn to its implications for the comparative study of Fichte and Marx. In view of the significance commonly attributed to the difference between idealism and materialism, it is of interest that Fichte and Marx both invoke the distinction in order to render plausible their respective theoretical approaches. In each case, indication of the inadequacy of the alternative procedure is taken as an argument in favor of an opposite perspective. Distinguishing idealism and realism, Fichte castigates the alleged inconsistencies of what, in his terminology, amounts to materialism. Conversely, Marx differentiates materialism and idealism in order to object to the latter. But although in each case there is a clear opposition between two sharply distinguished positions on the rhetorical level, the confrontation seems mainly to be confined to this plane. For as we shall see, in each case the "public" espousal of one side of what is portrayed as an irreducible opposition is in fact tempered by a "private" attempt in each position to propose and to defend a form of theory which is intermediate with respect to the extremes distinguished.

Fichte comments frequently on the idealism-materialism distinction, especially in the *First* and *Second Introductions* to the *WL*. These texts are of unequal value, since the former, which is explicitly directed to a public not versed in philosophy, is argued on a semipopular level not entirely faithful to the position Fichte elsewhere defends; whereas the latter, which is aimed at a philosophical audience, is more solidly defended and hence probably a more reliable indication of Fichte's own thought. But if one considers the importance of the idealism-materialism distinction for his thought, it is significant that he apparently feels that initial arguments for his position need to be made at this point.

Fichte explicitly distinguishes between theory and metatheory. He bases his own position on metatheoretical considerations concerning his normative understanding of the aim of philosophy and the type of theory best adapted to this purpose. Although he clearly holds that the philosophical goal is the explanation of experience, it is relatively easy to misunderstand the kind of theory he in fact favors due to his partially inconsistent presentation of his views. For although he offers at least three different arguments, from two of them one conclusion follows, whereas a different conclusion follows from the third and probably most important discussion.

In the two arguments Fichte makes on a semipopular level, he maintains, through separate lines of reasoning, that there are only two possible approaches to philosophy, idealism and realism. Idealism is the view that experience is to be accounted for through a theory of the person, or subject of experience. Realism, which Fichte also labels dogmatism, roughly corresponds to what Marx calls materialism. It is the position that experience is to be explained in terms of an independent given, the real or reality.

From this single argument, Fichte draws two separate and probably incompatible lessons. In the first discussion, he suggests that neither possible approach to experience can refute the other, since the quarrel is about first principles. He concludes, in an often cited passage, that the approach one elects is simply a function of one's own interests. "What sort of philosophy one chooses depends, therefore, on what sort of man one is; for a philosophical system is not a dead piece of furniture that we can reject or accept as we wish; it is rather a thing animated by the soul of the person who holds it. A person indolent by nature or dulled and distorted by mental servitude, learned luxury, and vanity will never raise himself to the level of idealism" (*WL*, p. 16). The evident weakness of this psychogenetic comment is that, if both approaches are of equal value, then it is not possible rationally to defend one choice as opposed to the other. But as is implicit in the *ad hominem* addressed to realists, Fichte is ultimately unwilling to acknowledge that the choice between the two approaches is to be effected on purely subjective grounds.

In a second discussion, Fichte maintains perhaps inconsistently that, although neither approach can refute the other, realism is inadequate to the task of explaining experience. It follows that if realism is not a viable theory, then idealism is the sole possible view. "Thus dogmatism can only repeat its principle, and then reiterate it under various guises: it can state it, and then state it again; but it cannot get from this to the explicandum, and deduce the latter. Yet philosophy consists precisely of this deduction. Hence, dogmatism even from the speculative viewpoint, is no philosophy at all, but merely an impotent claim and assurance. Idealism is left as the only possible philosophy" (*WL*, p. 19). But although this attempt to impugn the credentials of realism is an improvement over the weaker admission that the question of the preferability between the two alternatives cannot be adjudicated, this indirect argument for idealism is still unsatisfactory. For as it has not been shown that idealism and realism between them exhaust all the relevant possibilities, the alleged failure of realism as an adequate theoretical perspective can in no way be construed as a point in favor of idealism. Indeed, Fichte seems perfectly aware of this line of criticism, since in still a third discussion he proposed critical idealism as a theory which is neither idealism nor realism, but combines the virtues of both.

In the latter argument, Fichte provides the analysis on which he bases the position elaborated in the *WL*. As in the preceding arguments, idealism and realism are separate, self-consistent approaches, neither of which can refute the other since the quarrel is about first principles. Further, reason cannot choose between them, since each is directed as a different facet of experience. The proper view is a third alternative which combines the virtues of the a posteriori approach of realism and a priori attitude of idealism. In this way, realism is explained through idealism, but idealism is based on realism.

The idea behind this view is certainly less obscure than the terminology Fichte uses to refer to it. Terms such as "real-idealism," "ideal-realism," "critical idealism," and "transcendental idealism" abound in profusion and confusion. But the basic concept is quite simple, in that in any theory a distinction must be drawn between experience and the attempt to explain it. The role of speculation is not to replace experience, whatever that might mean, but rather to aid in understanding that which is not self-explanatory.

> The first standpoint is that of pure speculation; the second that of life and scientific knowledge. . . . The second is only intelligible on the basis of the first; realism has grounds, indeed, apart from that we are constrained to it by our own nature, but it has no *known* and *comprehensible* grounds: yet the first standpoint, again, exists only for the purpose of making the second intelligible. Idealism can never be a *mode of thought*, it is merely a *speculative* point of view. (*WL*, p. 31)

If the position Fichte finally wishes to defend is not idealism in any simple sense, but rather a proposed intermediate between idealism and realism, then one might expect him to be as critical of the former as he is of the latter. Indeed this is the case. Distinguishing in the *WL* the form of idealism he proposes from other varieties, Fichte attacks the latter for making unjustified and unjustifiable assumptions about the epistemological subject. It follows that neither idealism nor realism finds unqualified favor in a position which, although often consigned without qualification to the idealist camp, is understood by its author as an attempted mediation between two equally unacceptable extremes.

The task of ascertaining Marx's understanding of the idealism-materialism distinction is complicated by the inability of many, especially so-called orthodox Marxists, to distinguish between Marx's writings and Engels's own statements and hence to differentiate between Marx's position and Marxism. In his own writings, Engels described the distinction with great clarity, but it is less certain that Engels's rather schematic account of this problem represents Marx's own thinking on the subject. Indeed, when we turn to Marx's writings, here as elsewhere, we perceive a certain ambiguity in his position.

The sensitivity of Marx's reaction to different positions is sometimes undervalued. It would be an error to confuse Marx's often polemical criticism of forms of idealism with an inherent hostility to idealism itself. By the same token, one ought not to overlook his critical stance with respect to certain kinds of materialism. But if we are to grasp the "location" of his position with respect to other alternatives, it should be realized that Marx is by no means either wholly enamored of materialism, nor is he entirely repelled by idealism.

As a first step in this regard, it is important to note the qualitative difference in Marx's reaction to Hegel and to other idealists. This reaction to Hegel is by no means exclusively negative. Rather, it is a mixture of enormous respect for what he considers to be an important achievement and criticism where he believes criticism is due. Although a central theme in Marx's early writings is the struggle to come to grips with the Hegelian position, his criticism is associated with a balanced viewpoint. Marx is acutely aware of the positive aspects of the Hegelian synthesis, as witness the fact that he constantly returns to Hegelian themes in his own position. For example, in the *Paris Manuscripts* Marx professes admiration for what he terms Hegel's great law of negativity. Some time later in the *Grundrisse* he apparently endorses, as we shall see, a Hegelian theory of explanation. Further, it is common knowledge that the attempt in *Capital*, as Marx puts it, to set Hegel on his feet is in part carried out with Hegelian categories.

Marx is much more uncompromising in his attitude toward other forms of idealism, whether orthodox or tinged with materialism. As early as the *Dissertation* he distinguishes so-called liberals, who are later to be known as the Young Hegelians, from the more orthodox post-Hegelian idealists. Marx remarks that in a sense the two approaches are complementary and hence of equal value. For each of the adversaries in effect accomplishes what the other wants and not what he himself intends to accomplish. Still there is a difference to be observed, since the former, that is, the Young Hegelians, are at least critical in their desire to apply philosophy to the world, while the latter are content merely to theorize within the limits prescribed by philosophy with hardly a glance at external surroundings.

But it should be noted that Marx's reaction to his materialistically inclined contemporaries is, if anything, more severe than his objection to orthodox forms of idealism. The latter are after all guilty of nothing more serious than failing to consider the relation between their theories and the external world, whereas the former, who are aware of the problem, err still more grievously in thinking that criticism is by itself sufficient to change reality. *The Holy Family* is a direct attack on the Young Hegelian, critical approach and on its major representative, Bruno Bauer. According to Marx, Bauer's critical stance is really a concealed form of theology, and represents the failure of criticism alone to effect a change.

Marx uses the opportunity for some sharp polemics. A striking instance is his sharp attack on Franz Zychlin von Zychlinski, who under the pseudonym of Szeliga published a review of Eugène Sue's *Mystères de Paris*. Marx writes that "finite understanding, supported by my senses, distinguishes an apple from a pear and a pear from an almond, but my speculative reason declares these perceptual differences to be unessential and unimportant. My speculative reason sees in the apple *the same thing* as in the pear and in the pear the same thing as in the almond, namely 'the Fruit.' Particular, actual fruits are taken to be only apparent fruits whose true essence is 'the Substance,' 'the Fruit.'" [15] In other words, much as Feuerbach claims that within Christianity the relation of man to God is portrayed in an inverted manner, so Marx here accuses "critical theorists" such as Szeliga of mistaking the appearance for reality and conversely. And Marx closes the discussion in *The Holy Family* with the comment that the critical theory has failed to sublate the world, but has at least been successful in sublating itself, that is, in bringing about the disappearance of his own theoretical journal.

Unlike the Young Hegelians whose materialism is more or less hidden behind their critical attitude, in Feuerbach it is overt. In comparison with his treatment of the Young Hegelians, Marx's criticism of Feuerbach is certainly more restrained. His basic objection is that although Feuerbach correctly perceives that reality has an objective side, namely, a sense in which it exists independently of perception of it, he nevertheless fails to grasp its complementary, or subjective, side. Marx develops this point in the first of the "Theses on Feuerbach," where he notes that Feuerbach is unable to appreciate the role played by human activity. In this sense Feuerbach's materialism has no advantage over idealism, since both are too abstract to grasp human being. In fact, one could even maintain that Feuerbach's brand of materialism reduces to a species of idealism, since it understands man as a merely rational being, thus abstracting from his other characteristics.

As Marx is by turns critical of forms of both idealism and materialism, his own view cannot simply be equated with either if he is not to be guilty of radical inconsistency, which does not seem to be the case. But although Marx is generous in his specific criticism of others, he is sparing in his own self-characterization, and what few hints there are are often misleading. For these reasons, it seems appropriate to give more than normal weight to a rare passage in the *Paris Manuscripts* in which Marx seems to imply that what is needed is an intermediate position which combines the virtues of both extremes without the pitfalls associated with either of the exclusive alternatives embodied in the idealism-materialism distinction. Here Marx differentiates naturalism or humanism from materialism and idealism. He remarks that when developed, the former perspective is both the true unity of the alternatives in question and the only view appropriate for the understanding of world history. "We see here how consistent naturalism or humanism is distinguished from both idealism and material, and at the same time constitutes their unifying truth. We see also that only naturalism is able to comprehend the process of world history." [16]

If we compare Fichte's and Marx's attitudes to the idealism-materialism distinction, we can discern a parallel. One similarity is that in each position, the distinction aids in the selection and defense of a given form of theory. There is, of course, a difference in the degree of attention accorded to metatheory. Fichte, as indicated, is concerned at numerous points to justify from a metatheoretical perspective the form of theory he prefers. But with the exception of the important passage on "The Method of Political Economy" in the Introduction to the *Grundrisse* Marx accords little attention to the justification of the kind of theory he in fact employs. But despite this evident difference, the two metatheoretical views are further similar in that although Fichte is often simply described as an idealist and Marx as a materialist, both desire to circumvent the exclusive alternative which the idealism-materialism distinction represents through the adoption of a position intermediate between the two extremes. But since there is a parallel between Fichte's and Marx's understanding and use of the idealism-materialism distinction, it follows that whether or not this distinction can be defended it ought not to pose an obstacle for the comparative study of Fichte's and Marx's metatheoretical views.

METATHEORY

The point of raising the materialism-idealism distinction in the present context is twofold: to show the problematic nature of one of the basic distinctions in the philosophic arsenal, and to remove the obstacle posed by this distinction to the comparison between Fichte and Marx. It seems clear that if in the final analysis the distinction in question is tenable or if Fichte is an idealist and Marx a materialist in any simple sense, then the parallel I have tried to reveal between the two views would be of limited interest since there would be a difference in kind between the two theories. In order to forestall this kind of criticism I have tried to show that the distinction between idealism and materialism is fraught with difficulty and I have further argued that even if the distinction can be safely drawn, it is not the case that either Fichte or Marx is an idealist or a materialist in an unqualified sense.

But even if neither theory is an instance of unalloyed idealism or materialism, it is still possible that Fichte and Marx have basically different views of the nature of theory itself. I want now to redeem the promissory note implicit in the distinction between theory and metatheory by demonstrating an important parallel in the two views of the nature of theory. Since there has so far been little attention paid to either Fichte's or Marx's conceptions of metatheory, I shall be concerned more to indicate the outlines of the respective metatheories and the parallel between them than to provide an exhaustive analysis of either view.

If we turn now to a general characterization of the respective views of theory in general, two kinds of similarity can be described. One area of similarity lies in the concern with what may be called a "systematic" as opposed to a "nonsystematic," or pluralistic, approach to experience. In the Cartesian and post-Cartesian portion of the modern philosophical tradition, until approximately the middle of the nineteenth century, there is a heavy emphasis on the elaboration of a conceptual system based on one or at most several initial principles adequate for the analysis of any and all items of experience. Attention is consequently devoted more to what different forms of experience have in common on a higher level of abstraction than to what, in the more immediate, or concrete, sense tends to set them apart.

This interest in the systematic analysis of experience, broadly conceived, manifests itself in both Fichte's and Marx's conceptions of the nature of theory. The emphasis in Fichte's thought on system is one of its most evident features. We have already seen that his entire position is developed out of the hypothesis that the self is active plus the three quasi-logical rules descriptive of the manifestation of the self's activity. The combination of this hypothesis with the rules enables Fichte to perform his "deduction of presentation," in which all types of experience are reduced to the single paradigm of the subject-object interaction, analyzable from the twin perspectives of idealism and realism.

It is less commonly realized, perhaps because the intrinsic logic of Marx's position has not often been studied, that Marx shares with Fichte the idealistic tendency toward system. Although Marx's thought never exhibits the rigid structure typical of others in the philosophical tradition, the tendency toward system is evident in a variety of ways. Marx's tendency to explain all forms of social reality in terms of man's activity has already been discussed. The reductionist aspect of this approach is readily evident in Marx's propensity, in terms of his distinction between superstructure and base, to explain all other forms of social activity in terms of the underlying economic structure of society. The systematic side of Marx's position is further evident in his concern to elaborate a categorial theory, in which a small number of explanatory concepts or categories both exemplified in the social context and adequate for its analysis are isolated and combined in quasi-rigorous fashion. For example, in the Introduction to the *Grundrisse*, Marx defines the category of possession as a tool for social analysis, when he writes: "In the higher society it appears as the simpler relation of a developed organisation. But the concrete substratum of which possession is a relation is always presupposed." [17] The same kind of systematic tendency is again apparent in Marx's distinction, again in the same text, between specific categories, manifested in one kind of social context only, and more general or abstract categories, such as labor, which are to be found in different forms of society. [18]

A second feature common to both views, but less often discussed, is what may be called the "phenomenological" or first person approach to experience in general. In this approach, experience is to be understood from the perspective of the individual who in fact interacts with the external world, as opposed to the perhaps more common procedure in which experience is described from the "third person" perspective of the supposedly neutral observer. In Fichte's view, the first person perspective is evident in his definition of experience, referred to above, as the contents of consciousness accompanied by a feeling of necessity. It follows from this definition that experience is restricted to direct, conscious awareness of the interaction between the experiential subject and his surroundings. In the same way, Marx also emphasizes that the world is to be understood and explained through our conscious interaction with an object of experience which is known only as it impinges on us, although it must be assumed to exist independently of us. "The totality as it appears in the head, as a totality of thoughts, is a product of the thinking head, which appropriates the world in the only way it can. . . . The real subject retains its autonomous existence outside the head just as before. . . . Hence, in the theoretical method, too, the subject, society, must always be kept in mind as the presupposition." [19]

The two characteristics distinguished so far are not unique to Fichte and Marx, but rather are common to a number of thinkers. To a variable degree, the first person approach to experience is found in all forms of phenomenology, and the tendency toward system is even more widely represented in modern philosophy. But there is further a third characteristic, that is, the interest in ungrounded epistemology which, while not entirely specific to Fichte and Marx, tends to distinguish their conceptions of epistemology from that to be found in the mainstream of the modern philosophical tradition. In order to make this point, it will be helpful to make a general statement about the nature of modern philosophy and its relation to the wider philosophical tradition in order further to relate the positions of Fichte and Marx to both periods.

Although the modern problem of knowledge, in different form, is already to be found in Greek thought, the approach to this problem in terms of a ground or foundation arises only in the modern tradition. The modern concern with foundationalism was given a powerful push, and perhaps received its initial impetus, in the Cartesian position. After Descartes, this theme has become ever more important as philosophy has continued to turn inward upon itself in an inquiry into its own preconditions. Certainly since Descartes the problem of whether philosophy can be grounded has become a basic philosophical concern, and by the same token contemporary philosophical interest in anti-foundationalism continues to wrestle with the Cartesian problematic, even if its solution is now usually rejected.

It is helpful, to understand the problem of foundationalism, to set it in the historical context. Philosophy has, virtually since its inception, been preoccupied with the search for certain knowledge.[20] In Plato's thought, one finds a description of philosophy as the science of sciences, which justifies both itself and the other, special sciences. In the Platonic view, especially as stated in the sixth book of the *Republic*, epistemology depends on an underlying ontology, which can be directly given in philosophic intuition. The claim to knowledge cannot be doubted, since in this view reality is directly available to immediate intuition. But with the decline of the Greek ontology, it was no longer possible to argue for direct knowledge of the real, even if the criterion of certainty as the necessary condition for knowledge in the full sense was not abandoned.

Although in other respects Descartes's position may arguably be new, from the perspective of the traditional concern with certain knowledge its contribution is to propose an alternative means to attain the same goal. In the *Discourse on Method*, Descartes tells us that his dual purpose is to put an end to the conflict among different schools of thought and to protect against skepticism by providing certain knowledge. The *cogito* has a double function, as that point from which the remainder of the theory can be rigorously deduced, and further as that point which can be known to be true and which therefore confers certainty on the theory as a whole. Accordingly, Descartes can claim that the *cogito* can serve as the necessary Archimedean point which will ground or absolutely justify epistemological claims, and will also secure clear and distinct ideas which cannot err and whose veracity is grounded in the bedrock of the *cogito*. Thus Descartes hopes to attain the traditional Platonic goal. As we shall see, Fichte and Marx both reject the view that knowledge can be grounded and, in consequence, also reject the view that certainty is a necessary condition of knowledge.

As is so often the case in Fichte's writings, his comments about his intentions are misleading when compared with his own position. This is especially the case for his view of the nature of theory, which as a result has often been misunderstood. It has already been remarked that although Fichte agreed in general with the conclusions of the critical philosophy, he found the architectonic form in which Kant couched his thought to be unappealing. In order to carry to its conclusion, that is, fully to develop the kind of philosophical theory begun by Kant, Fichte felt impelled to restate the critical philosophy in "systematic" form. Hence, in a letter written shortly before he composed the first version of the *WL*, he remarks: "I have discovered a new foundation, from which the entire philosophy can easily be developed. Above all Kant has the right philosophy, but only concerning its results, not its grounds." [21]

This passage is however deceptive, since it leaves the clear implication that the manner in which the Kantian edifice is to be shored up requires it to be set atop a rationalist foundation. In other words, this passage and others like it create the impression that Fichte's strategy for the reconstruction of the critical philosophy required its unqualified restatement in Cartesian terms, and indeed even the most sensitive commentators have often understood this to be Fichte's intention. [22] But as we shall see, this is a fundamental misinterpretation of the position Fichte in fact describes.

Fichte signals his basic conception of theory in the opening paragraph of the *WL*, where he describes his task as the determination of the first and unconditioned ground (*Grundsatz*) of human knowledge. As unconditioned, or unlimited, the ground sought is not derivable from other propositions, and is hence not demonstrable. He writes: "Our task is to *discover* the primordial, absolutely unconditioned first principle of all human knowledge. This can be neither *proved* nor *defined*, if it is to be an absolutely primary principle" (*WL*, p. 93).

In the *WL* this claim appears as a conclusion, the argument for which is found in Fichte's metatheoretical discussion in *Über den Begriff der Wissenschaftslehre* (1794, 1798). In the latter work, Fichte sets out a normative view of theory in general. Knowledge is arrived at through science. A given science constitutes a whole, the truth of which depends on the initial proposition or set of propositions from which it derives. The primitive concepts of a science cannot be demonstrated within it, since they are presupposed by it. Philosophy is also a science, that is, the science of all particular sciences. It has as its task the grounding of all other sciences and hence of human knowledge in the widest sense. But like the particular sciences, philosophy must necessarily presuppose an initial proposition or set of propositions which cannot be shown to be true. For this reason, although one would normally expect Fichte to make the traditional claim for certain knowledge, he instead characterizes his own position as hypothetical. "The following investigation has no more than the status of an hypothesis." [23]

When we compare Fichte's view to Descartes's, it is apparent that although both employ a concept of ground, the concept is to be interpreted differently in the two positions. It has been mentioned that in Descartes's view, the *cogito* has a twofold function as a principle from which the remaining portion of the theory can be deduced and as that point whose demonstrable veracity imparts truth to the theory derived from it. There is clearly a rationalist dimension to the Fichtean position. Fichte follows the rationalist concept of rigorous theory half way by attempting to deduce his entire position from a single concept. But since he at the same time explicitly rejects the idea that a first or initial principle can be demonstrated or otherwise known to be true, he decisively parts company with the Cartesian conception of philosophy as a certain science, or science of certain knowledge.

Although exaggerated claims are often made for Marx's view of knowledge, it is less often described.[24] Marx does not provide more than isolated discussions of his view of the nature of theory, since his writing for the most part lacks the metatheoretical, or self-reflection, dimension found in Fichte's thought. It is hence to be regretted that the single substantial passage which does indicate Marx's metatheoretical views has not received adequate attention.[25] This passage occurs in the Introduction to the *Grundrisse*, especially in the third section, to which the editors have given the name "Method of Political Economy."

In this text, Marx argues that which kind of theory we defend depends on a choice among two alternative procedures, which supposedly exhaust all approaches to experience. In political economy, there are only two ways in which to understand the social context. It is incorrect to begin with "the real and the concrete, with the real precondition"[26] since in practice this requires us to analyze our terms further to determine their constituents. Rather than to employ high-level abstractions it is better to proceed directly from their simpler constituents, that is, from "simple relations such as labor, division of labor," and so forth.[27] This latter approach presents the advantage that its component parts are immediately transparent, and hence need not be further analyzed. It further enables us to reconstitute the concrete given through a combination of these elements. The concrete given thus assumes a double status, as "the concentration of many determinations, hence unity of the diverse" or result and accordingly the end point of the knowing process, although "it is the point of departure in reality and hence also the point of departure for observation and conception."[28]

Although Marx's argument is stated in the context of political economy, it is, I believe, quite general. Restated in other terms, the point seems to be that in order to understand the social context as given in experience and perhaps experience as such, we require concepts which function as explanatory factors. In terms of these factors we reconstitute the contents of experience, which can be considered as a whole initially composed of them, although the concepts are derived from experience. Hence, empirical knowledge is arrived at as the consequence of an inherently circular process which presupposes, if it is to result in knowledge, that the world reconstructed as the *terminus ad quem* preexist as the *terminus a quo*. It follows that, although the inference has not often been seen and Marx does not draw it explicitly, the Marxian view of epistemological circularity sets a limit to the strength of the claim which can be made for experiential knowledge.

The reason for this implicit conclusion can perhaps be reconstructed in the following way: As we have seen, explanatory concepts utilized by Marx are categories defined as simple relations of developed organization. In terms of this definition and the role of the category within Marx's view, his reasons in limiting his claims for knowledge can easily be inferred. There is, to begin with, the obvious point that if, as Marx holds, the categories are a posteriori and cannot hence be demonstrated in the strict sense, then incorrigible knowledge cannot result from their utilization. Just as geometry depends upon the indemonstrable validity of its initial axioms which cannot be proven through use, so Marx holds that theoretical knowledge is inherently speculative and by inference not knowledge in the full sense. Further, there is the unavoidable dependence of the categories upon the social context from which they derive. As the context changes, so must the categories descriptive of it. Experience cannot thus yield timeless truth, but only truth limited by time. Accordingly, although Marx agrees with Kant and Hegel that the interpretation of experience requires the utilization of a categorial framework, his emphasis on the historical variability of the framework in fact descriptive of the mutable social context requires him to deny that any such transhistorical explanatory scheme can be elucidated.

When we compare the conceptions of theory as such in Fichte and Marx, a basic parallel is evident. In each case the condition of the analysis of experience is the adoption of a set of explanatory principles in terms of which the explanatory framework is to be elaborated and experience understood, but which cannot themselves be proven in rigorous fashion either prior to or through experience. It follows that in both cases claims for certain knowledge in the traditional sense cannot be made, since epistemology cannot be grounded. Fichte and Marx thus stand opposed to the Platonic-Cartesian tradition in which only certain knowledge is knowledge fully worthy of the name. Further, if, as has been suggested, to refuse the claim to incorrigible knowledge is to make a turn away from the traditional conception of philosophy and toward pragmatism, then both Fichte and Marx can be said to make the pragmatic turn.[29]

If this point is correct, it would seem that to an unsuspected extent, the anti-Cartesian current in contemporary thought in effect commits many contemporary thinkers, such as Quine and Carnap, or Heidegger and the later Wittgenstein, to pragmatism broadly conceived. In this respect, the refusal of foundationalism in the positions of Fichte and Marx can be seen as an anticipation of a widespread but only rarely perceived development in contemporary thought. It would be beyond the compass of the present discussion to pursue either the relation between the views of theory as such in Fichte and Marx or their respective relation to contemporary philosophy. But three further parallels between the two views of metatheory, which follow from their shared anti-foundationalism, should be indicated.

1. Most philosophers strive to avoid any hint of epistemological circularity on pain of possibly falling into a *circulus vitiosus*, although there are some exceptions. In Greek thought, Aristotle[30] opposed the Socratic-Platonic emphasis on the inseparability of knowing and doing in his argument that there are certain kinds of

practical activity, such as playing the flute, for which we need prior knowledge which can, however, only be had through the activity itself. From a somewhat different perspective, epistemological circularity is central to Hegel's view of philosophical science as the circle of circles,[31] and, in related form, in the post-Husserlian, phenomenological interest in the so-called hermeneutical circle.[32]

A view of epistemological circularity arises in both Fichte's and Marx's positions in virtue of their respective denials of the possibility of an epistemological ground. Fichte, who unlike Marx, is explicitly aware of this consequence, distinguishes at least three kinds of epistemological circularity. One form is that which results from the interaction between subjectivity and objectivity. The result, according to Fichte, is the kind of circle which can be broadened but from which there is ultimately no escape on pain of falling into dogmatism. (See *WL*, p. 247.) Then there is the circularity in the relation between the twin perspectives, idealism and realism, from which experience is to be understood. (See *WL*, p. 147.) To illustrate, the activity of the finite individual, who is the subject of experience, can and in fact must be viewed both from the practical point of view as in fact limited, but ideally as potentially infinite. Finally, there is the circular nature of logic itself. (See *WL*, pp. 93–94.) Although the rules of logic need to be assumed in order for the discussion to progress, these same rules can only be established as a later result of the same discussion.

The Marxian concept of epistemological circularity is better known under the name of the so-called "progressive-regressive method."[33] Although Sartre specifically claims to borrow the method he uses from Lefebvre, his discussion seems to be largely based on the relevant passages in the *Grundrisse*. Further, the idea of an analysis which is both analytical and synthetic was anticipated by Hegel.[34] The relevant difference is that whereas Hegel took this method as a precondition to knowledge in the traditional philosophical sense, as we have seen, Marx resisted this conclusion. But as he did not apparently notice that the thrust of his view of knowledge is against the Cartesian conception of foundationalism, one should not expect him to be fully aware of the consequences that follow from his anti-foundationalism. It is thus not surprising that he neither distinguishes subtypes of epistemological circularity nor even identifies circularity as a characteristic of his own theory of knowledge. But the circularity implicit in his concept of knowledge should not for that reason be overlooked. It follows from his view of the category as both necessary for the explanation of experience and a posteriori. In this way experiential knowledge can be seen to require a categorial framework, although the categories utilized to explain experience are derived from it. Otherwise stated, the circularity is the consequence of the fact that a necessary element of the explanation of experience is only given in and through experience.

2. The loss of certainty that results from the inability to ground knowledge gives rise to a change in the conception of truth. The traditional conception of truth is truth now and forever or, in Spinoza's felicitous phrase, *sub specie aeternitatis*. In this view, an idea is true when it corresponds to an independent reality, as distinguished from the relation between thought and appearance which results in mere opinion. Truth in this sense depends upon two necessary distinctions. On the one hand, there is the epistemological difference between knowledge and opinion. When one has knowledge, one has true opinion, but the converse is not true since true opinion does not necessarily presuppose knowledge. For an opinion may be true, although the reasoning on which it rests is false. Or we can have true opinion today and only know tomorrow. Or we can have true opinion and never know. But reality is the object of knowledge. Thus in order to be able to make the epistemological distinction between knowledge and opinion, we must further be able to make the ontological distinction between reality and appearance. Accordingly, the epistemological claim to truth rests on the viability of a prior ontological distinction between appearance and reality. But if either of these distinctions cannot be made out, the claim to truth in the traditional sense cannot be maintained. Indeed, it has further been suggested that unless the wider claim to apodicticity can be maintained, the claim to truth cannot be made at all.[35]

Although he has little directly to say about the nature of truth, Fichte challenges both of the distinctions upon which the classical conception rests. From his perspective one cannot distinguish between opinion and knowledge. Although there are more or less rigorous forms of opinion, of which the most rigorous in his view is the science of knowledge developed in the *WL*, one cannot fully transcend opinion in order to claim knowledge. That this is his view is evident, for instance, in his description in a passage already quoted of his own discussion as hypothetical. The implication is that since philosophy has no access to certainty, it must remain speculative. Although one should certainly not confuse informed speculation with untutored opinion, philosophical speculation nevertheless cannot legitimately make the claim to certainty characteristic of knowledge in the traditional sense.

This result is consonant with the Fichtean approach to knowledge in terms of a first-person epistemology which depends on the interaction of subject and object of experience. Since objectivity cannot be encountered otherwise than through its effect upon the experiential subject, and not from some hypothetical neutral standpoint, the distinction between reality and appearance can have a philosophical use on the level of theory, although it cannot be met within experience. Fichte signals this conclusion in several ways, such as by his choice of terminology, for instance through his use of the term "not-self" to denote that which is given in experience, as opposed to the term "absolute not-self" which designates objectivity as it can be thought but not experienced and hence not known. But since in Fichte's position objectivity in the traditional sense can be thought, but neither experienced nor known, the claim to truth in the traditional sense cannot be made out within his view.

Unlike Fichte, Marx addresses himself directly to the question of truth, as well as the distinctions upon which it rests. As already noted, the second "Thesis on Feuerbach" contains the statement that the question of the truth of a theory cannot be settled theoretically, but only practically. The consequence of this claim for the traditional conception of truth is clear. Since no practical observation can result in incorrigible knowledge, there can be no legitimate claim to apodictic truth. Marx further clarifies his stand on this question through his implicit view of the relation between appearance and reality. His pronounced tendency is to eliminate all supraexperiential entities, as is apparent, for example, in his critique of Hegel for allegedly beginning from thought, whereas the correct procedure is to begin with being. But according to Marx, being in itself is not known. In experience we come in contact with a social context that can and indeed must be thought to be in a sense prior and therefore independent, despite the fact that in another sense the social context is merely the result of the social manifestation of human activity. But if truth is a practical question and if we do not experience an independent reality, the distinction between reality and appearance cannot be maintained.

A word must further be said about Marx's view of the distinction between knowledge and opinion. We have seen that it is difficult and perhaps impossible to defend this distinction unless the additional distinction between appearance and reality can also be defended, and we have further seen that the latter is not viable from the Marxian perspective. It could, however, be argued that the former distinction is represented in Marx's view by his conception of ideology, where ideology would be appearance and his own position would be knowledge. But on inspection this objection can be forestalled since although Marx no doubt believed his theory to be true, a claim for apodicticity cannot be made on its behalf within his position. Further, as Lukács has shown ideology is not true opinion, but rather a false belief which is accepted as true because of the absence of conscious awareness.[36] For these reasons, and though it might seem that one can make out a distinction between appearance and reality in Marx's position, in fact this is not the case.

3. A further effect of the refusal of apodictic knowledge is renewed interest in the relation between the process of knowledge and the subject of the process. In the traditional conception of truth as an objective relation between thought and being, stress was placed on the reduction or elimination of subjectivity as a condition of the claim to objectivity, which could in practice occur in several ways. One strategy was the requirement that in practice subjectivity be restricted to an absolute minimum in order to perceive objectivity. An example is Plato's view, as developed in the *Phaedo* and the *Republic*, that philosophy requires the elimination of all nonintellectual pursuits, so that philosophy becomes in effect a form of dying.[37] Another strategy is manifested by the tendency to abolish human subjectivity entirely as a factor in knowledge by replacing it with a quasi-logical concept, whose sole function is to provide objective knowledge. Examples can be found in the Kantian concept of the subject as a transcendental unity of apperception or in the Cartesian *cogito*.

Once again, it is helpful to view Fichte and Marx in contrast to prevailing practice. Moving against the grain of the philosophical tradition, both emphasize the unavoidable and fundamental relation of knowledge to subjectivity. In an important passage which has been already quoted, Fichte relates thought to human being in striking fashion. If the knowing process cannot be grounded, it follows that the kind of theory one chooses to defend cannot be justified wholly by an argument within that theory. Thus, a decision to opt for one among various kinds of theory cannot be separated from the person who makes this choice. This is not, of course, to commit the error of reducing the epistemological claim for the truth of a theory to psychological status. Rather, it is to say that in the final analysis personal factors cannot be wholly excluded in the choice of one kind of approach over another. In this way, Fichte calls attention to the ineliminable relation between thought and human being.

Marx makes a different but related point, although in seeming to except his own view from the restriction proposed he may be inconsistent. The relation of thought to human being in Marx's position can be illustrated by his view of ideology. Thought of all

kinds, according to this view, is influenced by the underlying social context, whether in the area of philosophy, law, art, and so
forth. This is a consequence of Marx's well known claim, referred
to above, according to which it is not thought which influences
being, but being which influences thought. Marx further suggests
that the form of self-understanding prevalent in capitalism is distorted by the bourgeois form of social life. In other words, capitalism is responsible for its own false apprehension. Marx's view,
which can be summarized as the double assertion that thought is
both limited and distorted by its relation to the social context, differs in two respects from Fichte's position. One aspect is Marx's
emphasis on the social context as a whole as opposed to Fichte's
more limited attention to the subjectivity of the isolated person.
Marx here displays a greater awareness of the organization of society into social classes. Marx further differs in his stronger claim
that thought is not only influenced, but is further distorted by its
relation to human subjectivity. Fichte stops short of making the
latter point and, although Marx's claim may arguably be correct,
it creates a problem within his own position. If this claim were
true, it would be difficult to avoid the objection that Marx's own
theory is similarly distorted. It thus seems that the stronger form
in which Marx makes his point concerning the relation of thought
to social being gives rise to a self-referential inconsistency within
his view.

To summarize the discussion, the aim of this chapter has been
to extend the parallel, already discussed, between the two theories, to the metatheoretical level, making use of the truism that
theory corresponds to a conception of metatheory, or theory as
such. I developed this point in two ways: to argue that the distinction between idealism and materialism is not an obstacle to the
comparison of the two views, and to extend the parallel previously interpreted through an analysis of similarities in the respective metatheories. The parallel between Fichte's and Marx's
positions has been explored on the three levels of Fichte's and
Marx's respective views of activity, concepts of man, and understanding of metatheory. It now remains to consider the origins of
this parallel within the German philosophical tradition. As we
shall see, the relation can be understood as due both to an influence of Fichte on Marx's thought as well as Fichte's and Marx's
shared desire, in reaction to Descartes and the philosophical tradition in general, to emphasize the concept of man as an active
being.

CHAPTER 7

ASPECTS OF THE

HISTORICAL RELATION

T HE discussion thus far has concentrated on identification and analysis of a parallel in the positions of Fichte and Marx on levels of theory and metatheory. If it is difficult to imagine that a similarity of such magnitude could simply be the result of chance, it is not easy to identify a single reason to account for the resemblance. Rather, as we shall see in a review of the historical material, a combination of several factors seems the most likely source of the parallel.

We might begin by noting that, since the similarity in question has not been widely perceived, little effort has been made to study the relation between the positions of Fichte and Marx within the context of the German tradition. Indeed, the few writers who recognize the presence of any resemblance confine their discussion for the most part to the elucidation of similar themes without an attempt to understand the genesis of the similarity. But two exceptions should be mentioned. Bernard Willms has indicated that the relation of Marx to Fichte is inexplicable solely through the former's relation to Hegel.[1] Roger Garaudy has gone further still in his suggestion that the influence of Fichte's *WL* is palpable in the young Marx.[2] Unfortunately, Garaudy does not follow up his remark with detailed analysis, but confines himself to vague thematic similarities. To the best of my knowledge, neither he nor any other writer has yet documented the various dimensions of the Fichte-Marx relation to the German intellectual context.

To be thorough, an account of the historical aspect of the relation should consider all possibilities, however remote, although at the outset at least some can be excluded. Thus, the question of an accidental similarity need not be raised, since it can serve only as a last resort in the event that no reasonable explanation is forthcoming, and this is not the case. A personal influence of Fichte on Marx can also be discounted, since as there is no chronological overlap they could not have known each other. This leaves a total of three possibilities for further study. As Fichte is known to have influenced the Young Hegelian movement to which Marx belonged, this avenue must be investigated. Second, Marx's biography and writings should be examined for traces of Fichtean influence. Finally the nature of Marx's position needs to be considered with respect to prevailing interests in the German tradition, since it is possible that his and Fichte's positions tend to converge around a common theme.

FICHTE AND THE YOUNG HEGELIANS

It is well known that Marx's relation to the Young Hegelians played a significant role in the genesis of his own position. Like the most illustrious member of their movement, the other Young Hegelians were concerned to come to grips with Hegel's ideas through an opposition to the orthodox emphasis on its theological dimension.[3] Perhaps better than anyone else, Heinrich Heine, the great German poet, summed up the mood of the times in his account of *Philosophie und Religion in Deutschland* (1834), which appeared at the beginning of this period. According to Heine, "thought wants to become activity, the concept wants to become flesh."[4] This interest in concrete concerns, as opposed to theoretical forms of explanation, led the Young Hegelians in two directions: toward practical philosophy and toward a concept of man as an active being. But since these elements were widely perceived as already present in a perhaps distorted form in Fichte's emphases on self and activity, the move in Young Hegelian circles away from the orthodox interpretation of Hegel was closely related to a step backward in the direction of Fichte.

The influence of Fichte on the Young Hegelians is easy to document and has already been discussed in the literature.[5] In one way or another, as Horst Stuke has suggested, almost all the Young Hegelians were affected by Fichte's thought.[6] In most instances through their common desire to turn philosophy into a practical force, they were attracted by the Fichtean view of man as an active being. For instance, in a remarkable work on historiosophy, the *Prolegomena zur Historiosophie* (1838), that influenced other Young Hegelians, a Polish count by the name of August von Cieszkowski made the claim that Hegel had resolved the outstanding problems on the level of thought and in the process carried philosophy to its ultimate conclusion. In partial anticipation of Marx, Cieszkowski went on to argue that what is now needed is a new form of philosophy become practical, or philosophy of practice.[7] Of interest for the present discussion is the strong emphasis placed on the Fichtean concepts of self and activity. Identifying the self as what he terms the great principle of movement in modern times, Cieszkowski maintains that the self's activity provides the means by which it can become concrete.[8] In other words, through his practical activity the individual has the capacity to put into practice the solutions achieved purely on the theoretical plane, and the future progress of philosophy depends on the practical application of essentially theoretically determined theses.

Another example is provided by Moses Hess, in a series of texts which appeared shortly after Cieszkowski's book. Hess remarks that at the present time the most important problem is to convert Hegel's philosophy of the spirit into what he terms a philosophy of activity. Hess further comments that although it may seem paradoxical since Fichte's position antedates Hegel's, the former has made more progress in this regard than even contemporary thinkers, such as the Young Hegelians who, according to Hess, are still caught up in theology.[9] In his own view, Hess placed heavy emphasis on the translation of Fichte's principle of activity, which he regarded as a mere theoretical concept, into practical activity. Following Fichte, Hess defined activity as the power through which all barriers can be sublated.[10] He further drew an explicit connection between the idealist view of activity and social progress. For the goal of socialism is, according to Hess, none other than the idealist aim of bringing about activity.[11]

The relation of Feuerbach's thought to Fichte's position is particularly complex, but important in view of the former's influence on Marx. We know that Feuerbach had an early, intense interest in Fichte's views. In 1835 in a letter to his fiancée, Berthe Löw, he reported strong admiration for Fichte as the result of reading a biography written by Fichte's son, I. H. Fichte.[12] Evidently the admiration for Fichte resulted in serious study of his writings, for several months later, in another letter to his fiancée, Feuerbach stated that he had recently been engrossed in the study of Fichte's posthumously published writings.[13] How serious was this study? We cannot know for certain, but it seems reasonable to assume that Feuerbach would not have gone to the trouble to undertake a serious study of Fichte's *Nachlass* prior to having worked through the generally more accessible and better known writings which appeared during his lifetime.

Although it seems quite likely that Feuerbach was deeply familiar with Fichte's thought, the question of its influence on his own thinking is controversial. In the nineteenth century a series of writers claimed to perceive Fichtean elements in Feuerbach's position. In what is probably the most detailed review of this ques-

tion, S. Rawidowicz lists the following commentators as represen-
tatives of the interpretation of the relation between the two
positions as positive: Karl Schwarz, V. Ph. Gumposch, C. L.
Michelet, J. E. Erdman, Julius Duboc, Adolph Cornhill, and
Rudolph Haym.[14] More recently the tendency in the literature has
been to point to Feuerbach's criticism of Fichte as evidence for the
view that the relation between them was negative. Rawidowicz
himself states that for Feuerbach Fichte's view represents no more
than a theory to be overcome.[15] In similar fashion, Johann Mader
has recently argued that in his attack on idealism Feuerbach's central theses were squarely directed against Fichte's position.[16] But
still more recently Mader has qualified his thesis in a discussion of
"Die Negation der Philosophie Fichtes und deren Folgen," in
which he argues that in the context of the struggle with Hegel's
position, Fichte's thought provided the basis for a new and nonidealistic anthropology.[17]

In fact the positive and negative interpretations of the relation
between Feuerbach and Fichte are largely compatible. There is
no contradiction between a Fichtean influence on Feuerbach's
thought and the fact that the latter devoted much attention toward overcoming the restrictions of the former's position. Indeed,
the relation of Marx and Hegel provides a similar case. We know
that Marx gave extensive study to the latter's position, in an attempt to overcome the limitations of the speculative philosophy,
but no one maintains that for this reason there is no Hegelian residue in Marx's position. On the contrary, there is a familiar, simplistic tendency to explain Marx's thought, as a result of a probably misleading hint in his own writings, as the "inversion" of
Hegel's position.

A brief look at Feuerbach's position reveals the compatibility of
a Fichtean influence in his thought with his criticism of Fichte's
views. Here the writings from the period 1839–43 contain some
precious hints.[18] Like the other Young Hegelians, Feuerbach desired to emphasize the practical dimension of philosophy. For the
transition from the ideal to the real can only occur through practical philosophy.[19] But in order to bring this about, philosophy
must be toppled from the empyrean heights on which it has been
placed by Hegel. To accomplish this, it is sufficient to apply the
same kind of criticism to philosophy that has been advanced
against religion. If we exchange the subject for the predicate, the
result is the disclosure of the pure and simple truth.[20] Now, the
initial step is to recognize that, Hegel notwithstanding, philosophy begins neither with God, nor the absolute, nor being as the
predicate either of the absolute or the idea. On the contrary,

Feuerbach is close to Fichte's view when he states that philosophy begins with the finite, the definite, and the real.[21] For the task of philosophy is to deal with the real, and the ideal can be invoked only in order to understand the real, and not conversely.

In order to relate philosophy to reality, it is necessary to recognize the intrinsic weakness of the speculative philosophy. But although Feuerbach is critical of Hegel, his approach to Hegel's thought is overly selective. He does not, for instance, give sufficient attention to the Hegelian view of substance as subject, which is a major theme in the speculative synthesis. But in the present context, it is less important to bring out the limits of the Feuerbachian interpretation of the Hegelian system than his understanding of the role of Fichte's thought in overcoming the system's inherent flaws.

According to Feuerbach, in order to go beyond the speculative philosophy, it is necessary to reintroduce the principle of subjectivity so lacking in Hegel's thought. Since Fichte's philosophy provides the most complete example of the needed concept, it is peculiarly relevant.[22] Indeed, Fichte's concept of the self can be regarded as the basis for a new approach to philosophy. But in virtue of its abstractness, the Fichtean idea of subjectivity is unsatisfactory as it stands. Rather, this idea must be utilized in a concrete, non-Fichtean sense, in which it is understood that all difference is not due to the self.[23] For the real source of subjectivity is man and not an abstract principle. By this intellectual itinerary, Feuerbach arrives at the position he will defend in all his later thought, that is, man is the basic principle of all philosophy.[24]

In view of the fact that Feuerbach's stated intention is to reformulate Fichte's principle of subjectivity as the basis of his own position, one should not be surprised to find a Fichtean residue in Feuerbach's thought. Now, I have repeatedly emphasized that the common tendency to interpret the Fichtean concept of the self as an abstract principle is an important error. But as Feuerbach commits the same interpretative mistake, it should not be surprising that his revised version of Fichte's concept is not unlike its original statement in Fichte's thought, at least as understood here. Although the two views are in some ways dissimilar, there is an important measure of agreement since Feuerbach shares with Fichte the belief that philosophy must be based on a theory of man as an active being.

Despite the abundant evidence demonstrating Fichte's influence on the Young Hegelians, most commentators are reluctant to view the relation in question as mediating a Fichtean influence on Marx. As already indicated, an important exception is provided by Engels, who, in his *Die Entwicklung des Sozialismus von der Utopie zur Wissenschaft*, states that German socialists are proud to be descended not only from Saint-Simon, Fourier, and Owen, but from Kant, Fichte, and Hegel as well. But curiously the reference to Fichte by someone particularly well placed to have insight into the genesis of Marx's position does not seem to have attracted much attention. Among the few writers to consider this possibility are Jürgen Habermas who, as already mentioned, perceives a superficial similarity in the conceptions of activity defended by Fichte and Marx,[25] and Thomas Meyer, who detects a Fichtean influence in the Marxian concept of the proletariat.[26] Interestingly, in Marxist circles, with the exception of Garaudy, Engels's remark does not seem to have found a sympathetic echo. Lukács, for example, while conceding Fichte's influence on the other Young Hegelians, expressly states that Marx and Engels are the only exceptions to the tendency of their contemporaries to appropriate Fichtean themes as they progressively withdraw from orthodox Hegelianism.[27] And Cornu, following Lukács, argues that Marx, unlike the other Young Hegelians, rejected Fichte's tendency to separate man from his context in favor of the Hegelian view of their profound union.[28]

The conviction, most widely held in Marxist circles, that unlike the other Young Hegelians, Marx was immune to Fichte's influence, seems improbable. When we consider Marx's critical relation to the other Young Hegelians, it seems likely that this would lead him toward, rather than away from, Fichte's thought. Although Marx was severely critical of his contemporaries, the basis of his criticism was usually either an alleged failure to transform philosophy into an active force, or a related failure to recognize the relation between theory and man. These are both standard Fichtean themes at least as interpreted by the Young Hegelians. In other words, Marx's criticism of the other Young Hegelians is directed not at their Fichtean tendencies, but rather at the fact that their theories do not measure up to their professed aims.

An instance is Marx's bitter critique of Bruno Bauer in *The Holy Family*. Bauer had developed a theory of pure criticism in which philosophy and its practical results, in consonance with Hegel's position, were regarded as one and the same.[29] For the same reason, Bauer felt justified in urging Marx not to undertake a practical career, since theory is itself the strongest form of practice.[30] It would seem that Marx was at first impressed by this neo-Hegelian view of the relation between philosophy and reality. There is reason to believe that he collaborated with Bauer in the composition of an inflammatory pamphlet on Hegel, *Die Posaune des jüngsten Gerichts über Hegel, den Atheisten und Antichristen*, which was published anonymously in Leipzig in 1841.[31] Here Hegel was defended against the criticism of other, unspecified Young Hegelians, who accused him of being interested only in theory. As the authors of this brochure point out, for Hegel theory is itself a form of practice.[32] Marx further echoes this view in his doctoral thesis when he writes that philosophy is a form of praxis, a point which again recurs in an article written soon after for the *Allgemeine Zeitung*, in which he maintains that theory is more dangerous than praxis.[33] But Marx later changed his mind, and in *The Holy Family* he subjected Bauer to a savage attack.

Marx addressed a related criticism to Feuerbach. Just as the latter had accused Fichte of presenting an abstract idea of human subjectivity, so in the first of the "Theses on Feuerbach," Marx objects to a supposed failure to understand that subjectivity is equivalent to man, when he writes that Feuerbach "does not conceive human activity as *objective* activity." [34] But although Marx was critical of Feuerbach, this is not of itself reason to assume, as has often been done, that at the same time Marx did not appropriate for his own ends the same anti-Hegelian weapon Feuerbach had earlier uncovered in Fichte's arsenal. In this sense, Klaus Hartmann is correct to point out that the Feuerbachian anthropology developed in independence of Marx was of great influence on his theory.[35] But one should add that although developed in independence from Marx, the Feuerbachian anthropology arose through his study of Fichte. Since Marx, like his Young Hegelian colleagues, was also interested in the same Fichtean themes of practical theory and man as the basis of theory, it seems entirely likely that an interest in Fichte may be demonstrable through study of his biography and writings.

FICHTEAN INFLUENCE IN MARX'S BIOGRAPHY AND WRITINGS

As it is the general topic of the present study, it seems superfluous here to enumerate Fichtean themes in Marx's thought. But if we are to surpass the level of discussion in which thematic parallels are identified without indication of their probable genesis, it is useful to discuss the extent to which Marx's biography and writings can provide indications of his interest in Fichte's thought. As we shall see, available evidence points strongly to an early and perhaps enduring Marxian interest in Fichte's position.

There seems to be little doubt that Marx was aware of Fichte's position. Although at the time Marx received his philosophical training, Fichte had already been eclipsed in importance by Hegel, he had at least briefly been the brightest star on the philosophical horizon, so that a student of philosophy was almost obliged to devote some study to his thought. Marx is likely to have been acquainted with Fichte's writings, since we know that he had a good grounding in philosophy and that he read widely. Yet, the extent of Marx's knowledge of Fichte's views is difficult to establish. We know from Marx's lecture notes as a student in Berlin that his program included lectures on Aristotle, Leibniz, Spinoza, and the Kantian School.[36] The latter was studied through Rosenkranz's *Geschichte der Kantischen Philosophie*. Section A, which is entitled "Uberwindung der Kantischen Philosophie," contains a brief, general account of Fichte's position, although whether in fact Marx read Rosenkranz's book or attended any of the lectures on it cannot be determined at this late date.

But examination of Marx's writings indicates knowledge of and at least passing interest in Fichte's thought. Although Fichte is never quoted, the writings contain a small, but chronologically diminishing number of references to him by name. These references indicate Marx's likely familiarity with various Fichtean writings. To take an example, Fichte's name occurs twice in the famous *Brief an der Vater* (November 10, 1837). Marx states that he has been trying to develop a theory of law based on a Fichtean model, an attempt later abandoned, which suggests that he had read the *Rechtslehre*. He further mentions that he has undertaken to work out a theory of philosophy in the style of Kant and Fichte, which indicates knowledge of Fichte's *Grundzüge*. But in the main the allusions to Fichte are increasingly negative in tone. A typical instance occurs toward the beginning of *Capital*, where Marx observes that man is like a commodity in that he comes into being neither as a mirror nor as a Fichtean philosopher, since on the latter's Pauline view one cannot separate man from animals.[37] Yet, despite the critical tone of this passage, there must have been some continuing interest in Fichte's thought, for several months after the appearance of the first volume of *Capital* Marx wrote to Engels to express his thanks for a series of quotations from Fichte's writings which had been sent to him by Lafargue.[38]

Although few in number, the direct allusions to Fichte in Marx's corpus reveal an acquaintance on his part with the former's thought. But if it were necessary to draw a conclusion merely on the basis of these scattered references, it would be hard to avoid the inference that after all Marx was little interested in Fichte's position, despite his knowledge of it. Yet if we dig a little deeper, we find that Marx was not only well acquainted with Fichte's thought, he further made important use of it in the course of his critique on Hegel. As we shall see, Marx's criticism of Hegel occurs in part from a Fichtean perspective and is further stated in Fichtean terminology.

An extremely interesting instance occurs in the third of the *Paris Manuscripts*, in the section known as the "Critique of Hegel's Dialectic and General Philosophy." In the course of a discussion of the relation of the object of consciousness to the external world, Marx maintains that it is as much an error to consider man under the aspect of self-consciousness as it is to reduce the object of consciousness to a purely mental creation. Apparently making use of Fichtean terminology against Fichte to make the latter point, Marx writes:

> When real, corporeal *man* . . . *posits* [*setzt*], . . . the *positing* [*das Setzen*] is not the subject of this act. . . . An objective being acts objectively. . . . It creates and establishes [*setzt*] only *objects*. . . . In the act of establishing it does not descend from its "pure activity" to the *creation of objects* [In dem Akt des Setzens fällt es also nicht aus seiner "reinen Tätigkeit" in ein *Schaffen* des *Gegenstandes*]; its *objective* product simply confirms its *objective* activity, its activity as an objective, natural being.[39]

In a word, in opposition to Fichte's view, which was widely understood as the belief that reality is *toto coelo* a product of thought, Marx insists on the objectivity of the external world.

But if the object is not solely created through mental activity, neither is man to be understood solely through his mental capacities. It is remarkable how close the view that Marx here urges presumably for the most part against Hegel, and perhaps Fichte as well, resembles Fichte's concept of man as it has been interpreted here. In order to bring this point out, it seems necessary to quote the relevant passage at some length. Marx writes:

> *Man* is directly a *natural being*. As a natural being, and as a living natural being he is, on the one hand, endowed with *natural powers* and *faculties*, which exist in him as tendencies and abilities, as *drives*. On the other hand, as a natural, embodied, sentient, objective being his is a *suffering*, conditioned and limited being, like animals and plants. The *objects* of his drives exist outside himself as *objects* independent of him, yet they are *objects* of his *needs*, essential

objects which are indispensable to the exercise and confirmation of his faculties. The fact that man is an *embodied*, living, real, sentient objective being with natural powers, means that he has *real, sensuous objects* as the objects of his being, or that he can only express his being in real, sensuous objects. . . . A being which does have its nature outside itself is not a *natural* being and does not share in the being of nature. . . . Man as an objective sentient being is a *suffering* being, and since he feels his suffering, a *passionate* being. Passion is man's faculties striving [*strebende*] to attain their object.[40]

This remarkable passage commands our attention for several reasons. Although hardly a complete theory of human being, to the best of my knowledge no other single passage anywhere in Marx's writings contains a more detailed statement of his conception of man. For this reason alone, the passage is doubly interesting, both in itself as a source of Marx's view of man and in reply to those who make a point of denying, regardless of the texts, that Marx ever had any such view. This passage is further fascinating for the remarkable resemblance between the conception of human being sketched here and Fichte's own view. When we examine the passage, we note that stress is placed on the natural existence of both man and the object of man's needs. Man is described as "natural," possessed of "drives," as "suffering" because limited, and as "passionate" due to his awareness of his limitations; the object which limits man is characterized as "indispensable" for his needs, as "real" and "sensuous," and as that toward which "striving" is directed. It would be repetitious at this point to show by detailed comparison the extensive parallel between Marx's conception of man and Fichte's own view, since this topic has already been discussed at length, but one should not ignore the similarities between the view proposed here and the language and content of Fichte's own view of man. To illustrate, specifically Fichtean are certain terms, such as "suffering," "passion," "drives," and "striving." Further Fichtean is the conception of man as essentially finite, as defined by his relation to the external world, and as meeting his needs within the latter relation. In short, in his argument against Hegel, and perhaps against Fichte as well, Marx both makes use of Fichtean language and further proposes a concept of man strikingly similar to Fichte's own concept, at least as interpreted in this discussion.

Although study of Marx's biography does not reveal a more than passing acquaintance with Fichte's thought, Marx's writings indicate both an awareness and a concern to combat what Marx apparently views as an erroneous conception of man as a non-natural being. But since Marx carries out this phase of his intellectual struggle in Fichtean language and in terms of Fichtean ideas, it follows that Fichte's influence on the other Young Hegelians is also visible in Marx's position, which hence does not differ significantly from those of the other Young Hegelians in this respect. It further follows that the parallel between the positions of Fichte and Marx studied above can at least partially be attributed to the general influence of Fichte on the thought of the Young Hegelians, including Marx. But from another perspective, the parallel can also be understood as a by-product of the anti-Cartesianism widespread in modern German philosophy.

MAN AS ACTOR AND CLASSICAL GERMAN PHILOSOPHY

So far the genesis of the parallel between the positions of Fichte and Marx has been considered in terms of Marx's relation to Hegel and the Young Hegelians. This procedure corresponds to the tendency, dominant since Lukács called attention to the Hegelian roots of Marx's thought, to understand Marx's position in relation to the Young Hegelians and Hegel only.[41] But although Marx's thought is certainly indebted to both Hegel and the Hegelian aftermath, it would be incorrect to restrict consideration of the genesis of Marx's thought merely to the Hegelian side of the tradition. This is not the sole influence on his position, as the parallel between the positions of Fichte and Marx demonstrates. Indeed, although it is no doubt conceptually easier to study Marx's thought merely in terms of the Hegelian heritage, the error inherent in this simplification can perhaps most easily be realized if it is remembered that the concerns of the Young Hegelians were by no means atypical of the interests prevailing in the mainstream German tradition. Accordingly, after having studied the historical origins of the Fichte-Marx parallel both through Marx's relation to the speculative philosophy and its consequences, as well as through the internal evidence of Marx's writings, it is necessary to emphasize that the relation in question is by no means a historical curiosity. On the contrary, it is one instance of a general concern in this period, in reaction to the Cartesian spectator theory of the subject, to formulate a view of man as the active subject of experience.

One is accustomed to the observation that through his discovery of the *cogito* Descartes is the founder of modern philosophy.

Heidegger, for instance, has claimed that the rise of modern anthropology is merely the fulfillment of the Cartesian project.[42] But if we are to lend any credence to this claim or others like it, it must be qualified in several ways. In the first place, it must be understood that although Descartes's thought has exercised a central influence on the development of modern philosophy, both in terms of those who accepted it and those who did not, many of the doctrines usually thought to originate in the Cartesian position, such as the *cogito* or the rationalist view of total freedom, were in fact anticipated by Augustine, as Etienne Gilson has shown.[43] It follows that although Descartes's conception of the subject was indeed an important influence in the rise of the modern "anthropological" philosophy, this form of philosophy arose less because the Cartesian theory was further developed than through a revolt against its strictures.

This is especially the case for the Cartesian concept of the subject. As is well known, Descartes draws a distinction between man as actor and as spectator in order to argue for the latter view.[44] But a strong current in modern philosophy, especially in the German side of the tradition, is the concerted attempt, which runs like a red thread through a number of otherwise diverse positions, to formulate a new and anti-Cartesian view of man as an active subject of experience.

Within the German tradition, concern with man as the active subject of experience connects numerous, otherwise disparate positions, as several examples will show. Leibniz understood activity as the monad's inherent tendency to change, unless otherwise prevented. Schelling saw the historical manifestation of activity as the crucial link between nature and God. And Schopenhauer included human activity in the fourth form of his principle of sufficient reason, namely, the law of motivation or *principium rationis sufficientis agendi*.

Although these few examples do not constitute a complete account of this phase of the German tradition, even in outline, they at least indicate the breadth of concern in this period with man as an active being and thus with an anti-Cartesian approach to human being. Indeed, a full account of the career of this idea within modern German thought would be difficult to offer and would fall outside the scope of the present inquiry. For present purposes, it is sufficient to demonstrate that from the historical perspective the parallel between the positions of Fichte and Marx is the result of the widespread, continuing attempt to state a theory of man as the experiential subject which becomes a central concern in the nineteenth century German tradition as the partial heritage of the critical philosophy. In this way, we shall see that the preoccupation of both Fichte and Marx with a concept of man as an active being, far from being eccentric, is closely tied to a central theme in this period of German philosophy.

Since Fichte's position arises out of his reaction to the critical philosophy, it seems appropriate to begin with Kant. The latter emphasizes kinds of activity as the precondition for kinds of experience, and there is further reason to believe that the concept of man was one of his enduring philosophical concerns. But despite considerable effort, Kant was unable to construct a view of man in terms of types of human activity, probably because this is not possible within the limits of the critical philosophy, although the attempt to do so remains a continuing theme in post-Kantian thought. Indeed, from this perspective the post-Kantian tradition in German philosophy can be regarded as a series of further attempts to remedy deficiencies perceived either in Kant's conception of man as the active subject of experience or in restatements of this view.

Insufficient attention seems to have been accorded to Kant's understanding of the Cartesian tradition. The epistemological problem Kant saw and his proposed solution of it have been often described, but their relation to Kant's reading of Descartes's position is not often studied. Despite the fact, for which we have Kant's testimony, that it was Hume who awakened him from his dogmatic slumber, we tend to forget that Kant was also concerned to argue against Descartes. In the *Prolegomena* Kant describes his intention in the *Critique of Pure Reason* as the desire to mediate between Cartesian dogmatism and Humean skepticism. "The *Critique of Pure Reason* here points out the true mean between dogmatism, which Hume combats, and scepticism, which he would substitute for it." [45] By the same token, although Kant's Copernican revolution is well known, its anti-Cartesian bias is perhaps less well understood. Kant's suggestion had, of course, been anticipated by Vico, one of the earliest, but most important, opponents of Descartes. Vico argued, as early as *De antichissima sapientia italiana* prior to his better known *New Science* (1725), that the condition of knowledge is that we make the object we know, a view which he later restated in its widely known form as *verum et factum convertuntur* in the latter work. Now there is no reason to believe that Kant read Vico, but the similarity between their epistemological views is striking. Kant, of course, did not agree to Vico's restriction of knowledge to the historical domain, nor did he recognize history as a science. But the manner in which he puts his case strongly echoes Vico. In the second Introduction to the

Critique of Pure Reason, Kant observes that "reason has insight only into that which it produces after a plan of its own."[46] In a word, for Kant, as for Vico, the possibility of knowledge is grounded in the activity through which the epistemological subject produces that which it knows. But by the same token, Kant's epistemological stance is relatively anti-Cartesian, since fundamental to his theory of knowledge is the assumption that if man is merely a spectator, then knowledge is impossible. Thus, from the epistemological perspective, subjectivity and activity are conjoined as the condition of knowledge.

Descartes was prevented by his spectator view of man from developing an ethical theory. But the anti-Cartesian tone in Kant's understanding of man as an active being is further apparent in his view of morality, which, since it makes use of distinctions borrowed from his epistemology, is an extension of his epistemological view. The condition of morality is that man is free to act, something which Kant simply assumes to be the case. Kant further distinguishes two kinds of moral activity. Pure moral activity has no relation to material considerations whatsoever. It is that moment in the moral process in which the individual determines the principle of his act according to universalizable rules. On the contrary, moral activity is that further moment in the moral process when the act so determined is actually put into practice. Kant's theory includes both aspects, and it follows that the moral subject is someone who subjectively determines his act according to duty and who objectively so acts.

So far we have noted the presence in Kant's position of a concern with the analysis of kinds of experience in terms of kinds of activity. This further suggests a general concern with man, which can easily be documented. There is evidence that Kant read widely on the topic, and we know that for over twenty years he taught a yearly course in anthropology at a time when such courses were quite unusual.[47] Indeed, in a letter from the critical period Kant remarks that nothing is more useful than consideration of the problem of man, if there is the least chance of making progress in this direction.[48] Kant further wrote a book, *Anthropologie in pragmatischer Hinsicht* (1798), based on his lectures.

This book is relevant to the present discussion. In the Preface Kant writes that although from one perspective man is only one creature among others in nature, from another perspective he is undoubtedly the most important being.[49] Kant further suggests that there are in fact only two ways to understand man. Either he must be studied from the physiological perspective, in order to see what nature has made of man; or, as Kant undertakes to do, he must be studied from the pragmatic perspective, under the presupposition that he is a freely acting being (*frei handelndes Wesen*), to grasp what man can, ought, or in fact does make of himself.

In the *Anthropologie* Kant studies man's rational capacity through a "faculty" psychology. He distinguishes three main faculties, or capacities: understanding, reason, and judgment.[50] Understanding is the capacity to generate rules, and to recognize as valid only those which the individual himself generates. This capacity is employed in two sectors. In the moral sphere, understanding is the faculty through which the individual generates a moral rule according to which he must act. In perception, understanding is the capacity through which the percept is produced as a result of the application of the categories, or rules of synthesis. Judgment is defined as the capacity to bring a particular under a general rule. This faculty is exercised in aesthetics, where in response to feelings of interest and disinterest (*Lust* and *Unlust*), the art object is evaluated. The same faculty is also exercised in attempts to judge events or situations in terms of an intrinsic purpose, which is attributed to them for purposes of their cognition, as in the supposition of purpose in biological evolution. Reason, the third capacity, is the ability to deduce the particular as necessary from the general rule. Examples are the deduction of the categories of the understanding from the rule that experiential knowledge is possible only if the form of the object of experience is supplied by the observer, or the deduction of geometric proofs from prior results or axioms assumed to be true. These three capacities, in Kant's view, constitute a complete inventory of rational human abilities.[51]

Despite Kant's interest in man, it is not immediately apparent where his view of human subjectivity is to be found. His response, if not the theory itself, is contained in a passage in his *Introduction to Logic* (1800), which appeared two years after the first edition of the *Anthropologie* (1798). In the *Critique of Pure Reason* Kant indicated that there are three topics of legitimate philosophic concern, which he summarized as a series of three questions.[52] In the *Logic* Kant adds a fourth question which both unites the other queries and suggests that in effect the required theory has already been stated, albeit in piecemeal fashion, in his other writings.

1. What can I know?
2. What ought I to do?
3. What may I hope?
4. What is man?

The first question is answered by *Metaphysics*, the second by *Morals*, the third by *Religion*, and the fourth by *Anthropology*. In reality, however, all these might be reckoned under anthropology, since the first three questions refer to the last.[53]

If the prior writings, as Kant suggests, are to be considered as stages in a theory of man, the argument can perhaps be reconstructed as follows: Man is a freely acting, or pragmatic, being. The kinds of activity of which he is capable are manifested in kinds of experience. The types of activity are grouped together as capacities within a faculty psychology. In order to construct a unitary image of man as the subject of experience, it is sufficient to relate the forms of activity of which man is capable among themselves.

One can discern two such attempts in Kant's writings. His initial approach is to unite man's epistemological and moral faculties in a single view of the subject. Kant here subordinates pure reason to its practical counterpart on the grounds that, as he observes, ultimately all reason is practical and even speculative reason is complete only in its practical usage.[54] Now, in the solution to the fourth antinomy in the first *Critique* Kant argues that, as he puts it in the *Prolegomena*, the subject can be considered from two perspectives, namely, as "free" inasmuch as it is a thing in itself, but as "subject to natural necessity," inasmuch as it is an appearance.[55] Following this suggestion, Kant goes on to maintain that moral activity is possible if the experiential subject can be considered from two perspectives, as either *noumenon* or *phenomenon*.

The weakness of this proposed solution is that although the subordination of pure to practical reason enables one to conceive their coexistence within a single subject, the practical possibility of moral activity cannot be demonstrated. Although the subject as *noumenon* can be held to determine its action freely in accordance with moral law, there is no provision for the action to be carried out. For if the phenomenal world is subject to necessity, man cannot act freely and moral activity is reduced to pure practical reason. Indeed, Kant, to his credit, was aware of this difficulty, as he indicates as early as the Introduction to the first edition of the *Critique of Judgment* (1790), in which he introduces judgment as a third faculty, that the attempt to create unity out of the diversity of human capacities is doomed to failure.[56]

Kant, however, rapidly changed his mind. For in the Introduction to the second edition of the *Critique of Judgment* (1793) he made use of the newly introduced third faculty in another attempt to unify human capacities. As before, Kant continues to maintain his phenomenon-noumenon analysis of the human subject in order to account for the coexistence of pure and practical forms of reason. But he now adds that these two forms of reason are related through judgment which, by bringing the particular under the universal, subordinates pure reason, or the capacity for the deduction of the particular, to practical reason, or the capacity to form rules.

If the argument seems plausible to this point, it is because the crucial difficulty of the possibility of moral activity has yet to be faced. Kant's strategy is to appeal to a concept of purpose as the regulative principle for the interpretation of natural phenomena, although it cannot be thought of as constitutive thereof. According to Kant, a tacit appeal to purpose is bound up with any and all judgment, since without this assumption the connection between particular and universal cannot be thought. In an extension of this argument, Kant now suggests that through the supposition of purpose as a final goal in nature the possibility of a harmony between moral decision and its performance can be thought.[57]

Although a full study of Kant's ingenious and influential view of purpose as a regulative idea is not germane to the present discussion, it should be noted that this suggestion is only partially successful with respect to a theory of man. Kant's move in a sense "saves the phenomena" by explaining the possible coexistence of theoretical and practical forms of reason at the minimal cost of adding a third faculty, or tertium quid, through which they are related. But purpose in nature cannot be invoked as an explanatory hypothesis without at least tacit appeal to a transcendental cause. It follows that, as Kant himself was aware, the price to be paid for the synthetic union of the faculties is the supposition of a divine agent. But unlike his rationalist predecessors, within the framework of his own position, Kant was unable to utilize a deus ex machina and remain consistent, since its existence can neither be proven nor assumed, but merely thought without contradiction. It follows that within the bounds of reason alone, the only limits Kant sets himself in his philosophy, he is unable to demonstrate the unity of the human faculties and hence does not achieve a satisfactory theory of the human subject.

This discussion of the critical philosophy may have seemed unnecessarily tedious, since it led to a theoretical impasse. But it was necessary to outline Kant's approach to the problem of man because post-Kantian thought relative to this problem can be viewed as a series of reactions to Kant. I have argued that although Kant's contribution is to correlate kinds of human activity with kinds of experience, he cannot relate the capacities for these types of activity within his "faculty" view of human nature without appealing to an absolute concept that is inadmissible as a constitutive principle within this view. In the post-Kantian German tradition, the anti-Cartesian approach to man as an active being remains an important theme, both for thinkers, such as Schopenhauer, who arguably stand outside the main line of the tradition, as well as for others, such as Fichte, Schelling, and Hegel, who fall within that strand of the tradition which leads to Marx. But Kant's analysis, with its tension between a finite being and a nonfinite explanatory principle, continues to exert its sway. As we shall see, the latter group can be further subdivided into those thinkers, such as Fichte and Marx, who attempt to conceive subjectivity wholly in terms of man, and those such as Schelling and Hegel, who invoke an absolute concept in order to understand a finite being.

Since the fundamentals of Fichte's position have already been stated, we can proceed directly to the analysis of the relation between Fichte's and Kant's views of man. As we shall see, the relation between the two views is the result of Fichte's understanding both of the disciple's role and of the nature of Kant's philosophical contribution.

Although Fichte was a professed disciple of Kant, it seems inaccurate to classify him as merely a Kantian, even if this has often been done. To begin with, the nature of the relation between Fichte and Kant was not unilinear. Although Fichte's position was sharply, albeit briefly, criticized by Kant, his influence on the founder of the critical philosophy is visible in the latter's *Nachlass*. Further, although Kantian assumptions are in evidence throughout Fichte's thought, as is always the case for an original thinker the concepts Fichte took over from Kant were considerably altered in his restatement of them. It follows that Fichte's thought must stand or fall on its own merits, and not through any claim of a privileged relation to Kant. But even if, as seems to be the case, it is necessary to evaluate Kant's and Fichte's positions independently, one should not therefore overlook the close relation between them. In particular one ought not to forget that Fichte's own stated intention is to reformulate the Kantian view of man.

As an aid in assessing Fichte's relation to Kant's thought, it is useful to comment on his own view of the relation of a disciple to an original body of thought. According to Fichte, the author of an original theory proceeds from a unitary vision which enables him to set out the various points of the theory, whereas the disciple's task is precisely to reconstruct retrospectively the central concept guiding the elaboration of the initial position. "The business of the followers is to synthesize what they still by no means possess, but are only able to obtain by the synthesis; the business of the inventor is to analyze what he already has in his possession" (*WL*, p. 57). Thus, while the original theory may consist of a series of isolated but important insights, the role of the disciple is to construct after the fact a theory which can contain them in systematic form.

The remaining piece of information needed to relate Fichte to Kant, Fichte's assessment of the central thrust of Kant's position, is already in hand. For we know, as has been mentioned, that according to Fichte the contribution of the critical philosophy is, in his terminology, the idea of the active self. But if the disciple's role is to reconstruct the unified theoretical view underlying the analytical presentation of it, then Fichte's task is, if he follows his own analysis, to synthesize the distinctions Kant utilizes in various discussions as a single view of man.

In fact, when we compare the two positions we note that Fichte's theory of the self is a reconstructed version of Kant's initial synthesis of two forms of human capacities. Striving corresponds to practical reason and positing to theoretical reason. The crucial difference is that while Kant's procedure is to relate capacities to types of experience before undertaking to unify these faculties within a single concept of subjectivity, Fichte begins with the assumption that man is an active being, thus invoking as his initial premise the goal which Kant was unable to attain within his own position. The problem then is not how to perceive unity in diversity, but rather to show that from the starting point employed it is possible to explain the different kinds of activity as correlated with types of experience. In this way Fichte's position can be seen as a concerted attempt to carry out in fact the Kantian desire, which within the critical philosophy remained unfulfilled, to construct a unified concept of man as an active being.[58]

We have seen that Marx was led in Fichte's direction by the latter's influence on the Young Hegelians and that he was himself familiar with Fichte's writings. Now, at least chronologically, within the mainstream of the German tradition the relation between Fichte and Marx is mediated by Hegel. With respect to the views of Kant and Fichte, Hegel's thought represents a new approach to the problem of man. Although Hegel shares Kant's and Fichte's respective interests in the general question of experience, for epistemological reasons closely related to his view of absolute knowledge (*absolutes Wissen*) he replaces man as an active subject by a transfinite concept, or absolute. Hegel hence adopts as the ultimate, and in his position constitutive, principle of subjectivity the transfinite concept to which Kant was driven by the logic of his analysis, but which remained within the critical philosophy a mere regulative idea. At least in this single respect, Hegel thus remains broadly within the Kantian tradition. But in another sense he differs radically from both Kant as well as Fichte, for in his position man is no longer the real actor on the historical stage as he is no longer defined in terms of himself.

In view of the complexity of Hegel's position, it is difficult to make general statements about it. Description frequently fails to do justice to his view, thus indirectly justifying the correctness of his belief that the truth is the whole. For example, we are used to being told that Hegel's position belongs to *Reflexionsphilosophie*, namely, the theory of consciousness, but one cannot emphasize enough that for Hegel the theory of consciousness is literally the theory of experience. This is evident, for instance, in the original title of the *Phenomenology of Mind* (*Phänomenologie des Geistes*) as the *Science of the Experience of Consciousness* (*Wissenschaft der Erfahrung des Bewusstseins*).[59] Indeed, Hegel never tires of pointing out that the limits of knowledge coincide with the limits of conscious experience. Hence, it would seem that, at least in the early stages, Hegel's main interest was the theory of experience.

We have seen that, following Kant, both Fichte and Marx approach experience through a concept of man as an active being. But although he does not entirely reject this procedure, following Schelling, for epistemological reasons Hegel feels obliged to invoke another concept as well. It has already been mentioned that Schelling criticized the supposed one-sidedness of Fichte's idealism, which he supplements through a theory of nature, or *Naturphilosophie*. This strategy raises, however, the epistemological problem of the relation of subjectivity and objectivity. Schelling's suggestion, which is based on a reinterpretation of the Fichtean concept of the absolute self, is that subjectivity and objectivity can only be seen to correspond if they both derive from a primitive unity, which he locates in a transfinite absolute or *Indifferenzpunkt*. This point is neither subjective nor objective, but rather the harmony between subjectivity and objectivity.

Hegel in turn appropriated and transformed Schelling's theory of the absolute for his own ends. In the *Differenzschrift* (1801), he restates Schelling's basic criticism of Fichte in similar form, although he generalizes it to apply to Kant as well. According to Hegel, neither Kant nor Fichte can explain knowledge since within their positions the transition from subjectivity to the objective perspective in which knowledge is grounded in nature cannot be made. It is well known that Hegel later broke with Schelling's view of the absolute when in the *Phenomenology* (1807) he compares it in a famous passage to the night in which all cows are black, implying that it is a completely undifferentiated and hence empty concept. But he continues to rely on another concept of the absolute for explanatory purposes. For instance, in the *Encyclopedia*, whose first edition appeared only ten years later in 1817, we find him claiming that the aim of philosophy is to achieve a fully articulated concept of the unity of subjectivity and objectivity in the form of the absolute, or fully adequate idea.[60]

The result of Hegel's reworking of an idea Schelling originally borrowed from Fichte is to be seen in the position which Hegel outlines in the *Phenomenology*, in which experience is to be understood from both finite and transfinite perspectives simultaneously. Although the details of Hegel's discussion are familiar, the relation of the different stages of the discussion and the intent of the discussion as a whole are still largely controversial. But it seems clear that Hegel makes a distinction between finite and nonfinite, or absolute, forms of subjectivity, and that he employs both perspectives in his description of experience. It further seems clear that in the final analysis, the real or ultimate subject of history is not finite human being, but transfinite and absolute.

To illustrate, from the finite perspective experience is analyzed in terms of human activity. On the one hand Hegel depicts the logical process through which an individual can and in fact does become aware and self-aware, and on the other he describes the historical process through which mankind has attained self-consciousness, culminating in the philosophic description of its moments viewed as successive stages in a unitary process in the *Phenomenology*. But from another perspective, the entire historical process is no more than the manifestation of the absolute in time and space, as a result of which, in Hegel's sybilline language, substance becomes subject. Indeed, the larger point of Hegel's ceaseless demonstration of the multiple levels of the unity of subject and object throughout the *Phenomenology* is to bring out the central relation underlying experience considered as a developmental process.

If experience is capable of analysis from both finite and transfinite perspectives, the problem arises of how they are to be related. Hegel's solution is to give ontological weight to Kant's concept of a regulative idea, which hence becomes immanent in the historical process. This point can be made in either of two ways, in terms of Hegel's interrelated views of knowledge and history.

With respect to epistemology, at the stage of absolute knowledge the discussion has in effect transcended any particular or finite approach in order to attain the synthetic vision which includes all relevant finite perspectives simultaneously as moments of an all-embracing totality. Absolute knowledge accordingly requires an absolute or transfinite perspective not associated with any particular individual, despite tension in this view due to the fact that an individual by the name of Hegel suggests it. A similar point can be made in terms of Hegel's concept of history. If there is an overarching or transfinite principle operative in the historical process, finite human being is dethroned as the central historical agent since, regardless of its accomplishments, it in turn depends on the absolute. Thus, although history is the record of man's activity, in the Hegelian view man is not himself the actor, but a false comedian or marionette, whose strings are pulled by the absolute, or process itself, which acts through man for its own purposes.

Hegel's emphasis on the absolute, as opposed to finite human subjectivity, has several consequences within his position, of which two should be mentioned. Despite the occasional and insightful discussions of man to be found in his writings, the result of Hegel's epistemological commitment to absolute knowledge is to remove man as the final explanatory factor in experience. Thus, we might say that, when Hegel throws his enormous conceptual net over all forms of experience, man as an active being slips through the holes in the netting. It can further be seen that Hegel's view in a sense represents a return to the Cartesian spectator theory, for if ultimate agency is lodged with the absolute man is not the actor at all.

Although perhaps incorrectly interpreted, Hegel's position was widely felt to reduce man to a mere place-holder in the historical process, for which he was necessary but on which he could have no voluntary effect. But in the post-Hegelian period, this doctrine was widely resisted. Numerous attempts were made to reduce or entirely to eliminate the transfinite perspective upon which Hegel relied and attention was focused ever more squarely on man. Although they are otherwise quite different, thinkers as diverse as Feuerbach, Kierkegaard, Marx, and Nietzsche are related through their concern with man.[61]

Although each of these thinkers was in revolt against the Hegelian position, the manner in which the revolt was carried out varied enormously. Among these thinkers, Marx stands out as the one perhaps most concerned to come to grips with Hegel's thought from inside the latter's system, through immanent critique, in order to explode it from within. In a sense, then, Marx's relation to Hegel is the opposite of Fichte's relation to Kant. Whereas Fichte consciously desired to carry out in a more radical manner the task Kant had undertaken, Marx suggests, especially in his early writings, that the main, contemporary, intellectual task is the overthrow of the speculative theory. But although in this sense Marx's position can be seen to arise from an immanent critique of Hegel's, one may wonder if Marx ever succeeds in escaping the voluminous folds of the latter's thought. It may be that despite Marx's best efforts, his own thought remains largely within the Hegelian compass. But by virtue of his avowed inten·tion there are ways in which Marx at least appeals to pre-Hegelian attitudes and, as we shall see, this is especially the case for the con-cept of man as an active being in his position.

Marx's early writings are studded with numerous, often weighty objections to Hegel's position. A recurrent theme is that Hegel, whom Marx views as the official representative of the German state, tends to overlook man, the real subject. As early as the *Introduction* to his *Contribution to the Critique of Hegel's Philosophy of Right* (1843), Marx states that "the German represen-tative of the modern state," namely, Hegel, "leaves out of account the *real* man." [62]

In subsequent writings Marx develops an analysis of the nature and source of Hegel's mistake. In the *Contribution to the Critique of Hegel's Philosophy of Right* (1843), he connects this error to Hegel's appeal to a transfinite explanatory principle. Discussing the Hegelian view of the state, he notes that Hegel's theory con-tains an unresolved tension between opposing perspectives. "Here Hegel poses an unresolved *antinomy*. On the one side, external necessity; *on the other side*, immanent aim." [63] In the context of the Hegelian discussion, the attribution of ultimate agency to the absolute has the effect of reducing reality to mere appearance. The result is that the explanatory concept becomes the real subject and the real subject in effect becomes a mere aspect of the mystical concept. "Hence the mystical substance turns into the actual sub-ject and the real subject appears as something else, as a moment of mystical substance." [64]

If man is merely a phenomenon, then human problems also lose their urgency. In the *Paris Manuscripts* (1844) Marx develops the consequences of Hegel's reduction of the real subject to merely phenomenal status in a discussion of his conceptions of man and nature. He praises Hegel's achievement in discovering the dialectic of negativity, but claims that Hegel's usage of this principle leads him into error, since he conceives of both man and nature in an abstract manner. Reality becomes merely mental and in consequence human problems such as alienation and reappropriation can be resolved on the mental level only. On the contrary, Marx objects that the various forms of human alienation are not merely mental, but are rather due to the structure of social relations.

According to Marx, the conception of man as an abstract being is not a contingent factor in the Hegelian position, since it is due to a fundamental misconception. In *The Holy Family* (1845), Marx maintains that Hegel misconceives the human capacity for self-consciousness, albeit man's distinguishing characteristic, as equivalent to man. But to reduce man to one of his capacities is in effect to overlook the fact that he lives within a real, external, social context within which his self-awareness can arise.[65]

We have seen that for epistemological reasons Hegel was driven beyond the finite perspective and that a central theme in Marx's criticism of the speculative philosophy is the concern to salvage man as the subject of experience. Now, it may well be that Marx is not entirely successful in his endeavor. It has been argued that his view of man is unsuccessful and that in his later writings there is a shift to a supraindividual perspective in the economic analysis of capitalism. But it seems nevertheless quite plain that the intent of his critique of the speculative theory leads him backward in the direction of pre-Hegelian attempts to understand man as the subject of experience, such as those of Kant and Fichte, and in this sense at least his theory belongs in the Kantian tradition.

In summary, the purpose of this chapter has been to inquire into the historical process of the Fichte-Marx parallel. This has been studied from three related perspectives: that of Fichte's impact on the Young Hegelians in general, in terms of the analysis of Marx's writings, and through the relation of Fichte and Marx in the context of the German philosophical tradition. The discussion has shown that Marx was aware of Fichte's position, that he may have been led in that direction through Fichte's widespread influence on the Young Hegelians in their revolt against Hegel, and that Marx's own criticism of Hegel led backward toward the pre-Hegelian concern with man as the subject of experience found in both Kant and Fichte. It is, however, not possible to "quantify" the relative importance of the three ways in which the genesis of the parallel in the positions of Fichte and Marx has been studied here. Whether the similarity considered above is explicable through a conscious move in Fichte's direction, through Fichte's influence on the Young Hegelians in general as well as on Marx, or through the intrinsic logic of certain problems of interest to Marx is difficult to determine. I believe that all three factors played a role in the genesis of Marx's position and hence in its resemblance to Fichte's. But whether this is the case or whether proportionately greater weight should be assigned to one factor rather than another, it seems clear that from the historical perspective there is ample evidence to account for the origin of the parallel described above.

CHAPTER 8

BEYOND FICHTE AND MARX

T HE purpose of the discussion so far has been to reveal and to explain the origin of a substantial parallel between the positions of Fichte and Marx. This parallel has been studied both through comparative analysis of the two positions and through consideration of their relations to others in the wider German context. At this point I would like to go beyond the positions of Fichte and Marx to consider two general issues which arise out of the preceding inquiry: the interpretation of the modern German philosophical tradition and the perennial philosophical problem of man.

In the first place, it is necessary to raise the question of why the parallel discussed here has not received more attention. As the modern German philosophical tradition has been extensively studied, any relation between two such important thinkers should already have come to light unless there were an intrinsic flaw in the manner in which such studies are carried out, which seems in fact to be suggested by the presence of the parallel demonstrated above. With this result in mind, I shall now proceed to identify and call into question the dominant view of the modern period in German philosophy. In particular, I shall argue that there is a common but mistaken paradigm which hides rather than helps to perceive the parallel in question.

It will further be necessary to address the problem of man. In disregard of the general tendency to regard Fichte and Marx as thinkers at opposite poles of the intellectual spectrum, I have tried to demonstrate a shared approach to man as an active being. It does not seem wise here to attempt to choose between the two positions, for that would properly be the topic of another study, although I have indicated in places that I do not consider either view to be above reproach. But this does not rule out consideration of the intrinsic worth of an approach to man as an active being. Indeed, such consideration seems indicated for at least two reasons. Probably no problem has received more attention throughout the history of philosophy than that of man. Further, the present discussion is relevant to this concern, since the approach to man as an active being found in the two positions implies that some version of it might in fact be a viable "solution" to the perennial question of the nature of human being.

A variety of reasons, only some of which seem philosophically relevant, can be adduced to explain the failure to notice the relation between the two positions. Fichte scholars are not often interested in Marx, which is understandable since, when judged by the standards Fichte invokes for philosophy, Marx's writings may seem to fall short of the mark. Conversely, Marx only rarely mentions Fichte, and one has to turn to his correspondence to note that at the same period as he was at work on the later volumes of *Capital* Marx was interested enough in Fichte to solicit quotations from his texts. Marx scholars are further even less concerned with Fichte, since he seems to epitomize the kind of sterile philosophy appropriately rejected by Marx in his quest for a new kind of theory.

But although there is some merit in each of these reasons, none of them seems overly compelling. Taken either singly or together, they do not explain the surprising failure to notice the parallel between the two positions, since nearly every conceivable angle of this period has been studied, often several times over. Further, although some students of the history of philosophy may be hindered by their preconceptions in understanding one or another aspect of the tradition, this is not universally the case. If there were even the slightest indication of a relation to be studied, such study would have been carried out. But the parallel in question is difficult to perceive, if indeed it is visible at all, when one accepts the usual approach to the interpretation of this period. Since this approach is to a great extent due to Hegel's influence, it would seem that it is in this direction that an inquiry into the disinterest in the similarity between the two positions must proceed.

It is only natural for the usual approach to the history of philosophy to reflect the imprint of Hegel, since more than any other thinker since Aristotle he sought insight through the study of the tradition. Although Aristotle frequently reported the views of previous thinkers, Hegel seems to have been the first to argue that there is a unity discernible in the apparently independent efforts of various thinkers, who are engaged in a common attempt to grasp reality through the medium of thought. In this regard, one can say that Hegel's accomplishment was to have made it possible to un-

derstand the different views as developing out of a dialectical interaction, and as constituting a single philosophical tradition. In
this way, Hegel almost single-handedly creates the concept of the
history of philosophy.

If this were all that Hegel had done, there might be few objections raised. Most philosophers since Hegel have been willing to
accept the idea that philosophical theories form a larger conceptual unity which develops through time. Of course an exception would have to be made for a recent "historian" of philosophy, Bertrand Russell, who was never able to view the history of
philosophy as anything other than a collection of unrelated theories, a view which, it has been argued, is most descriptive of his
own intellectual development. But Hegel further developed a conception of phiosophical progress. Succeeding theories are richer, in
that they build upon and profit from earlier views. In this sense,
philosophy is constantly moving forward. Since his own position
was both the latest and most complete, it follows that, as Hegel
sometimes seemed to suggest, for logical and chronological reasons the tradition comes to a peak in his own thought.

Hegel further implied that philosophy itself ends in his position,
although this may well be a misinterpretation. The aim of philosophy is to provide for the reconciliation of thought and being, or
reality. In Hegel's thought, reality as a whole, or in his language,
substance, becomes conscious of itself. This suggests that the
ongoing task of philosophy, which has been the excuse for im-
mense intellectual effort over a period of more than two and a half
millennia, comes to an end through its completion in the Hegelian
system. Now, it may well be that Hegel did not literally mean that
he had put a term to philosophy. For at the end of his *History of
Philosophy* he remarks significantly that "no philosophy transcends its own time." [1] This implies that even his own view is a
product of its historical moment and hence intrinsically limited.
Indeed, Hegel refers to the intrinsic limitation of his own reading
of the tradition when, several pages later, he observes that he has
now completed an account of the present stage of development.[2]
But it should be observed that whatever Hegel's view may have
been, he has often been thought to have argued that the tradition
both comes to a head and ends in his thought.

Hegel let slip few opportunities to state what may appear to be
a self-congratulatory view of the history of philosophy. In his first
publication, significantly entitled *Differenz des Fichte'schen und
Schelling'schen Systems der Philosophie* (1801), he adopted the
pose of a mediator whose role it is to study, from a neutral perspective, the proliferation of philosphical theories and whose task

it is to sort out and choose between the more nearly and the less nearly successful attempts to explain reality. Implicit in this attitude is that a standard is available, presumably the completely adequate philosophy, in terms of which all other views can be judged. Hegel maintained his pose in a number of other writings, such as *Glauben und Wissen* (1801), the Preface to the *Phenomenology* (1807), the various Introductions to the *Encyclopedia* (1817, 1827, 1830), and in elaborate detail in his *History of Philosophy* (1817). When in the Preface to the *Philosophy of Right* (1821) he made the famous remark that the actual (*wirklich*) is the rational and the rational the actual, to one familiar with his thought there is a clear, although perhaps mistaken inference to be drawn that beyond a specific doctrine relating epistemology and ontology, Hegel meant to imply that his own position constituted the final stage within the self-development of substance to a self-conscious subject.

It would be difficult to exaggerate the influence which the view commonly attributed to Hegel has had. This influence has made itself felt in two main ways, within the German tradition and in its interpretation. Although this may now seem inconceivable, to a surprising extent in the post-Hegelian tradition there was a tendency to accept the inference that not only a kind of philosophy but philosophy itself comes to an end in his thought.

From a distance of almost a century and a half since Hegel's death, it is difficult for us to grasp the impact of his thought on the intellectual life of his time. In an epoch when Hegel is frequently not taken seriously, it is hard to imagine that he was once taken so seriously that the implication that his position had in some sense put an end to philosophy seemed not only plausible but correct. The reaction of the great German poet, Heinrich Heine, is not untypical in this regard. Heine spent many years in exile in Paris. In an account of German philosophy and religion written for the French public shortly after Hegel's death, Heine sums up the course of German philosophy from its origins in German Protestantism, through the profound changes introduced by Kant, and then remarks that with Hegel philosophy has reached its end.[3] In other words, this student of Hegel and friend of Marx took seriously the view that in Hegel's thought philosophy had come to a close. At most certain small gaps in the edifice remained to be filled in, but the basic structure was now complete.

Heine was rather representative of a number of other thinkers, who also felt that philosophy had come to an end. An indication of the widespread conviction that the history of philosophy had been completed can be seen in the continued reticence of thinkers in the post-Hegelian period even to employ the term "philosophy" to designate their thought. This is not of course the case for either Schelling or Schopenhauer, each of whom considered himself an authentic representation of the grand tradition. But in a variety of ways others attempted to evade this designation. Examples are Bruno Bauer's description of his thought as criticism of Kierkegaard's presentation of his views as pseudonymous discourses of which he was not to be regarded as the author. Still more extreme is Nietzsche's attack on the philosophical enterprise itself in the guise of his critique of the possibility of epistemology which has long dominated the modern tradition.[4]

The idea that philosophy as a discipline can be brought to an end through resolution of its task is enticing but ultimately unacceptable. For any "solution" is itself controversial, which gives rise to further discussion and a continuation of philosophy. Further, any summary of the tradition inevitably belongs to it as only the most recent attempt of philosophy to consider its past. In the same way, even the most radical attacks on philosophy are not guaranteed that they can successfully evade becoming part of that to which they object. Indeed, the discipline's most radical critics have always been philosophers, although often against their own will. In fact, in the post-Hegelian period it is not correct that philosophy was given up or otherwise came to an end. Rather, new ways of doing philosophy were introduced because the old ways seemed to have lost their promise. So it is incorrect to hold that philosophy reaches its terminal point in Hegel's thought. At most a certain form of philosophy was no longer practiced because it no longer seemed possible.

One should further resist the inference, which Hegel sometimes seems to suggest, that by virtue of his masterly synthesis Hegel reproduces everything of importance that had already appeared in the tradition. Now, it is of course true that Hegel draws on an enormous number of important thinkers.[5] But although Hegel goes a long way toward reconciling many, often apparently disparate views, there is much of value in the history of philosophy that he does not take up in his own position. Despite the fact that his synthesis echoes many of the central concepts of the tradition, certain ideas are not and cannot be reproduced in Hegel's philosophy because they are contrary to the thrust of his thought. An example is the idea of man we have been considering here. Since Hegel, as has been pointed out, follows Schelling in the concern to understand man in terms of a transfinite absolute, despite some efforts in that direction he could hardly in the final analysis understand human being in terms of itself in the manner of the early Fichte and Marx.

Although the view of the relation between his own position and the history of philosophy often attributed to Hegel is beset with difficulties, one should not overlook the influence of this perhaps mistaken reading of Hegel's thought for the interpretation of modern German philosophy. This reading of Hegel has led to an interpretation of the classical German tradition as a chronological progression, which can be outlined as follows: The major figures in the German tradition are Kant and Hegel. Through the critical philosophy Kant initiates the great period of German thought. Fichte and Schelling are transitional figures, whose importance is circumscribed by the fact that they prepare the terrain for Hegel. In the latter's thought, the tradition reaches a new peak. After Hegel's death, his synthesis disintegrates in a conflict of interpretations among post-Hegelian thinkers. But these thinkers are of minor importance, since their views are one-sided and hence degenerate statements of Hegel's own thought.

Although I have stated this Hegelian-inspired reading of the modern German tradition in provocative and perhaps tendentious fashion, it should be observed that an analogous reading of the thought of this period is widely current among historians of philosophy. If we confine ourselves merely to the more orthodox historians of philosophy, similar views can be found in Erdmann, Fischer, and Windelband. Perhaps the definitive formulation of this way of reading the nineteenth-century German tradition occurs in Richard Kroner's comprehensive work, *Von Kant bis Hegel*. Further developing Kroner's approach, in *From Hegel to Nietzsche* Karl Löwith presents an influential discussion of the decline of the tradition after Hegel's death in a conflict of opposing tendencies. In his *Die Zerstörung der Vernunft* Georg Lukács further elaborated this thesis, arguing that the decline of the philosophical tradition is related to the transformation of rationalism into an irrationalism already adumbrated in the later Schelling.

This Hegelian-inspired reading of the history of philosophy is too simplistic to do justice to the entire tradition, much less to the complex nature of modern German thought. For this reason, it has come under increasing attack in the last decade.[6] The Hegelian paradigm has been identified and subjected to critical analysis. I have already suggested that despite Hegel's professed intentions it is too much to expect him to reproduce all important themes in his own thought, even if he seems to require that this be done as consonant with his aim. This in turn implies that it is not necessarily true that the latest philosophy is the best. Chronologically earlier views can sometimes be more advanced than theories that appear only later in the tradition, so one need not expect Hegel's position to be the most modern in all respects. It is further an error to overstate the extent to which all threads of the tradition are mediated through Hegel's thought. Although Hegel exerted a strong and continuing influence on the course of subsequent philosophy, there are nevertheless important relations between thinkers which simply bypass his thought.[7] Examples are the relations of Schopenhauer to Kant and of Schelling to Fichte, each of which contributed to the growth of a major position, but neither of which is mediated through Hegel's position.

It further seems that the frequent tendency to regard Hegel as the epitome of the German tradition can on occasion obscure the legitimate achievements of other members of that tradition. One tends to forget that Fichte and Schelling were major thinkers in their own right, whose ideas deserve to be considered for their intrinsic importance and not only for their input with respect to Hegel's thought. For this reason, an attempt is currently under way to rehabilitate Schelling. Walter Schulz has argued that German idealism reached its high-water mark not in Hegel's position, but rather in Schelling's further development after Hegel's death.[8]

The Hegelian influence on the interpretation of the nineteenth-century tradition has further contributed to distorted views of Fichte as well as Marx, and helped to retard identification of a parallel in their positions. Although a revival of Fichte scholarship is currently under way, Fichte has probably not received the attention to which he is entitled as a major thinker in the period which stretches from the first edition of the *Critique of Pure Reason* (1781) to the *Philosophy of Right* (1821), certainly one of the richest moments in the entire philosophic tradition. It should not be forgotten that Fichte was at one point widely acknowledged, not least of all by his younger contemporaries Schelling and Hegel, as the thinker who had carried Kant's critical philosophy to its logical conclusions. One can therefore deplore the fact that he is now widely regarded as a minor pre-Hegelian thinker. The ignorance of his position is probably greatest in English-speaking countries,[9] although it can be hoped that recent translations may in time ameliorate the situation. But even in Europe, especially in Germany where there is no language barrier, one must note an all too frequent tendency to view Fichte through Hegelian spectacles, which is no more justified than is interpreting Hegel through Marx's eyes.[10]

For a reason imputable to Hegel, Marx is also subject to neglect. This is by no means obvious, since there is no dearth of attention to his thought. On the contrary, there is a veritable Marx "industry" at work, as will be easily appreciated by anyone acquainted with the ever-burgeoning literature devoted to his thought. But as it is practically axiomatic that the area of general agreement regarding Marx is small, and perhaps extends no further than recognition of his importance, it may come as a surprise to some to learn that much of the discussion follows a paradigm based on the Hegelian-influenced view that philosophy ends in his thought. For if philosophy comes to an end in Hegel's thought, it follows that Marx's position cannot be philosophy, whatever else it may be.

The origins of this paradigm can in part be traced back to Marx's own writings, which are a source of somewhat imprecise and often misleading hints with respect to his own position, such as the famous comment that his own thought is the result of standing Hegel's position on its feet. The tendency to view Marx's theory as extraphilosophic received its first "official" formulation in the 1880s at the hands of Engels. In his book, *Ludwig Feuerbach and the Outcome of Classical German Philosophy* (1888), he apparently accepted without question Hegel's boast that the speculative philosophy constituted a high-water mark in the tradition. This impelled Engels to reason that if the problems remained, their "solution" was to be sought in an extraphilosophic realm. Marx's contribution was to have expelled philosophy from the interpretation of history. Marx's position was not philosophy, from which it differed in kind, but science.

The Engelsian interpretation of Marx's position as extraphilosophic received a trenchant reformulation in the first quarter of this century in Lukács's book *History and Class Consciousness*. Although in other ways critical of Engels, Lukács agreed with and developed his overall approach to Marx's relation to philosophy and the philosophical tradition. According to Lukács, the problems of modern philosophy cannot be resolved within it because of an inherent antinomy resulting from its bourgeois class standpoint. They can be resolved only on the extraphilosophical plane inhabited by Marx's theory, which is basically a form of political economy.

The Engels-Lukács approach has been as widely accepted as it is stultifying. Although the assumption is as erroneous as it is widespread, several generations of students of Marx have begun their discussions from the literally indemonstrable presupposition that his position is not and cannot be philosophy. Besides Engels and Lukács, other important students of Marx who follow this approach include Korsch, to varying degrees all the members of the Frankfurt School with the possible exception of Horkheimer, and more recently Althusser, the later Sartre, and even important non-Marxists, such as Hartmann. But this approach is stultifying because it inhibits the interpretation of Marx's position by posing as its condition an indemonstrable claim, which is probably due to a misinterpretation of Hegel's position and its relation to the tradition.[11]

Hegel's influence further tends to hide the parallel in the views of Fichte and Marx for two reasons. In the first place, as it tends to turn attention away from any possible contribution of Fichte other than his alleged mediation of the Kant-Hegel relation and further to locate Marx's position outside the philosophical tradition, it becomes more difficult to perceive the relation between what hence appear to be an unimportant philosopher and a non-philosopher. As a philosopher and a putative non-philosopher, Fichte and Marx would seem to have no common measure. Second, the inference that in his own position Hegel sums up all significant contributions to philosophy, despite the fact that he displayed little interest in man as such, directs attention away from the contributions of Fichte and Marx to this topic. But since, as has been shown, it seems probable that Marx was directed toward Fichte in virtue of the relative lack of such attention in Hegel's position, the result is that by an irony of the history of philosophy the very position whose perceived defects were arguably most important in bringing about the parallel between the two positions also contributed the most to prevent its recognition.

MAN: ACTOR OR SPECTATOR?

Since the inquiry into the nature of man has now been under way for more than two millennia, consideration of the appropriateness of the approach to man as an active being will have to be a compromise. Although it would be desirable to accord to this problem the attention it merits, this does not seem possible within the limits of the present discussion. If we limit ourselves to contemporary work on the question of Marx, four distinct lines of inquiry are currently under consideration.[12] Further, even to outline the major views raised so far with respect to man would require another book.[13] In view of the dimensions of this problem, it therefore seems appropriate to choose a path between omitting any evaluation and a full-scale inquiry, through a brief analysis of the present alternative.

As the parallel between the two positions has been presented within the perspective of the revolt against Descartes in nineteenth-century German philosophy, it seems permissible to evaluate the approach to man as an active being within the framework provided by the Cartesian dilemma, that is, the choice between rival views of man as actor or spectator. This strategy should not, of course, be interpreted as even an implicit claim that no other approach is possible. Although other factors would enter into a more complete discussion of the complex issues raised by the initial choice of an approach to human being, the Cartesian dichotomy will serve as a locus within which some, although by no means all, of the reasons that might lead one to prefer the actor theory can at least be stated.[14]

In his own discussion, Descartes implies but does not demonstrate that the two rival views mentioned by him exhaust the available possibilities. If for purposes of argument we provisionally grant this point, a strong, albeit indirect argument in favor of the actor theory can be made through successful criticism of the spectator view. Now, it might perhaps be thought that this latter view has in fact rarely been held and that it is merely a transitory moment in the history of philosophy associated only with Descartes. On the contrary, this approach to man neither originates in nor does it perish with the Cartesian position. As a brief look at the history of philosophy will show, Descartes merely made explicit a concept of man which was already rooted in the very conception of philosophy in its first flowering within the Greek tradition.

The origins of the spectator theory are already clearly to be seen within Plato's thought. At the same time as he enunciated the view of philosophy as the science of sciences which has since been the dominant paradigm in the philosophical tradition, Plato specified the nature of philosophic knowledge and accordingly the role of the subject in attaining knowledge. According to Plato, true knowledge, or knowledge worthy of the name, is to be attained only through definitive transcendence of the subjective or transient in favor of objectivity on the plane of reality. As has already been mentioned, philosophy thus entails a kind of dying, since it is only when we withdraw from the transient world of appearances that we can hope to accede to knowledge on the level of the real. But if the kind of knowledge we seek is to be untainted by any subjectivity whatsoever, then we cannot permit the subject to have any qualities other than the ineliminable rational capacity requisite to intellectual comprehension.

Plato, of course, never attempted any simple reduction of man to man's intellectual capacity, although the need for this kind of attempt would seem to follow from his theory. As is well known, within his faculty psychology he distinguished different capacities in virtue of his analogy between the individual and the state. But the implication remains that if knowledge is to be wholly objective, then subjectivity must be coextensive with intellectual capacity. In his spectator theory, Descartes merely rendered explicit the inference contained in the identification of knowledge with objectivity.

Descartes's conception of man as a spectator, or potentially wholly rational being, follows from the quasi-Platonic view of knowledge that he defends. For it is only if man can be considered as nothing but an intellectual spectator that error can be avoided, skepticism defeated, and the possibility of knowledge secured. The *cogito* founds knowledge because through the correct application of man's rational faculty the correctness of his perceptions can be guaranteed. But the consequence of this view is that man is defined as a thinking substance in virtue of the needs of epistemological theory.

In the modern tradition, the influence of the Cartesian approach is manifest. Just as the Cartesian form of the epistemological problem has widely dominated modern thought, even though there has probably been more resistance than assent to his view, in the same way a dominant tendency has been to understand man as the subject of his experience in terms of the apparent requirements of epistemology. The discussion of the concept of the subject which begins with Locke and terminates with Kant is centered around the form of subjectivity compatible with, if not actually derived from, the putative needs of the theory of knowledge. Locke's conception of man as a tabula rasa was meant to support his belief that all knowledge derives from experience. When Hume argued against Locke that the concept of the subject is a bogus entity, since its persistence in time cannot be demonstrated, he came to his conclusion on the basis of an epistemological view regarding the nature of substance and knowledge in general. In the same way, Kant's reply to Hume that the concept of a transcendental subject or "I think" must be able to accompany all my perceptions was the result, not the precondition, of his transcendental method of inquiry.

Despite its undoubted originality, modern philosophy retains many of the problems and approaches already manifest in the earlier tradition. In particular, the Cartesian strand of the modern tradition reproduces the earlier tendency to grasp human being in terms of the conditions posed by its view of knowledge, although the difference is that these conditions are now specified with respect to the Cartesian position. It should further be noted that although the Cartesian framework is no longer the dominant chord in contemporary thought, it remains a live option in both philosophy and science. In the latter, the desire to understand man as a purely rational being has led to the concept of the ideal observer. The justification for this attitude is perhaps clearest with respect to "natural" sciences, such as physics, where the pretension to quasi-mathematical certitude seems to require restriction of interest in the human individual only to the extent that his contribution to empirical observation must in principle either be eliminated entirely or pared down to an irreducible minimum. And in philosophy the Cartesian-inspired view of man as a source of total rationality lives on in the work of Husserl, who at least until his final period understood his own thought as the prolongation of the Cartesian approach to rigorous philosophy, and from another perspective in Heidegger's understanding of *Dasein*, or the essence of man, as the being who poses the question of the meaning of being, despite Heidegger's public hostility to Descartes.

There is further a new version of a form of neo-Cartesianism which is currently fashionable. The Cartesian theory is reductionistic, since for multiple human capacities is substituted rationality alone as the single characteristic. But writing in Descartes's wake La Mettrie quickly refused even this last human trait in his book, *L'Homme la machine* (1747). As if echoing La Mettrie, the minimal Cartesian view of man as a rational being has been challenged in recent years, not in the direction of a broader conception, but rather with the aim of eliminating even this last human trait. In science, behaviorists such as Watson and Skinner study man as if he were in principle completely explicable through a causal analysis of inquiry. In the same way, the desire, in behavioristic fashion, to eliminate human subjectivity, is a leading theme in English thought, visible not only in Ryle's attempt to exorcise what he conceives of as the Cartesian ghost in the machine, but also in the attacks on the moral nature of ethical discourse, culminating perhaps in Nowell-Smith's belief that ethical language is devoid of moral content.

So far we have been concerned to establish that the Cartesian approach to man as the spectator of all that is, far from being a merely transient incident in the history of thought, in fact is merely an explicit formulation of an implicit tendency found throughout the history of philosophy to understand man in terms of his rational capacity only, as seemingly dictated by the requirements of the theory of knowledge. Now we must raise the question: Is this an adequate approach to the understanding of man?

Although it is often assumed that man is a rational animal, we are entitled to ask, what speaks for human reason? If our conclusion is to follow from experience, that man is inherently rational is perhaps not entirely self-evident. If human history teaches us anything, it is perhaps that the exercise of rationality in a nontrivial sense has not been an overly frequent occurrence. Yet the understanding of man as a rational being is no mere unexamined assumption. Just as, according to Aristotle, the law of non-contradiction is a necessary condition of rational discourse, it would seem that man must be assumed to be rational as a condition of any inquiry into the nature of human being. For if we presume that man is not rational, the assertion cannot rationally be discussed, and for the same reason no investigation of human rationality in general can possibly come to a negative conclusion. This should not, of course, be taken to mean that all men are rational or that rationality is widely present in human existence, for the opposite seems closer to the truth. But although it is entirely possible to disagree with respect to the nature of rationality or the extent to which it is manifested, it would seem to be the case that human rationality cannot be denied without falling into an overt contradiction. For this reason, the widespread approach to man as a rational animal seems justified, because necessary.

But to admit that man is rational should not be taken to mean that he necessarily possesses the kind of rationality required by the Cartesian view of knowledge. For to be capable of reason on one or another level is not the same as in practice to manifest or even to possess the capacity for certain judgments based on experience. As Kant was aware, although the Cartesian epistemology is designed to combat skepticism, the extreme measures it requires may actually result in the result it combats. For it may well be that man is not capable of meeting the stringent requirements proposed as the condition of the defense of knowledge in the full sense. But I am less interested here in the inherent difficulties of the Cartesian epistemology in general than in the problems which arise from the Cartesian-inspired approach to man in terms of the needs of a prior epistemology rather than approaching epistemology in terms of a prior grasp of man's capacity for knowledge. The major difficulty in the indirect, Cartesian approach to man in terms of the theory of knowledge is that in according priority to epistemology and only then attempting to arrive at an appropriate conception of the subject there is no reason to believe that the resultant view of subjectivity corresponds with man as he can be known in experience. I would now like to make several brief comments about the Cartesian spectator theory of man in support of this observation.

It has been argued that one result of the Cartesian spectator view is to align philosophy with the belief current in science that the role of the observer is to be confined solely to gathering information. Since the rise of modern science in the sixteenth and seventeenth centuries, it has been increasingly thought that the objectivity of science depends on the fact that the observational results are untainted by subjectivity. But it is paramount not to confuse useful fiction, which results from the idealized understanding of the interaction between the observer and his world, with what in fact occurs. It may well be helpful and arguably essential in certain situations to postulate an ideal observer. But it would be an error therefore to infer that such an observer in fact exists. In the real world there are no such ideal individuals, just as there are no purely rational beings. As Heisenberg has shown in his uncertainty principle, an argument which is all the more interesting because it is stated from a position within physical science, the relation of the observer to the observed is necessarily an interaction. It follows that even in the scientific realm pure objectivity, or the total absence of subjectivity, is never in the principle to be attained. Aside from its importance in the purely scientific realm, this argument has a philosophic dimension, since it apparently contradicts a view, namely, the spectator theory, invoked by Descartes in order to transform philosophy into science.[15]

Another reason can be drawn from the area of depth psychology, especially psychoanalysis. The spectator view of man as capable of perfect rationality owes much to the enlightenment attitude toward reason as an independent faculty capable of wholly objective knowledge. But although we may and in fact need to continue to strive for this ideal, it seems questionable to employ the enlightenment conception as a pardigm for what human being in fact is. On the contrary, the depth psychology developed in this century has shown that conscious human rationality is merely the tip of a preconscious human iceberg. One hardly needs to accept the entire psychoanalytic theory to recognize a preconscious dimension to human personality, which influences both abnormal and normal human behavior. An example is the phenomenon of rationalization, from which none of us are immune, in which preconscious motives are hidden through elaborate conscious justifications. This indicates that the human mind is in fact and routinely influenced by other than the strictest form of reasoning, and that it is difficult and perhaps not wholly possible to exclude entirely the effect of the preconscious dimension on our conscious mental processes.

Further support for this last point can be found in the field of advertising, which is inextricably bound up with depth psychology. Unlike psychoanalysis, which directs its efforts at the reduction of the effects of preconscious processes on conscious behavior, the aim of the advertising industry is to exploit this relation for commercial gain. The advertising enterprise is predicated on the assumption, whose justification appears daily in the sale of the most useless and and varied products, that conscious human comportment can in fact be modified even against the individual's own desires or so-called better judgment in a direction determined through direct or indirect appeal to the preconscious mental level. The success habitually enjoyed by this branch of private industry suggests that rationality is not wholly divorced from the surrounding world. Taken together, psychoanalysis and advertising further serve as indications that the Enlightenment view of man as a source of wholly independent rationality is no longer acceptable without serious qualification, and perhaps no longer acceptable at all.

It should be emphasized that any criticism of the Cartesian view of subjectivity is not meant as an attack on the Cartesian epistemology as such. Although it may well be the case that if the Cartesian theory of subjectivity fails then his entire theory of knowledge is untenable, in criticizing Descartes's view of man my intention is merely to call into question the spectator theory. My basic point is that it is methodologically unsound to accord priority to epistemology prior to a view of the subject. But if it is fallacious to proceed by setting epistemological goals and then in consequence "adjusting" the conception of man to "fit" the theory of knowledge, it is equally incorrect to "evolve" a theory of human being in complete independence of epistemology. But there is a third option open to contemporary thought, which is to formulate theories of man and knowledge in interdependence. It is, I submit, incorrect to separate the logical conditions of knowledge from man's psychological capacities, because when this is done there is no assurance that a subject adequate for the epistemology in question in fact exists. On the contrary, it is only if psychology and epistemology are placed on the same level, in which neither enjoys exclusive priority, that a theory can be elaborated which does not by virtue of its procedure require one to do violence to man as the experiential subject.

Although my purpose is to argue for the actor theory in general, I have so far been criticizing the spectator view. To the extent that these two possibilities represent genuine alternatives, to infirm one is to affirm the other. But since it so far has not and perhaps cannot be demonstrated that these two possibilities exhaust all relevant ways to understand man, the inherent weakness of any study of subjectivity solely within the framework of the Cartesian dichotomy must be acknowledged. But this does not, however, mean that the Cartesian framework is without merit. The virtue of a fundamental choice between alternatives such as those found in the Cartesian dichotomy is that it provides us with a basic concept in terms of which a theory of great explanatory power can be elaborated. In this regard, perhaps the strongest argument in favor of the actor theory is that activity is a general capacity in terms of which other, less general capacities can be understood. Just as man is not a spectator only, so activity in general never occurs. Only specific forms of activity take place. But the advantage of the actor theory is that forms of activity can be grasped as aspects of the capacity for activity in general, which hence offers the basic framework for what may well be a viable theory of man.

CHAPTER 9

MAN AS AN ACTIVE BEING

THE overall goal of this study has been to demonstrate a significant parallel in the positions of Fichte and Marx, arising from their respective conceptions of man as an active being, and located on the levels of activity, man, and theory. Although counter to the thrust of much of the discussion of this period, the parallel between the two positions is initially suggested by their dual preoccupation with subjectivity. With the exception of Kant's attempt to grasp man, arguably unsuccessful within the limits of his own position, Fichte and Marx are perhaps the two thinkers in the modern tradition most concerned with the anti-Cartesian approach to man as an active being.

This study of the parallel between the two positions arising from the anti-Cartesian approach to human being was pursued here through several stages. I began by demonstrating that a conception of man as an active being is indeed central to the two positions, and further showed that in each case activity is understood on an Aristotelian model. I then suggested that the conceptions of man which follow from the respective views of activity are also alike. On a fourth level, I argued that the parallel can be further extended to include similar metatheoretical views of the nature of theory. I then marshaled historical evidence to explain the genesis of the parallel, which was further applied to the evaluation of the usual paradigm of the modern German tradition, prior to a brief discussion of the intrinsic value of the anti-Cartesian approach to man as such.

The results of this study fall into four definite areas, concerning the interpretation of the respective positions, their relation, the nature of classical German thought, and the theory of man. Recently it has become apparent how important Fichte's thought is for an understanding of subsequent developments in the German tradition, especially with respect to Schelling and Hegel. An unfortunate by-product of this late awareness is that problems which assume paramount importance in later thought, such as self-consciousness, are on occasion taken as Fichte's central interest. But one must avoid mistaking the part for the whole. For the theory of self-consciousness, to which Fichte undoubtedly makes an important contribution, is merely one facet of his more general attempt to, as he says himself, understand the nature and limits of man. But as this general aim has received little attention in the literature and as it is further obscured by the current interest in self-consciousness apart from human being, it is useful to focus on primary texts as one means of restoring perspective.

A similar comment can be made about Marx's position, although here the problem in the secondary literature is compounded by the fact that so many of those who write about Marx have a further end in view. As a result, the Marx literature has for many years been a theater of dispute that on occasion bears little resemblance to the original writings. One tendency, perhaps most important in recent French writing, consists in denying that man has a role to play in Marx's position, or in arguing that man is both basic to and absent from his theory. These two interpretations, although fundamentally opposed, are united in the belief that a theory of man is absent from Marx's position, although, as I have tried to suggest, study of the texts would seem to suggest the contrary. Thus, in drawing attention to Marx's own writings, my hope was to counter some of the more evident excesses in the secondary literature.

With respect to the parallel between the two views of man as an active being, a detailed discussion has been provided. But the extent to which it has been or in fact could be successful is difficult to evaluate. One cannot definitively prove a parallel between two positions. At best one can demonstrate a similarity with varying degrees of rigor. But as there are no standards for this kind of demonstration, one can never state with certainty that a convincing argument has been made. Further, it is common knowledge that if pushed far enough all analogies will ultimately fail, by virtue of the fact that the terms of the comparison are necessarily nonidentical in order for them to be comparable. But I think that on balance a credible case for the relation in question has been provided.

Turning now to the philosophical tradition, I have sought to show that Fichte's and Marx's respective preoccupations with man as an active being reflect the anti-Cartesian spirit which animates most of modern philosophy. Indeed, one must wonder whether to a certain extent philosophy has not finally been successful in bursting the bounds imposed on it by the Cartesian position. An example may be the view of man with which we have been concerned here. For in suggesting that both man and the cognitive relation are to be understood as facets of experience, it seems to me that modern philosophy is attentive to the Cartesian emphasis on subjectivity, but advances beyond the framework of Descartes's original problem.

A word should be said about Aristotelian activity. It is frequently suggested that Plato is the father of philosophy, and just as often we are told that Descartes is the father of modern philosophy. There is, of course, no contradiction in the two claims, since there is a great deal of intellectual continuity between these two thinkers. In Descartes's view of mind as the link between body and objective knowledge, one recognizes a revised form of the familiar Platonic dualism in which mind is situated between appearance and reality.

The restatement of Platonic themes in Descartes's thought is significant for the interpretation of the modern tradition. For the revolt against Descartes that is so characteristic of this period is in an important sense a revolt against the Platonic dualism which finds its restatement in his thought. In rejecting the Cartesian ontological framework, modern thinkers are also protesting against the concept of dualism itself, which found its first consequential statement in Plato's philosophy. In this sense, the modern tradition is merely the new arena for an old quarrel between dualistic and monistic world views which has divided philosophy into opposing camps ever since the golden age of Greek thought.

One should not be surprised at the recurrence of an Aristotelian conception of activity in the modern context. Aristotle's rejection of Platonic dualism is common knowledge. But since this point is rarely made, it is worth reemphasizing that the intellectual tool with which Aristotle overcomes the Platonic dualism is apparently none other than his conception of activity, which relates both potentiality and actuality in a manner which makes possible the avoidance of a two-worlds ontology. The reason that Aristotelian activity recurs in the aftermath of the Cartesian philosophy is that the latter's dualism presents in modern dress the ancient problem for whose solution the Aristotelian concept was arguably originally conceived.

A further comment should be made about the nineteenth-century German tradition. As it is usually understood, Fichte and Marx would seem to be unrelated. We are all used to hearing that Fichte is an idealist and Marx is a materialist and probably not a philosopher at all. But the result of this study has been to demonstrate a profound similarity in their two positions. It follows that, to the extent that the typical approach to this period would seem to preclude the relation in question, it needs to be rethought. For if the categories of our analysis prevent us from understanding, or at least correctly understanding, the period for which they are selected, then they need to be revised and a new set of categories chosen which will be more adequate to the task.

This same point bears restatement on a more general plane. The nineteenth-century German tradition is frequently discussed as if it were composed of a series of disparate thinkers, united mainly, if not solely, by their common use of the German language. But the extent to which the members of this tradition differed among themselves should not be allowed to obscure themes which connect their positions and which have the effect of creating a common tradition, as opposed to a collection of unrelated philosophical theories. One such theme, as discussed here, is the view of man as an active being, and others could be mentioned. In this sense, an aim of this volume is to contribute to a reconceptualization of this period as in fact a varied, diverse, but essentially continuous movement in the wider history of philosophy, and thereby to relativize oppositions often thought to separate thinkers in this period.

Finally, I would like to make a comment on the concept of man we have been considering. It would be repetitive to offer a defense of its merits, since in part this has already been undertaken through the argument of its intrinsic superiority to the spectator theory. But the list of rival theories is by no means exhausted. Other candidates include theories of man as *homo sapiens*, *homo ludens*, *homo faber*, and so forth. In comparison to such views, the advantage of the concept of man as an active being is its generality. For each of the other views listed here takes a facet of human activity as characteristic of human being. But although in each case a significant facet of human being is designated, any attempt to take the part for the whole must be unsatisfactory, because it will lead to the exclusion of other pertinent forms of human activity. Hence, an advantage of the present theory is that by virtue of its generality other, more specific views appear within it as special cases or aspects of the basic approach to man as an active being. The theory's generality thus turns out to be a relative strength and, I would like to suggest, a reason for its further study.

NOTES

SELECTED BIBLIOGRAPHY

INDEX

CHAPTER 1. *On Comparing the Positions of Fichte and Marx*

1. See especially Jean-Paul Sartre, *Search for a Method*, trans. Hazel Barnes (New York: Knopf, Vintage, 1968); Michel Henry, *Marx*, 2 vols. (Paris: Gallimard, 1976); and Leszek Kolakowski, *Main Currents of Marxism*, trans. P. S. Falla, 3 vols. (New York: Oxford University Press, 1978), in particular the first volume.

2. Among the discussions which deal in part with the comparison of one or more aspect common to the positions of Fichte and Marx, the following should be mentioned: Marianne Weber, *Fichtes Sozialismus und sein Verhältnis zur Marx'schen Doktrin* (Tübingen: Mohr, 1900); Manfred Buhr, *Revolution und Philosophie* (Berlin: V. E. B. Deutscher Verlag der Wissenschaften, 1965); Jürgen Habermas, *Knowledge and Human Interests*, trans. Jeremy J. Schapiro (Boston: Beacon, 1972); Arnold Gehlen, "Über die Geburt der Freiheit aus der Entfremdung," in *Studien zur Anthropologie und Soziologie* (Neuwied and Berlin: Luchterhand, 1971). To the best of my knowledge, a full-scale comparison of the two positions has not yet appeared in any language.

3. Karl Marx and Friedrich Engels, *Marx-Engels Werke*, 39 vols. (Berlin: Dietz Verlag, 1956–68), 19:188.

4. The tendency to relate Kant and Marx, according to Vranicki, was represented by R. Stammler, F. Staudinger, and K. Vorländer, and reached its most developed form in the writings of M. Adler. See Predrag Vranicki, *Geschichte des Marxismus*, trans. Stanislava Rummel and Vjekoslava Wiedmann, 2 vols. (Frankfurt: Suhrkamp, 1974), 1:287, 353–61.

5. See, for example, Giovanni Gentile, *La filosofia della prassi* (1899), rpt. *La filosofia di Marx* (Florence: Einaudi, 1974). According to Kolakowski, probably the initial attempt to treat Marxism as a theory of historical praxis was made by Labriola. See *Main Currents of Marxism*, 2:192.

6. See my "Marxian Praxis," *Philosophy and Social Criticism* 5 (1978).

7. A recent example is provided by Henry's *Marx*.

CHAPTER 2. *Fichte's Theory of Man as Active Self*

1. Johann Gottlieb Fichte, *Fichtes Werke*, ed. I. H. Fichte, 11 vols. (Berlin: Walter De Gruyter, 1971), 6, p. 294.

2. The signal exception is Wilhelm Weischedel, *Der Aufbruch der Freiheit zur Gemeinschaft* (Leipzig: Meiner, 1939). See also Heinz Heimsoeth, *Fichte* (Munich: E. Reinhardt, 1923).

3. "According to Fichte's verbal statements, which were not mentioned in his book, the self creates through its representations; and all reality is only in the self. The world is to the self like a ball, which the self has thrown out and then caught again through reflection [*Reflexion*]." Letter from Schiller to Goethe of October 28, 1794 in Johann Christian Friedrich Schiller *Briefwechsel zwischen Schiller und Goethe*, ed. H. Hauff, 2 vols. (Stuttgart: Cotta'sche Buchhandlung, 1856), 1:26. A more sophisticated, but similar interpretation is stated by Josiah Royce, *Lectures on Modern Idealism* (1919; reprint ed., New Haven: Yale University Press, 1964), p. 97: "That this self of philosophy is not the individual man of ordinary life appears from the very outset of Fichte's discussion. The individual man of ordinary life is one of the beings to be defined by philosophy, and is certainly not the principle of philosophy."

4. "In what sense does Fichte signify the beginning of something new? In that he begins from the intellectual intuition of the self, not however as a substance, a being, a givenness, but rather through this intuition, that is, he understands this striving for deepening (*diese angestrebte Vertiefung*) of the self in itself as life, activity, energy and, accordingly, the corresponding concepts of energy as opposition, etc., the realisation in itself." Wilhelm Dilthey, *Gesammelte Schriften* (Stuttgart: Tübner, 1961), 7:148.

5. Johann Gottlieb Fichte, *Fichte: Science of Knowledge (Wissenschaftslehre) with First and Second Introductions*, ed. and trans. Peter Heath and John Lachs (New York: Appleton-Century-Crofts, 1970). (Hereafter cited in text as *WL*.)

6. *Intelligenzblatt der Allgemeinen-Literatur-Zeitung*, no. 113 (October 1794).

7. For an example of the tendency to approach the *Wissenschaftslehre* apart from the wider context of Fichte's thought, see Dieter Henrich, *Fichtes ursprüngliche Einsicht* (Frankfurt: Vittorio Klostermann, 1966).

8. Letter from Fichte to Reinhold of March 1, 1794, in Johann Gottlieb Fichte, *J. G. Fichte. Briefwechsel*, ed. Hans Schulz, 2 vols. (Hildesheim: Georg Olms, 1967), 1 : 341.

9. Karl Leonhard Reinhold, *Beyträge zur Berichtigung bisheriger Missverständnisse der Philosophie*, 2 vols. (Jena: Manke, 1790, 1 : 267: "In consciousness the representation (*Vorstellung*) is distinguished from both subject and object, and related to both."

10. *Fichtes Werke*, 1 : 18.

11. Adolph Schurr makes a similar point when he writes, "During the process of working out [*Ausarbeitung*] the review of Aenesidemus Fichte conceived the foundation [*Fundament*] upon which his *Foundation [Grundlage]* was [later] built." *Philosophie als System bei Fichte, Schelling, und Hegel* (Stuttgart: Frommann-Holzboog, 1974), p. 12.

12. Martial Gueroult notes, "The effort towards totality is equalled only by the effort toward real and internal unity, which is opposed—even in a Schelling—to eclecticism or arbitrary syncretism." *L'Evolution et la structure de la doctrine de la science chez Fichte*, 2 vols. (Paris: Société d'éditions Les Belles Lettres, 1930), 1:3.

13. I have no intention of suggesting that Fichte was a phenomenologist *avant la lettre* in the sense this term has been given by such writers as Husserl and Heidegger. Here as elsewhere, unless otherwise specified, by "phenomenological" is meant the somewhat different, but not unrelated sense in which this term applies also, but not only, to Hegel. For a discussion, which however conflates the phenomenological sides of Husserl's and Hegel's positions, see Alexandre Kojève, *Introduction à la lecture de Hegel* (Paris: Gallimard, 1947).

14. "The absolute is neither knowledge, nor is it being, nor is it identity, nor is it the indifference of both; rather, it is throughout only and simply the absolute." *Fichtes Werke*, 2 : 13.

15. This point has frequently been misconstrued. On the whole, Wundt seems correct, when he writes, "The concept of God has no intrinsic place in the *Wissenschaftslehre* of 1794, but is only appealed to occasionally for purposes of comparison" (*sondern wird nur gelegentlich zum Vergleich herangezogen*). Wilhelm Wundt, *Fichteforschungen* (Stuttgart: F. Frommann, 1929), p. 275.

16. Schelling stated the need for a philosophy of nature as follows: "Fichte considered idealism from a fully subjective

perspective, and I considered it from a fully objective perspective. Fichte's idealistic principle remained on the reflective standpoint; on the contrary, I put forward the idealistic principle from the standpoint of production." *Darstellung meines Systems der Philosophie* in *Schellings Werke*, ed. Manfred Schröder (Munich: Beck and Oldenbourg, 1927), 3 : 5. For a recent study of the relation between Fichte and Schelling, see Reinhard Lauth, *Die Entstehung von Schellings Identitätsphilosophie in der Auseinandersetzung mit Fichtes Wissenschaftslehre, 1795–1801* (Munich: Alber, 1975).

17. For an account of Fichte's view of intellectual intuition, see Alexis Philonenko, "L'Intuition intellectuelle chez Fichte," in *Akten der Fichte-Tagung* (Proceedings of international conference at Zwettl, Austria, in press).

18. Letter from Fichte to Jacobi of August 30, 1795, from Osmannstadt in *J. G. Fichte. Briefwechsel*, 1 : 501.

19. The argument has been made that Fichte is a pioneer in the attempt to understand social interaction. See C. Hunter, *Der Interpersonalitätsbeweis in Fichtes früher angewandter praktischer Philosophie* (Meisenheim: a.M. Glan: Hain, 1973).

20. For the classic expression of this interpretation, see Richard Kroner, *Von Kant bis Hegel* (Tübingen: Siebeck, 1921–24) two volumes. For criticism of the Hegelian-inspired reading of Fichte's position, see Peter Baumanns, *Fichtes ursprüngliche System: Sein Standort zwischen Kant und Hegel* (Stuttgart: Frommann-Holzboog, 1972).

21. For a recent, general introduction to Fichte's thought as a whole, see Pierre-Philippe Druet, *Fichte* (Namur: Seghers, 1977). For a more specialized, recent discussion, see Wolfgang Janke, *Fichte: Sein und Reflexion. Grundlagen der kritischen Vernunft* (Berlin: Walter De Gruyter, 1970). For the most detailed analysis of the structure of the *Wissenschaftslehre* of 1794, see Alexis Philonenko, *La Liberté humaine dans la philosophie de Fichte* (Paris: Vrin, 1966).

22. *Fichtes Werke*, 3 : 39.

23. Ibid., p. 55.

24. Ibid., 10 : 498. Marianne Weber's failure to note this correction leads her unfortunately to perceive an analogy on this point between the positions of Fichte and Marx, when in fact there is none. See *Fichtes Sozialismus und sein Verhältnis zum Marx'schen Doktrin.*

25. Letter from Fichte to Struensee of November 9, 1800, in
    J. G. Fichte. Briefwechsel, 2:288.

CHAPTER 3. *Philosophy and Political Economy:
Marxian Theory of Man*

1. See Henry, *Marx*. See also Kolakowski, *Main Currents of
   Marxism*.
2. See Agnes Heller, *La Théorie des besoins chez Marx* (Paris:
   Union générale des éditions, 1978), p. 35.
3. The retrospective kind of reconstruction to be undertaken
   here in order to determine the outlines of Marx's position
   should be distinguished from a prospective form of reconstruction, currently in fashion, in which the aim is to improve on the original position. For a description of this
   latter form of reconstruction, see Jürgen Habermas, *Zur Rekonstruktion des historischen Materialismus* (Frankfurt:
   Suhrkamp, 1976), p. 9.
4. A recent, typical instance is found in a book by Bertell Ollman, who writes: "Engels is usually taken as a co-equal
   spokesman with Marx for the theories of Marxism. For
   most purposes, this procedure is perfectly justified." *Alienation: Marx's Conception of Man in Capitalist Society* (New
   York and London: Cambridge University Press, 1973),
   p. xv.
5. For an early discussion, see Anton Pannekoek, *Lenin als Philosoph*, ed. Alfred Schmidt (1938; reprint ed., Frankfurt:
   Europäische Verlagsanstalt, 1969). For a more recent account, see Kolakowski, *Main Currents of Marxism*, vol. 1,
   chap. 16.
6. Anselm Feuerbach, *Fundamental Principles of the Philosophy of the Future*, trans. Manfred H. Vogel (Indianapolis
   and New York: Bobbs-Merrill, 1966), p. 3.
7. Karl Marx, *Karl Marx: Early Writings*, trans. and ed. T. B.
   Bottomore (New York: McGraw-Hill, 1964), p. 44. (Hereafter cited as Marx, *Early Writings* [Bottomore].)
8. Ibid., p. 44.
9. Ibid., p. 63.
10. Bruno Bauer, *Die gute Sache der Freiheit und meine eigene
    Angelegemheit* (1842; reprint ed., Aalen: Scientia Verlag,
    1972), pp. 224 f.
11. Karl Marx and Friedrich Engels, *The German Ideology*,

trans. C. J. Arthur (New York: International Publishers, 1970), p. 123.

12. Marx, *Early Writings* (Bottomore), p. 50.

13. Letter to Oppenheim (25 August 1842) in *Marx-Engels Werke*, 27:408.

14. For instance, in an otherwise excellent study, Klaus Hartmann has argued that Marx's position combines unrelated views of man and political economy. Noting that if the politico-economic side of the theory were grounded in a concept of man, then the position would be philosophic, he suggests that Marxian political economy must be developed immanently. See *Die Marx'sche Theorie: Eine philosophische Untersuchung zu den Hauptschriften* (Berlin: Walter de Gruyter, 1970), pp. 253–54.

15. This point has been made by Althusser and his followers. See Louis Althusser, *For Marx*, trans. Ben Brewster (New York: Knopf, Vintage, 1970), esp. chapter 7: "Marxism and Humanism." Althusser's recent admission that his theoretical anti-humanism was inspired as much by his desire to counter "dangerous tendencies" as his reading of the texts seriously weakens his interpretation.

16. *Marx-Engels Werke*, 16:362.

17. The Marxian concept of need has been further developed by Jean-Paul Sartre in his *Critique of Dialectical Reason*, trans. Alan Sheridan-Smith (Atlantic Highlands, N.J.: Humanities Press, 1976). For an attempt to base the interpretation of Marx's whole position on this concept, see Heller, *La théorie des besoins chez Marx*.

18. Karl Marx, *Writings of the Young Marx on Philosophy and Society*, ed. and trans. Lloyd D. Easton and Kurt H. Guddat (Garden City: Doubleday, 1967), p. 409. (Hereafter cited as Marx, *Writings of Young Marx*.)

19. Marx, *Early Writings* (Bottomore), pp. 164–65.

20. For example, Richard J. Bernstein maintains that the concept of species-being is absent in Marx's later thought (see *Praxis and Action* [Philadelphia: University of Pennsylvania Press, 1971], pp. 68–70), while Bertell Ollman sees it as the foundation of Marx's theory of man (see *Alienation*, p. 76).

21. Marx and Engels, *German Ideology*, p. 122.

22. Karl Marx, *Capital*, ed. Friedrich Engels, trans. Samuel Moore and Edward Aveling, 3 vols. (New York: International Publishers, 1967), 1:609.

23. Marx, *Early Writings* (Bottomore), p. 158.

24. Marx and Engels, *German Ideology*, p. 50. According to

Bertell Ollman, *Alienation*, this is the central concept in Marx's position.

25. Marx, *Writings of Young Marx*, p. 431.

26. Among the first to make this observation were Georg Lukács in *History and Class Consciousness* (1923), trans. Rodney Livingston (Cambridge: MIT Press, 1971) and Karl Korsch, *Marxism and Philosophy* (1923), trans. Fred Halliday (London: New Left Books, 1970). For more recent discussions, see also Lucien Goldmann, *Recherches dialectiques* (Paris: Gallimard, 1959) and Karel Kosik, *Dialectic of the Concrete*, trans. Karel Kovanda and James Schmidt (Boston: Reidel, 1976).

27. For further discussion, see the specialized literature on this topic. The first discussion of alienation in Marx's position, which appeared in Lukács's *History and Class Consciousness*, is vitiated by a celebrated confusion between alienation and objectification. The first discussion of alienation in the *Paris Manuscripts* is in Herbert Marcuse's review, "The Foundations of Historical Materialism" (1931), reprinted in his *Studies in Critical Philosophy*, trans. Joris de Bres (Boston: Beacon Press, 1972). Among more recent studies, see especially Istvan Mészáros, *Marx's Theory of Alienation* (London: Merlin, 1970), and H. Popitz, *Der entfremdete Mensch: Zeitkritik und Geschichtsphilosophie des jungen Marx* (Basel: J. Springer, 1953). For a study of alienation in general, see Richard Schacht, *Alienation* (Garden City: Doubleday, 1971).

28. Marx, *Early Writings* (Bottomore), p. 125.

29. Ibid., p. 127.

30. See Mészáros, *Marx's Theory of Alienation*, pp. 222–27, 328–31.

31. For the full exposition of the concept of fetishism, see Marx, *Capital*, 1, chap. 1, pt. 4. For earlier occurrences of this term in Marx's writing, see the lead article of the *Kölnischer Zeitung* (no. 179), reprinted in Marx, *Writings of Young Marx*, p. 115; *Towards the Critique of Hegel's Philosophy of Law*, in Marx, *Writings of Young Marx*, p. 259; *Paris Manuscripts*, in Marx, *Early Writings* (Bottomore), pp. 342–44, 364. For an earlier formulation of the concept without mention of the term "fetishism," see Marx, *Grundrisse: Foundations of the Critique of Political Economy*, trans. Martin Nicolaus (Baltimore: Penguin, 1973), p. 157.

32. Marx, *Capital*, 1:72.

33. This interpretation is to be found in the writings of Althusser and his followers. See Louis Althusser, *For Marx*, and Louis Althusser and Etienne Balibar, *Reading Capital*, trans. Ben Brewster, 2 vols. (New York: Pantheon Press, 1970). For a recent criticism of this approach, see Leszek Kolakowski, "Le Marx d'Althusser," in *L'Esprit révolutionnaire* (Brussels: Editions complexes, 1978), pp. 158–86.

34. See Mészáros, *Marx's Theory of Alienation*, and Alfred Schmidt, *Geschichte und Struktur: Fragen einer marxistischen Historik* (Munich: Hansa Reihe, 1971).

35. See Schlomo Avineri, *The Social and Political Thought of Karl Marx* (New York: Cambridge University Press, 1968). Avineri errs however in his concern to show that Marx's entire later development is already implicit in his early criticism of Hegel.

36. An interesting argument has been made that Marx's inability to complete his major writings is due to an inherent tension between his a priori method and the a posteriori material he gathered to illustrate his theoretical conclusions. See Bertram D. Wolfe, *Marxism: 100 Years in the Life of a Doctrine* (New York: Dell, Delta, 1965), pp. 319 ff.

37. For a larger overview, see Ernest Mandel, *Traité d'économie politique marxiste* (Paris: Union générale d'éditions, 1962), 4 vols. For a specialized discussion of the labor theory of value, see Joan Robinson, *An Essay on Marxian Economics* (London: Macmillan, 1947). For a representative, recent study, see M. C. Howard and J. E. King, *The Political Economy of Marx* (New York: Longmans, 1975), and for a more critical perspective, Werner Becker, *Die Achillesferse des Marxismus, der Widerspruch Von Kapital und Arbeit* (Hamburg: Hoffmann and Campe, 1974). For recent discussions from a philosophical perspective, see Henry, *Marx*, vol. 2, and Kolakowski, *Main Currents of Marxism*, 1, chaps. 12–14.

38. Marx, *Early Writings* (Bottomore), p. 69.

39. See Marx, *Capital*, 1:35 ff.

40. Ibid., pp. 35 ff., 49 ff.

41. Kolakowski makes the interesting point that the labor theory of value presupposes the theory of alienation, when he writes, "Exchange value is nothing other than the 'living work' of man transformed into a foreign force in a market [governed by] anonymous laws." *L'Esprit révolutionnaire*, p. 170.

42. Marx, *Writings of Young Marx*, p. 454.

43. *Marx and Engels: Basic Writings on Politics and Philosophy*, ed. Lewis S. Feuer (Garden City: Doubleday, Anchor Books, 1959), p. 20. (Hereafter cited as Marx and Engels, *Basic Writings.*)
44. Ibid., p. 44.
45. See Herbert Marcuse, *One Dimensional Man* (Boston: Beacon, 1964), especially the discussion of sur-repression.
46. Marx, *Capital*, 1:8.
47. Ibid., p. 763.
48. For a study of the concept of dictatorship and the dictatorship of the proletariat in the Marxist tradition, see H. Draper, "Marx and the Dictatorship of the Proletariat," in *Etudes de marxologie* (Paris, Sept. 1962), supplement to *Cahiers de l'Institut de sciences économiques appliquées.*
49. See Wolfe, *Marxism*, chaps. 10 and 11.
50. See Marx, *Grundrisse*, pp. 704 ff. For a discussion of this passage, see Jürgen Habermas, *Knowledge and Human Interests*, trans. Jeremy J. Shapiro (Boston: Beacon Press, 1972), pp. 48 ff.
51. Marx, *Capital*, 3:820.
52. Hannah Arendt takes Marx to task on this score. See her *The Human Condition* (Chicago: University of Chicago Press, 1971), chap. 3.
53. Marx, *Capital*, 3:820.
54. *Theorien über den Mehrwert*, in *Marx-Engels Werke*, vol. 26, pt. 3, p. 255.
55. For this interpretation, see Lucien Sève, *Marxisme et théorie de la personnalité* (Paris: Editions sociales, 1969). For a contrary reading, see Adam Schaff, *Marxism and the Human Individual*, trans. O. Wojtasiwicz (New York: McGraw-Hill, 1970).
56. Marx, *Early Writings* (Bottomore), p. 159.

CHAPTER 4. *Activity in Fichte and Marx*

1. "Marxism demands for its class [that is, the proletariat] the advantages heretofore enjoyed by privileged ranks. . . . Work remains however important in its role as a necessary evil. . . . On the contrary, Fichte demands its virtual abolition in favor of a comfortable life of ease and enjoyment." Peter Coulmas, *Fichtes Idee der Arbeit* (Hamburg: Hansischer Gildenverlag, 1939), p. 73.
2. Habermas, *Knowledge and Human Interests*, p. 44.

3. "The following exposition will seek to show that pure consciousness, which in the system is an absolute identity of subject and object is a subjective identity of subject/object." G. W. F. Hegel, *Differenz des Fichte'schen und Schelling'schen Systems der Philosophie* (Hamburg: Meiner Verlag, 1962), p. 38.

4. See Emil Lask, *Fichtes Idealismus und die Geschichte* in *Gesammelte Schriften*, ed. Eugen Herriegel (Tübingen: Mohr, 1923–24), vol. 1, passim.

5. Johann Gottlieb Fichte, *Fichte: Science of Knowledge (Wissenschaftslehre) with First and Second Introductions*, ed. and trans. Peter Heath and John Lachs (New York: Appleton-Century-Crofts, 1970), p. 119. (Cited in text as *WL* with page number.)

6. Marx, *Early Writings* (Bottomore), p. 126.

7. Marx, *Capital*, 1:177.

8. For an interesting attempt to distinguish between work and labor in general, see Arendt, *The Human Condition*, chap. 3.

9. Marx and Engels, *The German Ideology*, p. 94.

10. See Karel Kosik, *Die Dialektik des Konkreten*, trans. Marianne Hoffmann (Frankfurt: Suhrkamp, 1970), p. 208, "Human activity, which is limited only through inner purpose and not through natural necessity of social duty, is not work [*Arbeit*], but rather free creation, independently of its domain."

11. Marx, *Writings of Young Marx*, p. 94.

12. *The Republic of Plato*, trans. F. M. Cornford (New York: Oxford University Press, 1973), pp. 38–39.

13. See Aristotle *Metaphysics* Book *Theta*. 1050a21–23.

14. Most general discussions of Aristotle's thought have little to say about his concept of activity. See, for example, W. D. Ross, *Aristotle* (New York: Meridian Press, 1960) and Ingemar Düring, *Aristoteles: Darstellung und Interpretation seines Denkens* (Heidelberg: C. Winter, 1966). This is further the case for specialized discussions of the Aristotelian concept of being. See, for example, Joseph Owens, *The Doctrine of Being in the Aristotelian Metaphysics* (Toronto: Institute of Pontifical Studies, 1951) and Pierre Aubenque, *Le Problème de l'être chez Aristote; essai sur la problématique aristotélicienne* (Paris: Presses universitaires de France, 1962).

15. See Aristotle *Metaphysics* Book *Theta*. Esp. 1048b18–35.

16. See J. L. Ackrill, "Aristotle's Distinction between *Energeia*

and *Kinesis*," in *New Essays on Plato and Aristotle*, ed. Remford Bambrough (New York: Humanities Press, 1967). For a reply to Ackrill, see Terry Penner, "Verbs and Identity of Action: A Philosophical Exercise in the Interpretation of Aristotle," in *Ryle*, ed. G. Pitcher and O. Wood (Garden City: Doubleday, Anchor Books, 1970).

17. For a rather different analysis of unity in diversity, see Martin Heidegger, *Identity and Difference*, trans. Joan Stambaugh (New York: Harper and Row, 1969).

18. See Josef Stallmach, *Dynamis und Energeia* (Meisenheim: Hain, 1959), p. 11.

19. See Emerson Buchanan, "Aristotle's Theory of Being" (Ph.D. diss., Columbia University, 1962). For a more recent, related study, see James P. Etzwiler, "Being as Activity in Aristotle: A Process Interpretation," *International Phiosophical Quarterly* 18, no. 3 (September 1978).

20. An analogous point is developed at length in Ernst Bloch, *Das Materialismusproblem* (Frankfurt: Suhrkamp, 1972).

21. "In this way the whole of Aristotle's philosophy, both in construction and in its critical aspects, may be enunciated in the one word, 'Energeia.'" F. C. S. Schiller, "Activity and Substance," in *Humanism: Philosophical Essays* (London: Macmillan, 1912), p. 208. See also Jacob Klein, "Aristotle, an Introduction," in *Ancients and Moderns*, ed. Joseph Cropsey (New York: Basic Books, 1964).

22. "The original definition of activity (*energeia*) has, as actuality (*actualitas*) become being." Martin Heidegger, *Nietzsche*, 2 vols. (Pfullingen: Neske, 1961), 2:412.

23. "Since the definition of being as actuality (*actualitas*) is all history . . . accordingly in multiple ways Roman and no longer Greek." Heidegger, *Nietzsche*, 2:413.

24. H. F. Hallett puts this point well. "By 'action' is signified this distinction in unity of 'potency' and its 'actuality.'" *Benedict de Spinoza* (London: Athlone Press, 1957), p. 9.

25. See Aristotle *Nichomachean Ethics* 1. 7.

26. Ibid. 10. 4. 1175a11–15.

27. Aristotle *Nicomachean Ethics*, trans. Martin Ostwald (Indianapolis: Bobbs-Merrill, 1962), pp. 17–18. (Aristotle *Nicomachean Ethics* 1. 7. 1098a18–20.)

28. Buchanan, "Aristotle's Theory of Being," p. 60.

29. See Aristotle *Metaphysics* Book *Theta*. 1050a23–27.

30. See *Über die aesthetische Erziehung des Menschen in einer Reihe von Briefen*.

31. For a good account of the related view of "expressionism" in

Herder, Hegel, and the German tradition, see Charles Taylor, *Hegel* (Cambridge: Cambridge University Press, 1975), esp. chap. 1.

CHAPTER 5. *Activity and Man*

1. For a recent discussion, see John Passmore, *The Perfectibility of Man* (London: Duckworth, 1970).
2. "Causalität des Begriffs." *Fichtes Werke*, 4:9.
3. *Fichtes Werke*, 7:7.
4. An argument has recently been made that Marx was not opposed to religion as such, but rather to the reactionary form it assumed in the nineteenth century. See Philippe Warnier, *Marx pour un chrétien* (Paris: Mame-Fayard, 1977), chap. 3.
5. *Fichtes Werke*, 7:240–41.
6. *Studien zur Anthropologie und Soziologie* (Neuweid and Berlin: Luchterhand, 1971).
7. *Fichtes Werke*, 3:11.
8. Ibid., p. 401.
9. Fichte claims to perceive and to comprehend a distinction in Rousseau between the latter's concepts of *volonté générale* and *volonté de tous*. See *Fichtes Werke*, 3:106–7. For a discussion of the problem of the will in Fichte and Rousseau, see Alexis Philonenko, *Théorie et praxis dans la pensée morale et pratique de Kant et Fichte en 1793* (Paris: Vrin, 1968), chap. 19.
10. Karl Marx, *Karl Marx: Early Writings*, trans. T. R. Livingstone and G. Benton (New York: Random House, 1975), p. 278.
11. Marx and Engels, *Basic Writings*, p. 29.
12. Marx, *Grundrisse*, p. 708.
13. Marx, *Capital*, 3:820.
14. See Marx, *Capital*, vol. 1, esp. chaps. 8 and 13.
15. Marx, *Early Writings* (Bottomore), p. 161.
16. Immanuel Kant, *Religion within the Limits of Reason Alone*, trans. T. M. Greene and H. H. Hudson (New York: Harper and Row, 1960), p. 5.
17. Johann Gottlieb Fichte, *The Vocation of Man*, trans. R. M. Chisholm (Indianapolis: Bobbs-Merrill, 1956), p. 134.
18. See, for example, the analysis of the relation of reason and faith in Hegel's discussion of the "*Aufklärung*" in the *Phänomenologie des Geistes*, chap. 6.

19. Fichte, *Vocation of Man*, pp. 88–89.
20. Ibid., p. 98.

CHAPTER 6. *Theory and Metatheory*

1. See, for example, Friedrich Engels, *Ludwig Feuerbach and the Outcome of Classical German Philosophy*, ed. C. P. Dutt (New York: International Publishers, 1941), chapter 4. An exception is provided by the following passage in Theodor Adorno, *Negative Dialectics*, trans. E. B. Ashton (New York: Seabury Press, 1973), p. 197. "It was Marx who drew the link between historical materialism and the popular-metaphysical kind. He thus involved the former in the problematics of philosophy, leaving popular materialism to cut its capers this side of philosophy. Since then, materialism is no longer a counter-position one may resolve to take; it is the critique of idealism in its entirety, and of the reality for which idealism opts by distorting it."
2. For Ayer's admission of defeat, see "Phenomenalism," in *Proceedings of the Aristotelian Society* 47 (1946–47), pp. 163 ff.
3. See W. V. O. Quine, "Two Dogmas of Empiricism," in *From a Logical Point of View* (Cambridge: Harvard University Press, 1953), pp. 20 ff.
4. See Avineri, *The Social and Political Thought of Karl Marx*, p. 65.
5. See *Dictionary of Philosophy*, ed. Dagobert D. Runes (New York: Philosophical Library, Alliance Corporation, 1942), articles on "Idealism" and "Materialism"; and *Philosophisches Wörterbuch*, ed. Georg Klaus and Manfred Buhr (Leipzig: Bibliographisches Institut, 1970), articles on "Idealismus" and "Materialismus."
6. See Georg Lukács, *Ontologie: Marx* (Darmstadt and Neuwied: Luchterhand, 1970), p. 38.
7. *Enciclopedia Filosofica*, ed. N. Abbagnano (Turin: Unione Tipografico, 1961), articles on "Idealismo" and "Materialismo."
8. See *Baldwin's Dictionary of Philosophy and Psychology*, ed. James Baldwin (London: Macmillan, 1902), articles on "Materialism" and "Idealism."
9. G. E. Moore, *Philosophical Studies* (London: Routledge and Kegan Paul, 1965).
10. See Norman Kemp Smith, *Prolegomena to an Idealist The-*

ory of Knowledge (London: Macmillan, 1924); and H. B. Acton, articles on "Materialism," "Idealism," and "Dialectical Materialism," in *Encyclopedia of Philosophy*, ed. Paul Edwards (New York:Macmillan, Free Press, 1967).

11. See G. W. F. Hegel, *Wissenschaft der Logik*, ed. Georg Lasson, 2 vols. (Hamburg: Meiner Verlag, 1967), 1:145.

12. See George Santayana, *Realm of Matter* (London: Constable, 1930), esp. chap. 10, "The Latent Materialism of Idealists."

13. See Bernard Bosanquet, *The Meeting of Extremes in Modern Philosophy* (London: Macmillan, 1921).

14. See Richard Rorty, "The World Well Lost," *Journal of Philosophy* 59, no. 19 (October 1972), pp. 649 ff.

15. Marx, *Writings of Young Marx*, p. 370; *Marx-Engels Werke*, 2:60.

16. Marx, *Early Writings* (Bottomore), p. 206.

17. Marx, *Grundrisse*, p. 102.

18. Ibid., p. 104.

19. Ibid., pp. 101–2.

20. It has been argued that the requirement for perfect knowledge is already present in Parmenides. See Pierre Aubenque, *La Prudence chez Aristote* (Paris: Presses universitaires de France, 1963), pp. 169–70: "For it is not only Aristotle's project, but that of all philosophy, to rival with the gods for the possession of wisdom. Since Parmenides all philosophers have attempted, although in different ways, to rise above finite thought . . . in order to arrive at absolute wisdom, free from human characteristics or limitations, namely, as the gods must possess it."

21. Fichte to Stephani (December 1793), in *J. G. Fichtes Briefwechsel*, 1:319.

22. See Reinhard Lauth, *Zur Idee der Transzendental-Philosophie* (Munich and Salzburg: A. Pustet, 1965), p. 44: "Kant left behind the preparation for the development of the first philosophical system. It was reserved for Fichte . . . to develop the philosophy, based on the transcendental principle of the *cogito*." Lauth further writes (p. 51), "The essential reductive and deductive steps in the philosophies of Fichte and Descartes essentially correspond." But although it may well be the case that, as Lauth further maintains, there is a substantial parallel in the *Gotteslehre* of the two thinkers, in his argument against the possibility of the epistemological ground Fichte clearly opposes a main idea in the Cartesian theory of knowledge.

23. *Fichtes Werke*, 1:30.
24. See Lukács, *History and Class Consciousness*, p. 83, "For at this stage in the history of mankind there is no problem that does not ultimately lead back to that question [that is, the analysis of commodities] and there is no solution that could not be found in the solution to the riddle of commodity-*structure*."
25. For a discussion in many ways more obscure than the original text, see Althusser and Balibar, *Reading Capital*, vol. 1, Introduction, pars. 10–20.
26. Marx, *Grundrisse*, p. 100.
27. Ibid.
28. Ibid., p. 101.
29. This suggestion is implicit in John E. Smith, *Purpose and Thought: The Meaning of Pragmatism* (London: Hutchinson, 1978), p. 115. "For Peirce, no less than for James and Dewey, tentativeness belongs essentially to all inquiry, and cannot, in principle, be overcome. One has simply to live with it, and accept the risk which tentativeness entails both in belief and action."
30. See Aristotle *Nicomachean Ethics* 2. 1.
31. This theme recurs throughout Hegel's thought, but see especially the *Enzyklopädie der philosophischen Wissenschaften* in G. W. F. Hegel, *Sämtliche Werke*, ed. Hermann Glockner, 4:75: "The essential for science is not so much that the beginning be purely immediate, but that the whole of it be a circle [*Kreislauf*] in itself in which the first is also the last and the last also the first."
32. See Martin Heidegger, *Being and Time*, trans. John Macquarrie and Edward Robinson (New York: Harper and Row, 1962), par. 32, and Hans-Georg Gadamer, *Truth and Method*, trans. Garrett Barden and John Cumming (New York: Seabury Press, 1975), pt. 2, chap. 2 passim.
33. Jean-Paul Sartre, *Search for a Method*, trans. Hazel Barnes (New York: Knopf, Vintage, 1968), pp. 151–52.
34. See *The Logic of Hegel*, translated from the *Encyclopedia of the Philosophical Sciences*, trans. William Wallace (New York: Oxford University Press, 1968), par. 238, *Zusatz* (p. 376): "Philosophical method is analytical as well as synthetical."
35. See Leszek Kolakowski, *Husserl and the Search for Certainty* (New Haven: Yale University Press, 1975), p. 14: "It turned out that once we gave up the idea of an apodictically certain (and not analytical) truth, we did not need, and we

were not capable of building, any concept of truth at all. . . .
when absolute truth and metaphysical certainty disappear
the truth *tout court* disappears as well. . . . To be sure, the
distinction remains between what is *acceptable* and what is
not, but to be acceptable does not mean 'to be acceptable as
true.' It means 'to accord with experience,' rather than 'to
accord with the world as it really is.'"

36. See Lukács, *History and Class Consciousness*, esp. "Class
Consciousness," pp. 46–83.

37. For example, in the *Phaedo* (64a), trans. R. S. Black (Indianapolis: Bobbs-Merrill, 1955), p. 47, Plato writes that
"those who apply themselves correctly to the pursuit of philosophy are in fact practicing nothing more nor less than
dying and death."

CHAPTER 7. *Aspects of the Historical Relation*

1. "The relative significance of Marx's relation to Fichte is not
understood in terms of the simple [*eindeutigen*] Hegel-Marx
relation." Bernard Willms, *Die totale Freiheit* (Cologne:
West Deutsches Verlag, 1967), p. 53.

2. "It is Fichte's *Doctrine of Science*, with its reflections on the
creative action of man, on the primacy of action, on the necessity of the transcendance of the individual in the rational
totality, which left its mark on young Marx." Roger Garaudy, *Karl Marx: The Evolution of His Thought*, trans. Nan
Aptheker (New York: International Publishers, 1967), p. 35.

3. For an account, see David McLellan, *The Young Hegelians
and Karl Marx* (New York: Praeger, 1969).

4. Heinrich Heine, *Sämtliche Werke*, ed. E. Elster, 4 vols.
(Leipzig and Vienna: Bibliographisches Institut, 1887–90),
4:248.

5. For a general account, see Hans Speier, "Die Geschichtsphilosophie Lassalles I," *Archiv für Sozialphilosophie und
Sozialpolitik* (1929), esp. pp. 118–19.

6. "In one way or another all [the Young Hegelians] have either directly or indirectly fastened on to Fichte." Horst
Stuke, *Philosophie der Tat* (Stuttgart: E. Klett, 1963), pp.
80–81.

7. "Thus philosophy needs to come down from the heights of
theory to the land of practice. The practical philosophy is—
or better said, the philosophy of practice [*Praxis*]. . . . this is
in general the future destiny of philosophy." August von

Cieszkowski, *Prolegomena zur Historiosophie* (1838; reprint ed., Posen: J. Leitgeber, 1908), pp. 125–26.

8. "The self is really the great moving principle, which has been brought forth by recent times. . . . The self must become concrete, and this can occur in the first place through the process of activity." Cieszkowski, *Prolegomena*, pp. 125–26.

9. "At the present time the task of the philosophy of mind is to become philosophy of activity. . . . In this connection Fichte has gone much further than the most recent philosophy. However paradoxical it may seem, the young Hegelians still remain in theological consciousness." Moses Hess, *Philosophische und sozialistische Schriften*, ed. A. Cornu and C. Mönke (Berlin: Akademie Verlag, 1961), p. 219.

10. "In the philosophy of activity *every* external limitation is to be removed." Hess, *Philosophische*, p. 241.

11. "The goal of socialism is none other than that of idealism; it is thus, to leave nothing from the old rubbish [*Plunder*] other than activity." Hess, *Philosophische*, p. 219.

12. See letter to Berthe Löw, Saturday morning, Nov. 1835, in Carl Grün, *Ludwig Feuerbach in seinem Briefwechsel und Nachlass sowie in seiner philosophischen Charakterentwicklung* (Heidelberg: Carl Winter Verlag, 1874), p. 260.

13. "Since then my work has been particularly [concerned with] Fichte's posthumous writings." Letter to Berthe Löw, Feb. 1836, in Grün, *Feuerbach*, p. 262.

14. For the details, see Simon Rawidowicz, *Ludwig Feuerbachs Philosophie: Ursprung und Schicksal* (Berlin: Reuther and Reichard, 1931), esp. section on "Feuerbachs Stellung zu Fichte."

15. Rawidowicz, *Feuerbachs Philosophie*, p. 272.

16. "It will be shown that the central and fundamental theses of L. Feuerbach, which are in general directed against idealism, are [particularly] turned against J. G. Fichte's transcendental, critical, subjective idealism." Johann Mader, *Fichte, Feuerbach, Marx: Leib, Dialog, Gesellschaft* (Vienna: Herder, 1968), p. 94.

17. "The rejection of philosophy, conceived in the context [*Horizont*] of the controversy with Hegel, initiated a new, nonmetaphysical and nonidealistic anthropology." Johann Mader, *Zwischen Hegel und Marx: Zur Verwirklichung der Philosophie* (Munich: Oldenbourg, 1975), p. 54.

18. For the early evolution of Feuerbach's position and the influence of Fichte on it, see especially *Christian Kapp und*

seine literarischen Leistungen (1839), *Über den Anfang der Philosophie* (1841), *Vorläufige Thesen zur Reform der Philosophie* (1842), and *Grundsätze der Philosophie der Zukunft* (1843)—all in vol. 2 of *Ludwig Feuerbach: Sämtliche Werke*, ed. Wilhelm Bolin and Friedrich Jodl, 10 vols. (1903–11; reprint ed., Stuttgart and Bad Lannstatt: Frommann, 1959).

19. "The transition from the ideal to the real can occur only in the practical philosophy." *Feuerbach: Samtliche Werke*, 2:231.

20. "We ought always to take the predicate for the subject, and the subject as object and principle. . . . [For] in thus inverting the speculative philosophy we have the unveiled, pure, shining truth." *Feuerbach: Sämtliche Werke*, 2:224.

21. "The beginning of philosophy is neither God, nor the absolute, nor being as the predicate of the absolute or of the idea—the beginning of philosophy is the finite, the limited, the critical." *Feuerbach:Sämtliche Werke*, 2:230.

22. "In its whole foundation the contrary to the Hegelian philosophy has no other principle than the principle of subjectivity, which in its whole energy and most perfect form has been realized in Fichte." *Feuerbach: Sämtliche Werke*, 2:147.

23. "To be sure, one can also . . . turn the self into a universal principle of deduction. But this is possible only on the condition that in general one not discover and prove in the self a non-self, differences, [and] contradictions." *Feuerbach: Sämtliche Werke*, 2:214.

24. "The new philosophy . . . declares that only the human is the true and real, for only the human is the rational; man is the measure of reason." Feuerbach, *Fundamental Principles of the Philosophy of the Future*, p. 67.

25. See Habermas, *Knowledge and Human Interests*, esp. chap. 2, pp. 40 ff.

26. "As is clear in the course of his further development and in comparison with his, at this point well-prized, young-Hegelian friends of opinion [*Gesinnunsfreunden*] . . . in terms of his demands for realization [*Realizierungsdesiderat*], directed against the Hegelian philosophy, Marx accomplishes a *turn back [Rückwendung] to the Fichtean philosophy of desire and activity*." Thomas Meyer, *Der Zwiespalt in der Marx'schen Emanzipationstheorie: Studie zur Rolle des proletarischen Subjekts* (Kronberg: Scriptor Verlag, 1973), p. 12.

27. See Georg Lukács, *Lukács Werke*, 14 vols. (Darmstadt and Neuwied: Luchterhand, 1964–73), 2:165.

28. See August Cornu, *Karl Marx et Friedrich Engels*, 2 vols. (Paris: Presses universitaires de France, 1955–70), 2:294.

29. See Hegel's Letter to Niethammer (October 10, 1808). "Daily I am more convinced that theoretical work is more productive [*bringt mehr zustande in der Welt*] than practical work; if the realm of appearance [*Vorstellung*] is basically altered [*revolutioniert*] reality cannot resist." *Briefe von und an Hegel*, ed. J. Hoffmeister, 4 vols. (Hamburg: Meiner Verlag, 1952), 1:253.

30. "It would be nonsense for you to dedicate yourself to a practical career. Theory is now the strongest form of practice [*Praxis*]." Letter from Bauer to Marx of March 31, 1841, in Karl Marx and Friedrich Engels, *Historisch-kritische Gesamtausgabe*, ed. D. Rjazanov and V. Adoratskij (Frankfurt and Berlin: Marx-Engels Verlag, 1927–32), vol. 1, pt. 1, sec. 2, p. 250. (Hereafter cited as MEGA.)

31. For a judicious discussion of this question, see Gustav Meyer, "Karl Marx und der zweite Teil der 'Posaune,'" *Archiv für die Geschichte des Sozialismus und der Arbeiterbewegung* 4 (1916):332–63. Meyer cautiously concludes that "with the textual criticism we do not reach a clear result [*festen Ergebnis*]" (p. 362).

32. "The band of Young Hegelians would like to convince us that only Hegel immerses himself in the shamefulness of theory and has not thought to continue theory to practice. . . . His theory in itself was the most dangerous, all-embracing and destructive practice [*Praxis*]." [Bruno Bauer and Karl Marx?], *Die Posaune des jüngsten Gerichts über Hegel, den Atheisten und Antichristen* (1841; reprint ed., Aalen: Scientia Verlag, 1969), p. 81.

33. "We have the firm conviction that not the *practical attempt* but the *theoretical continuation* of communist ideas reflects the *essential* danger." *Marx-Engels Werke*, 1:108.

34. Marx and Engels, *The German Ideology*, p. 121.

35. "It is important that in independence of Marx and in temporal priority an anthropology directed against Hegel was developed, and in particular by L. Feuerbach. It [that is, this anthropology] is known to have been an important, also restrictive influence on Marx." Klaus Hartmann, *Die Marx'sche Theorie* (Berlin: Walter de Gruyter, 1970), pp. 43–44.

36. See *MEGA*, vol. 1, pt. 1, p. 113.

37. See Marx, *Capital*, vol. 1, ch. 1, sec. 3, p. 52, fn. 18. Since Fichte's so-called Pauline period only begins in 1804, this comment may indicate Marx's familiarity with lesser known, later versions of the *WL*.

38. See Letter to Engels of 19 October 1867. *Marx-Engels Werke*, 31:308.

39. Marx, *Early Writings* (Bottomore), p. 206.

40. Ibid., pp. 206–8; *Marx-Engels Werke Ergänzungsband*, pt. 1, pp. 577–79.

41. This is the case even for the occasional writer on Marx who also possesses a good grounding in the history of philosophy, such as Nicholas Lobkowicz in his *Theory and Practice: History of a Concept from Aristotle to Marx* (Notre Dame: University of Notre Dame Press, 1967).

42. "With the interpretation of man as subject Descartes creates the metaphysical presupposition for futher anthropology of all kinds [*jeder Art und Richtung*]. In the rise of anthropology, Descartes celebrates his greatest triumph." Martin Heidegger, *Holzwege* (Frankfurt: Vittorio Klostermann, 1950), pp. 91–92.

43. See Etienne Gilson, *La Liberté chez Descartes et la théologie* (Paris: Alcan, 1913), and *Etudes sur le rôle de la pensée médiévale dans la formation du système cartésien* (Paris: Vrin, 1930).

44. For ten articles on this theme, see *The Monist* (April 1965). See also Lewis White Beck, *Actor or Spectator* (New Haven: Yale University Press, 1976).

45. Immanuel Kant, *Prolegomena to Any Future Metaphysics*, trans. Lewis White Beck (Indianapolis and New York: Bobbs-Merrill, 1950), pp. 108–9.

46. Kant, *Critique of Pure Reason*, B. xiii.

47. See letter to Stäudlin (April 4, 1793): "Anthropology, on which I have taught a course yearly for more than twenty years." *Briefe von und an Kant* in *Immanuel Kants Werke*, ed. Ernst Cassirer, 11 vols. (Berlin: Bruno Cassirer, 1923), 10:205.

48. *Immanuel Kants Werke*, ed. Ernst Cassirer, 10:98. See letter to Beck (Oct. 27, 1791): "What can be more fitting in addition to that and in fact for an entire lifetime, than to be concerned with the entire vocation [*Bestimmung*] of man, if one only had hope . . . that the least progress could be made in that regard."

49. "All outward progress . . . has the goal of applying the acquired knowledge and skills to the world, but the most im-

portant object in the world, on which all others can be utilized, is man." Kant, *Anthropologie, Vorrede.*

50. For definitions, see Kant, *Anthropologie*, par. 40.
51. "A correct understanding, a practical judgment, and a profound [faculty of] reason constitute the entire scope of the intellectual capacity of knowledge." Kant, *Anthropologie*, par. 39.
52. See Kant, *Critique of Pure Reason*, A805–B833.
53. *Kant's Introduction to Logic*, trans. Thomas Kingsmill Abbott (1885; reprint ed., New York: Philosophical Library), p. 15. This passage is the basis of F. van de Pitte's recent, interesting attempt to argue that Kant's entire enterprise falls under philosophical anthropology. See *Kant as Philosophical Anthropologist* (The Hague: Martinus Nijhoff, 1971).
54. See Kant, *Critique of Practical Reason*, par. 31.
55. Kant, *Prolegomena*, pp. 94–95. See also Kant, *Critique of Pure Reason*, B566.
56. See Kant, *Critique of Judgment*, par. 3.
57. Ibid., par. 9.
58. Habermas makes an analogous point (*Knowledge and Human Interests*, p. 37), when he writes that "Fichte covers Kant's path in reverse," but he is incorrect in his claim, probably influenced by Hegel, that Fichte's interest is to "prove the identity of ego and non-ego," since it is in fact to construct a view of the active subject.
59. For a discussion of the *Phenomenology* as a theory of experience, see Martin Heidegger, "Hegels Begriff der Erfahrung," in *Holzwege.*
60. See par. 213: "The *Idea* is truth in itself and for itself—the absolute unity of the notion and objectivity. . . . The definition, which declares the Absolute to be the Idea, is itself absolute. All former definitions come back to this." *The Logic of Hegel*, trans. William Wallace, p. 352.
61. For a discussion of the respective views of man, see Karl Löwith, *From Hegel to Nietzsche*, trans. David E. Green (Garden City: Doubleday, Anchor Books, 1967), pt. 2, chap. 4.
62. Marx, *Early Writings* (Bottomore), p. 51.
63. Marx, *Writings of Young Marx*, p. 154.
64. Ibid., p. 166.
65. "Hegel makes man into a *man of self-consciousness* instead of making self-consciousness into the *self-consciousness of man*, of the real man who also lives in the real, objective world and is defined by it." *Marx-Engels Werke*, 2:204.

CHAPTER 8. *Beyond Fichte and Marx*

1. Hegel, *Sämtliche Werke: Jubiläumsausgabe*, 19:185.
2. This is now the standpoint of the present time, and the realms of spiritual shapes are for now closed. Hegel, *Sämtliche Werke*, 19:690.
3. "Our philosophical revolution is ended. Hegel has closed its great circle." Heinrich Heine, *Philosophie und Religion in Deutschland* in *Werke und Briefe*, ed. Hans Kaufmann, 10 vols. (Berlin: Aufbau Verlag, 1961), 5:303.
4. "One must know what being is in order to decide whether this or any other is real (for instance, 'the facts of consciousness'); in the same way for certainty, for knowledge and such like [*dergleichen*].—Since we don't know it, a critique of the capacity of knowledge is senseless; how might this instrument [*Werkzeug*] criticize itself, since it uses itself for criticism? It cannot even define itself." *Friedrich Nietzsche: Werke*, ed. Karl Schlecta, 5 vols. (Frankfurt, Vienna, and Berlin: Ullstein, 1972), 4:91.
5. Rosenkranz, Hegel's first biographer, was scarcely overstating the case when he remarked, "It is just as true that Hegel owes a powerful impulse to Schelling's system and has in the deepest sense taken it into itself, as it is true that he has made not less Fichte's, not less Spinoza's, Plato's, and Aristotle's systems his own living property [*Eigenthum*]." Karl Rosenkranz, *Hegels Leben* (Berlin: Duncker and Humblot, 1844), p. 62.
6. For an account, see Xavier Tilliette, "La nouvelle image de l'idéalisme allemand," *Revue philosophique de Louvain* 71 (February 1973): 46 ff.
7. For a contrary claim that in its main lines the post-Hegelian tradition can be largely seen as a series of reactions to and continuation of Hegel's thought, see Richard J. Bernstein, *Praxis and Action* (Philadelphia: University of Pennsylvania Press, 1971).
8. In his account of Schelling, Walter Schulz writes, "He is the perfector of German idealism insofar as he radicalizes its basic problems, the self-mediation, to a grasp of the ungraspableness of pure being." *Die Vollendung des deutschen Idealismus in der Spätphilosophie Schellings* (Stuttgart: Kohlhammer, 1955), p. 8. For a masterly study of Schelling's entire thought, see Xavier Tilliette, *Schelling: Une philosophie en devenir*, 2 vols. (Paris: Vrin, 1970).
9. An extreme example is a recent reference to "G. W. Fichte"

[*sic*] as belonging to a group of "somewhat obscure philosophers," including Brentano, Meinong, and Reid. See Richard Taylor's "Tribute" in *Analysis and Metaphysics: Essays in Honor of R. M. Chisholm*, ed. Keith Lehrer (Dordrecht and Boston: Reidel, 1975), p. 7.

10. There has been much recent criticism of the Hegel-influenced reading of Fichte. See especially Peter Baumanns, *Fichtes ursprüngliche System: Sein Standort zwischen Kant und Hegel* (Stuttgart: Frommann-Holzboog, 1972).

11. There are some important exceptions. Recent studies of Marx which both prescind from this widespread presupposition and even deny it include Henry, *Marx*, and Kolakowski, *Main Currents of Marxism*.

12. Dietmar Kamper, *Geschichte und menschliche Natur: Die Tragweite gegenwärtiger Anthropologiekritik* (Regensburg: Hansa Verlag, 1973), pp. 29–30: "In the *first* place, one is concerned with a situational analysis, concerning the recognition of the nature of man, his particular position in the 'Realm of the living.' The presumed 'stratification,' 'gradation,' . . . and 'multi-dimensionality' of man is sought, in the *second* place, through an integration of all relevant science, through a 'basic anthropology.' In the *third* place, anthropology is studied from the 'pragmatic perspective,' which means the desire to work out a theory of acting [*Handlungslehre*]. . . . From a *fourth* perspective finally anthropological interest is concentrated on the phenomenon of expression, in which one wants to grasp the specific [character] of human self-presentation from play to speech."

13. See Michael Landman, ed., *De Homine: Der Mensch im Spiegel seines Gedankens* (Freiburg: Alberts, 1962).

14. For a somewhat different discussion, see John Macmurray, *The Self as Agent* (London: Faber and Faber, 1969).

15. John Dewey puts this point well in his book, *The Quest for Certainty* (1929; reprint ed., New York:G. P. Putnam's Sons, 1960). "The principle of indeterminacy thus presents itself as the final step in the dislodgment of the old spectator theory of knowledge. It marks the acknowledgment, within scientific procedure itself, of the fact that knowing is one kind of interaction which goes on within the world." Pp. 204–5.

SELECTED BIBLIOGRAPHY

Several brief observations regarding quotations and texts are necessary. We do not possess complete editions of the writings of either Fichte or Marx in any language. Few of Fichte's writings have been translated into English. With the exception of the recent excellent translation of the *Wissenschaftslehre* of 1794 and the two *Introductions* (1797), none of Fichte's major writings are accessible in acceptable English-language versions. When necessary, I have quoted from the readily accessible *Fichtes Werke* (edited by I. H. Fichte), which has long been a standard source. Although this edition is by no means complete, it is more nearly so than the more recent six-volume edition edited by Fritz Medicus. The monumental definitive edition now in preparation, edited by Reinhold Lauth and Hans Jacob, will eventually be the standard source, but as it is as yet neither complete nor widely available, it seemed preferable to rely on the edition mentioned.

Marx's writings exist in a variety of editions of varying degrees of completeness and accuracy, in various languages. Work on a complete edition, to run concurrently with a similar German effort, is now in the initial stages. The best editions currently available are those published by Cotta and by Dietz Verlag. The latter is based on the earlier, also incomplete edition, commonly known as *MEGA*. As for Fichte, for Marx I have made it a practice to quote from English translations as much as possible. When necessary, I have relied on the Dietz edition, despite the fact that it has a number of important faults, such as the omission of the *Grundrisse*, since it is at present the most nearly complete source of Marx's writings.

Both Fichte and Marx use frequent emphases, which have been reproduced as in the original writings. Unless otherwise indicated, all translations are my own.

Ackrill, J. L. "Aristotle's Distinction between *Energeia* and *Kinesis*." In *New Essays on Plato and Aristotle*, ed. Remford Bambrough. New York: Humanities Press, 1967.

Adorno, Theodor. *Negative Dialectics*. Trans. E. B. Ashton. New York: Seabury Press, 1973.

Althusser, Louis. *For Marx*. Trans. Ben Brewster. New York: Knopf, Vintage, 1970.

Althusser, Louis, and Etienne Balibar. *Reading Capital.* 2 vols. Trans. Ben Brewster. New York: Pantheon Press, 1970.

Arendt, Hannah. *The Human Condition.* Chicago: University of Chicago Press, 1971.

Aristotle. *Metaphysics.* Trans. Richard Hope. Ann Arbor: University of Michigan Press, 1968.

———. *Nicomachean Ethics.* Trans. Martin Ostwald. Indianapolis: Bobbs-Merrill, 1962.

Aubenque, Pierre. *Le Problème de l'être chez Aristote: essai sur la problématique aristotélicienne.* Paris: Presses universitaires de France, 1962.

———. *La Prudence chez Aristote.* Paris: Presses universitaires de France, 1963.

Avineri, Shlomo. *The Social and Political Thought of Karl Marx.* New York: Cambridge University Press, 1968.

Ayer, Alfred Jules. "Phenomenalism," *Proceedings of the Aristotelian Society* 47 (1946–47).

Baldwin's Dictionary of Philosophy and Psychology. James Baldwin, ed. London: Macmillan, 1902.

Bauer, Bruno. *Die gute Sache der Freiheit und meine eigene Angelegenheit.* 1842. Reprint ed. Aalen: Scientia Verlag, 1972.

[Bauer, Bruno, and Karl Marx?] *Die Posaune des jüngsten Gerichts über Hegel, den Atheisten und Antichristen.* 1841. Reprint ed. Aalen: Scientia Verlag, 1969.

Baumanns, Peter. *Fichtes ursprüngliche System: Sein Standort zwischen Kant und Hegel.* Stuttgart: Frommann-Holzboog, 1972.

Beck, Lewis White. *Actor or Spectator.* New Haven: Yale University Press, 1976.

Becker, Werner. *Die Achillesferse des Marxismus, der Widerspruch von Kapital und Arbeit.* Hamburg: Hoffman and Campe, 1974.

Bernstein, Richard J. *Praxis and Action.* Philadelphia: University of Pennsylvania Press, 1971.

Bloch, Ernst. *Das Materialismusproblem.* Frankfurt: Suhrkamp, 1972.

Bosanquet, Bernard. *The Meeting of Extremes in Modern Philosophy.* London: Macmillan, 1921.

Bourgeois, Bernard. *L'Idéalisme de Fichte.* Paris: Presses universitaires de France, 1968.

Buchanan, Emerson. "Aristotle's Theory of Being." Ph.D. diss., Columbia University, 1962.

Buhr, Manfred. *Revolution und Philosophie.* Berlin: V. E. B. Deutscher Verlag der Wissenschaften, 1965.

Cieszkowski, August von. *Prolegomena zur Historiosophie.*
1838. Reprint ed. Posen: J. Leitgeber, 1908.

Cornu, Auguste. *Karl Marx et Friedrich Engels.* 2 vols. Paris:
Presses universitaires de France, 1955–70.

Coulmas, Peter. *Fichtes Idee der Arbeit.* Hamburg: Hansischer
Gildenverlag, 1939.

Dewey, John. *The Quest for Certainty.* 1929. Reprint ed. New
York: G. P. Putnam's Sons, 1960.

Dictionary of Philosophy. Ed. Dagobert D. Runes. New York:
Philosophical Library, Alliance Corporation, 1942.

Draper, H. "Marx and the Dictatorship of the Proletariat." In
Etudes de marxologie. Paris, Sept. 1962. Supplement to
Cahiers de l'Institut de sciences économiques appliquées.

Druet, Pierre-Philippe. *Fichte.* Namur: Seghers, 1977.

Düring, Ingemar. *Aristoteles:Darstellung und Interpretation
seines Denkens.* Heidelberg: C. Winter, 1966.

Enciclopedia Filosofica. Ed. N. Abbagnano. Turin: Unione Tipografico, 1961.

Encyclopedia of Philosophy. Ed. Paul Edwards. New York: Macmillan, Free Press, 1967.

Engels, Friedrich. *Herr Eugen Dührings Revolution in Science.*
Trans. Emile Burns. New York: International Publishers,
1970.

———. *Ludwig Feuerbach and the Outcome of Classical German Philosophy.* Ed. C. P. Dutt. New York: International
Publishers, 1941.

Etzwiler, James P. "Being as Activity in Aristotle: A Process Interpretation," *International Philosophical Quarterly* 18 (September 1978).

Feuerbach, Ludwig. *The Essence of Christianity.* Trans. George
Eliot. New York: Harper and Row, 1957.

———. *Fundamental Principles of the Philosophy of the Future.*
Trans. Manfred H. Vogel. Indianapolis and New York:
Bobbs-Merrill, 1966.

———. *Ludwig Feuerbach: Sämtliche Werke.* Ed. Wilhelm Bolin
and Friedrich Jodl. 10 vols. 1903–11. Reprint ed. Stuttgart
and Bad Cannstatt: Frommann, 1959.

Fichte, Johann Gottlieb. *Addresses to the German Nation.* Ed.
George Armstrong Kelly. New York: Harper and Row,
1968.

———. *Fichte: Science of Knowledge (Wissenschaftslehre) with
First and Second Introductions.* Ed. and trans. Peter Heath
and John Lachs. New York: Appleton-Century-Crofts,
1970.

———. *Fichtes Werke*. Ed. I. H. Fichte. 11 vols. Berlin: Walter de Gruyter, 1971.

———. *J. G. Fichte. Briefwechsel*. Ed. Hans Schulz. 2 vols. Hildesheim: Georg Olms, 1967.

———. *The Vocation of Man*. Trans. Roderick M. Chisholm. Indianapolis: Bobbs-Merrill, 1956.

Gadamer, Hans-Georg. *Truth and Method*. Trans. Garrett Barden and John Cumming. New York: Seabury Press, 1975.

Garaudy, Roger. *Karl Marx: The Evolution of His Thought*. Trans. Nan Aptheker. New York: International Publishers, 1967.

Gehlen, Arnold. "Über die Geburt der Freiheit aus der Entfremdung." In *Studien zur Anthropologie und Soziologie*. Neuweid and Berlin: Luchterhand, 1971.

Gentile, Giovanni. *La filosofia della prassi* (1899). Rpt. *La filosofia di Marx*. Florence: Einaudi, 1974.

Gilson, Etienne. *Etudes sur le rôle de la pensée mediévale dans la formation du système cartésien*. Paris: Vrin, 1930.

———. *La Liberté chez Descartes et la théologie*. Paris: Alcan, 1913.

Goldmann, Lucien. *Recherches dialectiques*. Paris: Gallimard, 1959.

Grün, Carl. *Ludwig Feuerbach in seinem Briefwechsel und Nachlass sowie in seiner philosophischen Charakterentwicklung*. Heidelberg: Carl Winter Verlag, 1874.

Gueroult, Martial. *L'Evolution et la structure de la doctrine de la science chez Fichte*. 2 vols. Paris: Société d'éditions les belles lettres, 1930.

Habermas, Jürgen. *Knowledge and Human Interests*. Trans. Jeremy J. Schapiro. Boston: Beacon Press, 1972.

———. *Zur Rekonstruktion des historischen Materialismus*. Frankfurt: Suhrkamp, 1976.

Hallett, H. F. *Benedict de Spinoza*. London: Athlone Press, 1957.

Hartmann, Klaus. *Die Marx'sche Theorie: Eine philosophische Untersuchung zu den Hauptschriften*. Berlin: Walter de Gruyter, 1970.

Hegel, G. W. F. *Briefe von und an Hegel*. Ed. J. Hoffmeister. 4 vols. Hamburg: Meiner Verlag, 1952.

———. *Differenz des Fichte'schen und Schelling'schen Systems der Philosophie*. Hamburg: Meiner Verlag, 1962.

———. *Enzyklopädie der philosophischen Wissenschaften*. Ed. F. Nicolin and O. Pöggeler. Hamburg: Meiner Verlag, 1959.

———. *G. W. F. Hegel. Sämtliche Werke: Jubiläumsausgabe*.

Ed. H. Glockner, 20 vols. Stuttgart: F. Fromman, 1927–40.

———. *Hegel's Phenomenology of Mind.* Trans. J. B. Baillie. London and New York: George Allen and Unwin–Macmillan, 1961.

———. *Hegel's Phenomenology of Spirit.* Trans. A. V. Miller. Foreword by J. N. Findlay. Oxford and New York: Oxford University Press, 1979.

———. *The Logic of Hegel.* Trans. William Wallace. New York: Oxford University Press, 1968.

———. *Phänomenologie des Geistes.* Ed. J. Hoffmeister. Hamburg: Meiner Verlag, 1952.

———. *Wissenschaft der Logik.* Ed. Georg Lasson. 2 vols. Hamburg: Meiner Verlag, 1967.

Heidegger, Martin. *Being and Time.* Trans. John Macquarrie and Edward Robinson. New York: Harper and Row, 1962.

———. *Holzwege.* Frankfurt: Vittorio Klostermann, 1950.

———. *Identity and Difference.* Trans. Joan Stambaugh. New York: Harper and Row, 1969.

———. *Nietzsche.* 2 vols. Pfullingen: Neske, 1961.

Heimsoeth, Heinz. *Fichte.* Munich: E. Reinhardt, 1923.

Heine, Heinrich. *Zur Geschichte der Religion und Philosophie in Deutschland.* Vol. 7 in *Werke und Briefe*, ed. Hans Kaufmann. 10 vols. Berlin: Aufbau Verlag, 1961.

———. *Sämtliche Werke.* Ed. E. Elster. 4 vols. Leipzig and Vienna: Bibliographisches Institut, 1887–90.

Heller, Agnes. *La Théorie des besoins chez Marx.* Paris: Union générale des éditions, 1978.

Henrich, Dieter. *Fichtes ursprüngliche Einsicht.* Frankfurt: Vittorio Klostermann, 1966.

Henry, Michel. *Marx.* 2 vols. Paris: Gallimard, 1976.

Hess, Moses. *Philosophische und sozialistische Schriften.* Ed. A. Cornu and C. Mönke. Berlin: Akademie Verlag, 1961.

Howard, M. C., and J. E. King. *The Political Economy of Marx.* New York: Longmans, 1975.

Hunter, C. *Der Interpersonalitätsbeweis in Fichtes früher angewandter praktischer Philosophie.* Meinsenheim: Hain, 1973.

Intelligenzblatt der Allgemeinen-Literatur-Zeitung. No. 113 (October 1794).

Janke, Wolfgang. *Fichte: Sein und Reflexion. Grundlagen der kritischen Vernunft.* Berlin: Walter de Gruyter, 1970.

Kamper, Dietmar. *Geschichte und menschliche Natur: Die Trag-*

weite gegenwärtiger Anthropologiekritik. Regensburg: Hansa Verlag, 1973.

Kant, Immanuel. *Anthropologie in pragmatischer Hindsicht.* Vol. 10 in *Kant Werke*, ed. W. Weischedel. 10 vols. Frankfurt: Insel Verlag, 1956–64.

———. *Briefe von und an Kant.* Vols. 9 and 10 in *Immanuel Kants Werke*, ed. Ernst Cassirer. 11 vols. Berlin: Bruno Cassirer, 1912–22.

———. *Critique of Judgment.* Trans. J. H. Bernard. New York: Hafner, 1951.

———. *Critique of Practical Reason.* Trans. Lewis White Beck. Indianapolis, Bobbs-Merrill, 1956.

———. *Critique of Pure Reason.* Trans. Norman Kemp Smith. New York: St. Martin's Press, 1961.

———. *Kant's Introduction to Logic.* Trans. Thomas Kingsmill Abbott. 1885. Reprint ed. New York: Philosophical Library, 1963.

———. *Prolegomena to Any Future Metaphysics.* Trans. Lewis White Beck. Indianapolis and New York: Bobbs-Merrill, 1950.

———. *Religion within the Limits of Reason Alone.* Trans. T. M. Greene and H. H. Hudson. New York: Harper and Row, 1960.

Klein, Jacob. "Aristotle, An Introduction." In *Ancients and Moderns*, ed. Joseph Cropsey. New York: Basic Books, 1964.

Kojève, Alexandre. *Introduction à la lecture de Hegel.* Paris: Gallimard, 1947.

Kolakowski, Leszek. *L'Esprit révolutionnaire.* Brussels: Editions complexes, 1978.

———. *Husserl and the Search for Certainty.* New Haven: Yale University Press, 1975.

———. *Main Currents of Marxism.* Trans. P. S. Falla. 3 vols. New York: Oxford University Press, 1978.

Kölnischer Zeitung. No. 179.

Korsch, Karl. *Marxism and Philosophy.* Trans. Fred Halliday. 1923. Reprint ed. London: New Left Books, 1970.

Kosik, Karel. *Die Dialektik des Konkreten.* Trans. Marianne Hoffmann. Frankfurt: Suhrkamp, 1970.

Kroner, Richard. *Von Kant bis Hegel.* 2 vols. Tübingen: Siebeck, 1921–24.

Landman, Michael, ed. *De Homine: Der Mensch im Spiegel seines Gedankens.* Freiburg: Alberts, 1962.

Lask, Emil. *Fichtes Idealismus und die Geschichte in Gesam-*

melte Schriften. Ed. Eugen Herriegel. Vol. 1. Tübingen: Mohr, 1923–24.

Lauth, Reinhard. *die Entstehung von Schellings Identitäts-philosophie in der Auseinandersetzung mit Fichtes Wissenschaftslehre, 1795–1801.* Munich: Alber, 1975.

———. *Zur Idee der Transzendental-Philosophie.* Munich and Salzburg: A. Pustet, 1965.

Lobkowicz, Nicholas. *Theory and Practice: History of a Concept from Aristotle to Marx.* Notre Dame: University of Notre Dame Press, 1967.

Löwith, Karl. *From Hegel to Nietzsche.* Trans. David E. Green. Garden City: Doubleday, Anchor, 1967.

Lukács, Georg. *History and Class Consciousness.* Trans. Rodney Livingstone. 1923. Reprint ed. Cambridge: MIT Press, 1971.

———. *Lukács Werke.* 14 vols. Darmstadt and Neuwied: Luchterhand, 1964–73.

———. *Ontologie: Marx.* Darmstadt and Neuwied: Luchterhand, 1970.

———. *Die Zerstörung der Vernunft.* 3 vols. 1954. Reprint ed. Darmstadt and Neuwied: Luchterhand, 1973–74.

McLellan, David. *The Young Hegelians and Karl Marx.* New York: Praeger, 1969.

Macmurray, John. *The Self as Agent.* London: Faber and Faber, 1969.

Mader, Johann. *Fichte, Feuerbach, Marx: Leib, Dialog, Gesellschaft.* Vienna: Herder, 1968.

———. *Zwischen Hegel und Marx: Zur Verwirklichung der Philosophie.* Munich: Oldenbourg, 1975.

Mandel, Ernest. *Traité d'économie politique marxiste.* 4 vols. Paris: Union générale d'éditions, 1962.

Marcuse, Herbert. "The Foundations of Historical Materialism" (1932). In *Studies in Critical Philosophy,* trans. Joris de Bres. Boston: Beacon Press, 1972.

———. *One Dimensional Man.* Boston: Beacon Press, 1964.

Marx, Karl. *Capital.* Ed. Friedrich Engels. Trans. Samuel Moore and Edward Aveling. 3 vols. New York: International Publishers, 1967.

———. *Grundrisse: Foundations of the Critique of Political Economy.* Trans. Martin Nicolaus. Baltimore: Penguin, 1973.

———. *Karl Marx: Early Writings.* Trans. and ed. T. B. Bottomore. New York: McGraw-Hill, 1964.

————. *Karl Marx: Early Writings*. Trans. T. R. Livingstone and G. Benton. New York: Random House, 1975.

————. *Werke, Schriften, Briefe*. 5 vols. Stuttgart: Cotta, 1960–71.

————. *Writings of the Young Marx on Philosophy and Society*. Trans. and ed. Lloyd D. Easton and Kurt H. Guddat. Garden City: Doubleday, 1967.

Marx, Karl, and Friedrich Engels. *The German Ideology*. Trans. and ed. C. J. Arthur. New York: International Publishers, 1970.

————. *Historisch-kritische Gesamtausgabe*. Ed. D. Rjazanov and V. Adoratskij. 12 vols. Frankfurt and Berlin: Marx-Engels Verlag, 1927–35. Cited as MEGA.

————. *Marx and Engels: Basic Writings on Politics and Philosophy*. Ed. Lewis S. Feuer. Garden City: Doubleday, Anchor Books, 1959.

————. *Marx-Engels Werke*. 39 vols. Berlin: Dietz Verlag, 1956–68.

Mészáros, Istvan. *Marx's Theory of Alienation*. London: Merlin, 1970.

Meyer, Gustav. "Karl Marx und der zweite Teil der 'Posaune,'" *Archiv für die Geschichte des Sozialismus und der Arbeiterbewegung* 7 (1916).

Meyer, Thomas. *Der Zwiespalt in der Marx'schen Emanzipationstheorie: Studie zur Rolle des proletarischen Subjekts*. Kronberg: Scriptor Verlag, 1973.

Monist, The. (April 1965).

Moore, G. E. *Philosophical Studies*. London: Routledge and Kegan Paul, 1965.

Nietzsche, Friedrich. *Friedrich Nietzsche: Werke*. Ed. Karl Schlecta. 5 vols. Frankfurt, Vienna, and Berlin: Ullstein, 1972.

Ollman, Bertell. *Alienation: Marx's Conception of Man in Capitalist Society*. New York and London: Cambridge University Press, 1973.

Owens, Joseph. *The Doctrine of Being in the Aristotelian Metaphysics*. Toronto: Institute of Pontifical Studies, 1951.

Pannekoek, Anton. *Lenin als Philosoph*. Ed. Alfred Schmidt. 1938. Reprint ed. Frankfurt: Europäische Verlagsanstalt, 1969.

Passmore, John. *The Perfectibility of Man*. London: Duckworth, 1970.

Penner, Terry. "Verbs and Identity of Action: A Philosophical Exercise in the Interpretation of Aristotle." In *Ryle*, ed. G. Pitcher and O. Wood. Garden City: Doubleday, Anchor Books, 1970.

Philonenko, Alexis. "L'Intuition intellectuelle chez Fichte." In *Akten der Fichte-Tagung*. Proceedings of international conference at Zwettl, Austria, in press.

——. *La Liberté humaine dans la philosophie de Fichte*. Paris: Vrin, 1966.

——. *Théorie et praxis dans la pensée morale et pratique de Kant et Fichte en 1793*. Paris: Vrin, 1968.

Philosophisches Wörterbuch. Ed. Georg Klaus and Manfred Buhr. Leipzig: Bibliographisches Institut, 1970.

Plato, *Phaedo*. Trans. R. S. Black. Indianapolis: Bobbs-Merrill, 1955.

——. *The Republic of Plato*. Trans. F. M. Cornford. New York: Oxford University Press, 1973.

Popitz, H. *Der entfremdete Mensch: Zeitkritik und Geschichtsphilosophie des jungen Marx*. Basel: J. Springer, 1953.

Quine, W. V. O. "Two Dogmas of Empiricism." In *From a Logical Point of View*. Cambridge: Harvard University Press, 1953.

Rawidowicz, Simon. *Ludwig Feuerbachs Philosophie: Ursprung und Schicksal*. Berlin: Reuther and Reichard, 1931.

Reinhold, Karl Leonhard. *Beyträge zur Berichtigung bisheriger Missverständnisse der Philosophie*. 2 vols. Jena: Manke, 1790.

Robinson, Joan. *An Essay on Marxian Economics*. London: Macmillan, 1947.

Rockmore, Tom. "Marxian Praxis," *Philosophy and Social Criticism* 5 (1978).

Rorty, Richard. "The World Well Lost," *Journal of Philosophy* 59, no. 19 (October 1972).

Rosenkranz, Karl. *Hegels Leben*. Brlin: Duncker and Humblot, 1844.

Ross, W. D. *Aristotle*. New York: Meridian Press, 1960.

Royce, Josiah. *Lectures on Modern Idealism*. 1919. Reprint ed. New Haven: Yale University Press, 1964.

Santayana, George. *Realm of Matter*. London: Constable, 1930.

Sartre, Jean-Paul. *Critique of Dialectical Reason*. Trans. Alan Sheridan-Smith. Atlantic Highlands, N.J.: Humanities Press, 1976.

——. *Search for a Method*. Trans. Hazel Barnes. New York: Knopf, Vintage, 1968.

Schacht, Richard. *Alienation*. Garden City: Doubleday, 1971.

Schaff, Adam. *Marxism and the Human Individual*. Trans. O. Wojtasiwicz. New York: McGraw-Hill, 1970.

Schelling, F. W. J. *Darstellung meines Systems der Philosophie*. Vol. 3 in *Schellings Werke*, ed. Manfred Schröder. 6 vols. Munich: Beck and Oldenbourg, 1927.

Schiller, F. C. S. "Activity and Substance" in *Humanism: Philosophical Essays*. London: Macmillan, 1912.

Schiller, Johann Christian Friedrich. *Briefwechsel zwischen Schiller und Goethe*. Ed. H. Hauff. 2 vols. Stuttgart: Cotta'sche Buchhandlung, 1856.

————. *Über die aesthetische Erziehung des Menschen in einer Reihe von Briefen*. In *Schriftren zur Philosophie und Kunst*. Munich: Goldmann, 1964.

Schmidt, Alfred. *Geschichte und Struktur: Fragen einer marxistischen Historik*. Munich: Hansa Reihe, 1971.

Schulz, Walter. *Die Vollendung des deutschen Idealismus in der Spätphilosophie Schellings*. Stuttgart: Kohlhammer, 1955.

Schurr, Adolph. *Philosophie als System bei Fichte, Schelling, und Hegel*. Stuttgart: Frommann-Holzboog, 1974.

Sève, Lucien. *Marxisme et théorie de la personnalité*. Paris: Editions sociales, 1969.

Smith, John E. *Purpose and Thought: The Meaning of Pragmatism*. London: Hutchinson, 1978.

Smith, Norman Kemp. *Prolegomena to an Idealist Theory of Knowledge*. London: Macmillan, 1924.

Speier, Hans. "Die Geschichtsphilosophie Lassalles I," *Archiv für Sozialphilosophie und Sozialpolitik* (1929).

Stallmach, Josef. *Dynamis und Energeia*. Meisenheim: Hain, 1959.

Stuke, Horst. *Philosophie der Tat*. Stuttgart: E. Klett, 1963.

Taylor, Charles. *Hegel*. Cambridge: Cambridge University Press, 1975.

Taylor, Richard. "Tribute." In *Analysis and Metaphysics: Essays in Honor of R. M. Chisholm*, ed. Keith Lehrer. Dordrecht and Boston: Reidel, 1975.

Tilliette, Xavier. "La nouvelle image de l'idéalisme allemand," *Revue philosophique de Louvain* 71 (February 1973).

————. *Schelling: Une philosophie en devenir*. 2 vols. Paris: Vrin, 1970.

van de Pitte, F. *Kant as Philosophical Anthropologist*. The Hague: Martinus Nijhoff, 1971.

Vranicki, Predrag. *Geschichte des Marxismus*. Trans. Stanislava

Rummel and Vjekoslava Wiedmann. 2 vols. Frankfurt: Suhrkamp, 1974.

Warnier, Philippe. *Marx pour un chrétien*. Paris: Mame-Fayard, 1977.

Weber, Marianne. *Fichtes Sozialismus und sein Verhältnis zur Marx'schen Doktrin*. Tübingen: Mohr, 1900.

Weischedel, Wilhelm. *Der Aufbruch der Freiheit zur Gemeinschaft*. Leipzig: Meiner, 1939.

Willms, Bernard. *Die totale Freiheit*. Cologne: West Deutsche Verlag, 1967.

Wolfe, Bertram D. *Marxism: 100 Years in the Life of a Doctrine*. New York: Dell Publishing Co., Delta Books, 1965.

Wundt, Wilhelm. *Fichteforschungen*. Stuttgart: F. Frommann, 1929.

INDEX

Absolute, 12, 90, 94, 136, 138–41

Ackrill, J. L., 176n, 177n

Activity: Aristotle's view of, 4, 54, 62–71, 163

—Fichte's view of: absolute, 56; independent, 13, 25; and Marx's view of, 56–62; positing and fundamental principles, 14; positing and imagination, 57; positing and knowledge, 56, 80; positing and *Paris Manuscripts*, 128; positing and striving, 58, 61; positing as nonconscious, 21; positing defined, 13; practical vs. theoretical, 21, 22, 25; striving and fulfillment, 80, 88; striving and Kant's position, 20, 138; striving and Marx's critique of Hegel, 139; striving and parallel with Marx, 56–58, 61, 63; striving and self-development, 19–21; striving as basic form of activity, 13

—Kant's view of, 132–36

—Marx's view of: free human activity, 60, 61, 83, 84; labor, 59, 60, 113; labor power, 46, 47, 50, 59; labor theory of value, 47. *See also* Work

—as neutral term, 4, 5. *See also* Man, as problematic concept

Acton, H.B., 100, 180n

Adler, Max, 167n

Adorno, Theodor, 179n

Aenesidemus. *See* Schulze, G. E.

Agency, 4, 38, 73, 95; and development, 91–94

Alienation, Marxian view of, 40–43; and Fichte/Marx comparison, 70, 79; and fulfillment, 84; and Hegel's view, 143; and Marxian view of man, 34, 37; and political economy, 44, 46; and Young Hegelians, 32, 33

Althusser, Louis, 28, 153, 172n, 174n, 181n

Anti-Cartesian. *See* Cartesian philosophy

Arendt, Hannah, 175n, 176n

Aristotelian: activity, 54, 64, 161, 163; activity and Fichte/Marx comparison, 67–71; view of development, 76; view of potentiality, 89

Aristotle: on activity, 54, 62–66, 163, 176n, 177n; and Fichte/Marx comparison, 68; and Fichte's view of politics, 75; and fulfillment, 80; and Hegel, 99, 146, 188n; on logic, 15, 157; and Marx's education, 127; and Marx's view of society, 44

Armstrong, David M., 99

Atheismusstreit, 12, 24, 58, 82

Aubenque, Pierre, 176n, 180n

Augustine, 131

Autonomy, 20

Avineri, Shlomo, 99, 174n, 179n

Ayer, Alfred Jules, 98, 179n

Balibar, Etienne, 174n, 181n

Bauer, Bruno: and criticism, 32, 105, 125, 149; criticized by Marx, 126

Baumanns, Peter, 170n, 189n

Beck, J. S., 186n

Beck, Lewis White, 186n

Becker, Werner, 174n

Bernstein, Richard J., 172n, 188n

Bloch, Ernst, 177n

Bosanquet, Bernard, 100, 180n

Bourgeois society, 40, 44, 46, 49

Index

view of activity, 61; and Fichte's
views of idealism and realism,
102–4; and Fichte's views of
man, 22, 23; and Fichte's views
of philosophy, 10, 11, 14–19,
80; and first person approach,
109, 116, 117; and Hegel's philosophy, 139–41; and Kant's
philosophy, 132, 138; and
Marx's epistemology, 113, 114

Fetishism, 42, 43
Feuerbach, Anselm: criticized by
Marx, 106, 126; and Marx's
terminology, 5, 37; and Marx's
"Theses," 4, 32; and Marx's
view of religion, 77; as student
of Fichte's views, 122–24,
183n, 184n; and view of man,
141
Fichte, I. H., 122
Fichte, Johann Gottlieb: historical
background, 8–10; as influence
on Feuerbach, 122–24; as influence on Marx, 126–30; interpretative tendencies, 6, 7; and
Kant, 8–10, 137, 138; on philosophy, experience, and self,
10–12; on self and activity,
12–22; and Young Hegelians,
121–26
First person epistemology, 109
Fischer, Kuno, 150
Foundationalism, epistemological,
110, 111. *See also* Ground,
epistemological
Fourier, Charles, 2, 125
Freedom, 51, 76, 131; and neces-
sity, 50, 84, 135
Free time, 51, 55, 83, 84
Freud, Sigmund, 31
Fulfillment, 20, 72, 80–89
Function, 62
Fundamental principles, 14–16

Gadamer, Hans-Georg, 181n
Garaudy, Roger, 120, 125, 182n

Gehlen, Arnold, 79, 167n
Gentile, Giovanni, 167n
German philosophical tradition:
and actor view of man,
130–44; and Aristotelian view
of activity, 64; and genesis of
Fichte/Marx parallel, 1, 3,
119–43; and its Hegelian interpretation, 101, 146–53, 163,
164; and Marx's position, 56,
97; and problem of man, 145,
154, 161
Gilson, Etienne, 131, 186n
Goethe, Johann Wolfgang, 1,
168n
Goldmann, Lucien, 173n
Ground, epistemological, 19,
110–12, 115
Grün, Carl, 183n
Gueroult, Martial, 169n
Gumposch, V. Ph., 123

Habermas, Jürgen: on activity in
Fichte and Marx, 55, 56; on
Fichte's relation to Kant, 187n;
on Fichte's relation to Marx,
125, 167n; on reconstruction,
171n
Hallett, H. F., 177n
Harmony, 20
Hartmann, Klaus, 126, 153,
172n, 185n
Haym, Rudolf, 123
Hegel, Georg Wilhelm Friedrich:
and Aristotelian view of man,
65; criticized by Marx,
128–30; and Fichte interpretation, 7, 55; and Fichte's philosophy, 8, 25, 92, 93, 124; and
genesis of Marx's thought, 2,
93, 94, 125, 126, 174n; and
idealism/materialism distinction, 99, 100; and interpretation of German philosophy, 24,
137, 146–53, 161; and Krug,
69; and Marx's views of capitalism and communism, 50; as

Index

Weischedel, Wilhelm, 168n
Willms, Bernard, 120, 182n
Windelband, Wilhelm, 150
Wittgenstein, Ludwig, 114
Wolfe, Bertram, 174n, 175n
Work: Marx's view of, 41, 59, 60;
    parallel in Fichte's and Marx's
    views of, 54, 55, 67
Wundt, Wilhelm, 169n

Young Hegelians: criticized in the
    Posaune, 126; and Feuerbach,
106; and Fichte's influence on,
2, 121–26, 138, 143, 182n,
183n; and genesis of Marx's
view, 125, 130, 138; and
Marx's view of theory, 31–33,
105

Zychlinski, Franz Zychlin von, 106

ECHEANCE   DATE DUE

UNIVERSITY OF SUDBURY
UNIVERSITE DE SUDBURY